OUT OF UNIFORM

OUT OF UNIFORM

Your Guide to
a Successful
Military-to-Civilian
Career Transition

Tom Wolfe

Potomac Books
Washington, D.C.

Library of Congress Cataloging-in-Publication Data
Wolfe, Tom, 1950–
  Out of uniform : your guide to a successful military-to-civilian career transition / Tom Wolfe. — 1st ed.
     p. cm.
  Includes index.
  ISBN 978-1-59797-715-9 (hardcover)
  ISBN 978-1-59797-720-3 (electronic edition)
  1. Career changes—United States. 2. Retired military personnel—Employment—United States. 3. Veterans—Employment—United States. 4. Job hunting—United States. 5. Vocational guidance. I. Title.
  HF5384.W64 2011
  650.14086'970973—dc23
                                                                        2011024809

Printed in the United States of America on acid-free paper that meets the American National Standards Institute Z39-48 Standard.

Potomac Books
22841 Quicksilver Drive
Dulles, Virginia 20166

First Edition

10 9 8 7 6 5 4 3 2 1

To my mom
a lifelong educator and lover of books,
for her encouragement and support.

To my dad
a veteran of Omaha Beach, Normandy, and Orange Beach, Okinawa,
whose service both in and out of uniform has been an inspiration.

CONTENTS

Preface   xi
Introduction   xiii

SECTION I. TRANSITION READINESS

1. Life Is Like a Roller Coaster   3
2. The Education of Self   6
3. Stereotypes   8
4. Master of Change   10
5. The Four Profiles   11
6. Filters, Part One (Employer's)   14
7. When Can You Start?   17
8. Travel—Are Your Bags Packed?   18
9. Grade Point Average   20
10. How Much Are You Worth?   22
11. Will You Relocate?   25
12. Filters, Part Two (Yours)   28
13. Quality of Life vs. Quality of Work   30
14. Educational Background Check   31
15. Transition Timeline   34

SECTION II. THE SELF-DISCOVERY ZONE

16. From Trees to Toilet Paper   39
17. Lifetime Tasks and Skills Inventory   41

18. What Size Company Is Best for You?   43
19. The Classifieds—More Than Meets the Eye   46
20. What's Behind Curtain Number Three?   48
21. Experience or Potential?   49
22. The Best Job for You?   51
23. Job Hunting from a Remote Location   53
24. The Geographically Restricted Job Search   56

SECTION III. THE OTHER SIDE OF THE FENCE

25. What's Out There?   61
26. I Want to Work with People   62
27. I Want to Be a Manager   64
28. Operations Management   65
29. Engineering   67
30. Is Consulting Right for You?   69
31. Government Contractors   71
32. Additional Options   73
33. The Boss of Me   75
34. The S Word   77
35. Your SQ Number   81
36. The Audition   83

SECTION IV. PREPARATIONS (MECHANICAL)

37. Your *BENCHMARK* Company and Decision Matrix   89
38. The Six Ps   91
39. Documentation   93
40. Creating Your Résumé   95
41. Cover Letters   105
42. Your Reference List   108
43. Application Forms—Thank Goodness I Made a Copy   110
44. Uniform of the Day   113
45. Finding Uncle Harry or Aunt Mary   115
46. Headhunters   121
47. An Employment Perfect Storm   123
48. The Runaway Résumé   125

SECTION V. PREPARATIONS (MENTAL)

49. The Power of Questions   131
50. Researching Companies   133
51. Knowledge Is Power   135
52. Wallflowers and Cheerleaders   138
53. Weaknesses—Use Them to Your Benefit   141
54. Camaraderie and the Power of People   142
55. Tell 'Em What They Want to Hear   145

SECTION VI. INTERVIEWS—TIPS AND TECHNIQUES

56. Body Language   151
57. Interviewers: The Good, the Bad, and the Ugly   155
58. What's with That Tie?   156
59. From Adversary to Advocate   159
60. All of My Questions Have Been Answered   161
61. Please Leave a Message at the Beep   165
62. Be Memorable   166
63. Extra Preparations   170

SECTION VII. INTERVIEWS—VARIETY AND FUNCTION

64. Interview and Etiquette Checklist   177
65. Interviews—Purpose, Process, and Form   179
66. Can You Hear Me Now?   183
67. Let's Do Lunch   185
68. Post-Interview Follow-Up Procedures   187
69. Until the Paperwork Is Done   189
70. Dear John   191
71. Your Decision Matrix (Part Two—Usage)   196

SECTION VIII. OFFER, DECISION, AND LAUNCH

72. Learning How to Swim   201
73. The Power Shift   202
74. Job Offer—The Message and the Makeup   204

75. The REV Factor   206
76. The High Jumpers   208
77. Will You Marry Me?   211
78. One-offer-itis   214
79. Salary Negotiation   216
80. Responding to Offers—the Right Way   220
81. Lift Off and Stay on Course   222
82. A Personal Trainer for Your Career   225
83. Has the Ride Lost Its Thrill?   227

Afterword   231
Acknowledgments   233
Keyword Index   235
About the Author   239

PREFACE

My first civilian career lasted four weeks. I was just about to start week five when the president of the company called me to his office to tell me that I was not a good match for the job. He explained that although I had done nothing wrong, he was letting me go.

Dazed and confused, I found my way to my car. My wife had yet to make the move from Virginia Beach so I packed up what few things I had with me and headed home. That five-hour drive gave me plenty of time to think. My emotions were all over the place—shock, disbelief, anger, embarrassment, sadness, fear, and uncertainty. However, by the time I pulled into my driveway, what I was mostly feeling was relief.

I had not been happy in that job, something I sensed during my second week. I had very little interest in the company's products, and I had very little in common with the people who worked there. In fact, I was the first veteran they had ever hired. So, why in the world did I accept the offer in the first place?

For all the wrong reasons, of course, but how was I to know that at the time? I was twenty-seven years old, and the last time I had a civilian job was when I was a plumber's helper at the age of sixteen. Since then the navy had eliminated any need for a résumé, a suit, or an interview. I was a successful, confident naval officer and I felt bulletproof. In reality, I was a babe in the woods. I took that offer because of the title (southeast regional sales manager) and the money. Big mistake.

Being fired was a humbling experience, but I landed on my feet. I knew I needed help, so I checked out several of the military-to-civilian placement firms. One stood out from the rest. In addition to a notable list of client companies, the people who worked there were impressive, and most of them were veterans. They took an interest in me as a person and did their best to help me find the right job. After a dozen interviews and multiple offers, the placement company asked me to work for them, and I accepted their offer. Fortunately I got it right the second time around. I made partner and retired from that company thirty years later.

During those thirty years I assisted thousands of service men and women as they transitioned from the military to civilian employment. In addition to providing technical guidance (on résumés, wardrobe selection, and interview skills), I made it my mission to help every one of them avoid the mistakes I had made. I emphasized the importance of identifying what really matters to them and taking the time to develop an awareness of personal strengths and motivators. A frequent reaction to my guidance and counseling was encouragement to write a book, to which I would respond by saying, "Someday."

Someday is now. The standard advice for aspiring writers is to write what you know. Having dedicated my professional life to assisting those in military-to-civilian career transition, that is what I know. I wrote this book in order to share this information and lessons learned with current and future veterans.

INTRODUCTION

More than 200,000 military personnel transitioned to civilian status last year. Millions more made that journey before them. About 200,000 or more will do so this year. All of them share a single common denominator: wearing the uniform in the service of our country. Almost all of them share a second common denominator: when they leave the military, they look for civilian employment.

How about you? Why are you reading this book? Let me guess. You are in transition from a military to a civilian career and you are thinking:

I want a fast-paced career with a growing, dynamic company where compensation is aligned with work ethic and results, where the environment and people are positive and supportive, and where there is an opportunity for rapid professional growth commensurate with proven performance.

Or maybe:

I want a nice house in a safe, quiet neighborhood with access to good schools, and a personal life that allows me to spend time with my family, play golf, coach Little League, and get involved in community service activities.

Or perhaps:

I want a career opportunity that allows me to balance the requirements of my personal and professional lives.

Or simply:

I need a job.

No matter what your goals or aspirations may be, I am here to help. I am a veteran, and I know what it is like to get out and look for a job. For over thirty years I have had the privilege of guiding thousands of men and women as they transitioned from military to civilian occupations. I am very familiar with that process and fortunate to have worked with many professionals and subject matter experts over the years.

This guide will help military personnel as they prepare for and adjust to civilian employment, regardless of service, branch, rank, rating, time in service, or specialty. Although all of you share the common denominators mentioned earlier, each of you brings something unique to the job market, and each of you wants something different from a job search.

While those differences make a one-size-fits-all guide impossible, you can tailor the use of the material to suit your needs. Some of you will absorb the information cover to cover, while others will use the table of contents or keyword index to focus on exactly the information and guidance needed at the moment. Throughout this book you will encounter the words "tool," "tools," and "toolbox" many times. Keep track of them. Not only will you use them throughout your job search and interviews, but you will also carry them with you as your career continues to develop.

You will also notice that I use the names of companies and individuals throughout the book. The company names spelled in all capital letters and italicized (*ALLCAPS*) are pseudonyms. The names of individuals are also fictitious, although their stories are either factual or based on composite characters or combined events.

So, grab a pen, paper, and a highlighter, find a comfortable chair, and get started. Remember—sometimes the hardest part of getting there is taking the first step. This book is designed to make that first step an easier one.

SECTION I.
TRANSITION READINESS

A successful military-to-civilian transition and job search requires not only an overall plan but also the tactics to implement it. Before you start worrying about the nuts and bolts of interview preparation, you need to determine what is really important to you. It is counterproductive to conduct a search only to end up in a job that does not meet your needs. It is also important to balance the quality of your work with the quality of your life.

This section will help you get a handle on the big picture and map out your strategy. You will be equipped with information and tools to better define and implement your overall plan and enhance your chances of success. The tactics come later. Here you will:

- Take the first step.
- Gain some perspective.
- Discover the influence of stereotypes.
- Learn about the profiling process.
- Discover the impact of training and performance.
- Become aware of the importance and use of filters.
- Compare quality of life and quality of work.
- Construct a timeline.

1. Life Is Like a Roller Coaster

Career transition is part of the journey called *your life*. It occurs more than once and differs each time it happens. Major changes are a challenge, but you can take comfort in knowing you are not alone. Thousands of people have gone through this before, and thousands more will do so in the future. Every one of those people has a story to tell. Here is one you might like.

One of my favorite ways to get to know the person I am interviewing is to ask this question:

> I want you to ignore whether or not you are qualified to do it, whether or not the job is out there, whether or not the associated quality of life would make your family happy, and whether or not you could even earn a living doing it. Now, tell me—what would you really like to do for a living?

I do not ask this question because I expect to help the person find that job, but rather to gain some insight into his or her motivators and perhaps even passion. Although that particular job might be unrealistic, maybe we can find one that can satisfy some of those motivators and tap into that passion.

Several years ago I met a navy lieutenant named Mark. He was stationed in the D.C. area, working as a facilities manager at the Patuxent River Naval Air Station. A carrier-based F/A-18 pilot, he was on shore duty after almost two years at sea. For reasons dealing with quality of life and family separation, Mark had made the decision to resign his commission. He was seeking civilian employment and I was assisting him in his career transition and job search. During our initial meeting I asked Mark my favorite question. Many people struggle with an answer, but not Mark: "That's an easy one, Tom. I would design roller coasters." I laughed. I had heard some interesting responses over the years, but that one surprised me. I asked him to explain.

Throughout his childhood he had loved riding roller coasters. He grew up in Cleaves, Ohio, a Cincinnati suburb that was only a short drive from the Kings Island Amusement Park. Mark begged his parents to take him there, and as soon as he was tall enough he rode the park's assortment of roller coasters almost non-stop. When he turned sixteen he would drive himself to the park several times a month. He eventually got a job there so he could pay for gas and, better still, ride the coasters for free.

A few years later Mark received a navy ROTC scholarship and chose to attend Ohio State University, in part because of the proximity of Columbus to Cincinnati. He could keep his job at Kings Island and work some weekends and summers. Mark graduated with a mechanical engineering degree in his hand and ensign's bars on his collar. His training as a naval aviator and his early assignments as an F/A-18 pilot took him all over the country—Florida, Mississippi, Texas, California, Virginia, and D.C. No matter where he was stationed he always found the amusement parks and the roller coasters. In fact, after our meeting he was going to head down Interstate 95 to Kings Dominion for his first ride on a coaster that had just opened the previous weekend.

Unlike many of the dream jobs that had been described to me, the one that Mark had in mind might actually be feasible. I asked him what was stopping him from going after that job. Turns out he had done much in the way of research on that profession. Although his job at the park had given him considerable operational experience and his passion as a fan made him an expert as a user, he was missing the academic credentials necessary to get hired by one of the amusement park ride design firms. Furthermore, even if he could get hired in that field the starting salary was about half of what he was making as a naval officer, and with a wife and two children, that was not acceptable.

I could see the disappointment in his eyes, but he was also smiling. He explained to me that as long as there was a roller coaster close by he would be happy. Although he would not be able to design them there was nothing stopping him from continuing to ride.

Mark completed his job search and accepted an offer from the *RDPM* Corporation, a major real estate development and property management company based out of Chicago. After a year of training and a year of rotational development assignments, he was assigned to the company's regional office in Orlando, Florida, as a facilities engineering manager. The job was a nice fit for his educational background, his naval officer leadership and management experience, and his shore duty tour as a facilities manager. The location of the job was the icing on the cake—the Orlando area is home to some of the best roller coasters in the world.

We stayed in touch. I remained curious about his career and he continued to solicit my guidance as a career coach. Mark did very well at *RDPM*, so well in fact that after just three years he was offered a promotion to operations manager. He called me to share the news but he did not sound all that happy. This promotion, like most promotions, required a sacrifice. It was one he was not willing to make: moving his family to Chicago.

He and his family loved living in Orlando. His kids were doing well in school, his wife was happy in her job as a teacher, they had just moved into a new home, and they were surrounded by roller coasters. I asked him if the operations manager position could be done out of Orlando or if another promotion—one that would let him stay in Orlando—might come along. He answered no and no. The corporate culture at *RDPM* was not one that liked to be told no, especially when it came to career advancement. In fact, declining a promotion meant career stagnation at best, looking for a new job at worst. We talked it over and Mark decided to investigate the job market in the greater Orlando area.

A few days later we had our next career coaching session. I initiated the conversation by once again asking about the dream job. Mark replied, "That's an easy one, Tom. I would design roller coasters."

I laughed and replied that some things never change. Although the design side remained unlikely, maybe we could get a little closer this time. Mark did his homework. We explored his existing network and discussed how to utilize and expand it. He researched potential employers in the area. We both made some phone calls. I encouraged him to select four or five likely targets and he picked two. Given his passion, his choices did not surprise me—two of the largest entertainment companies in the world, both of which had a significant presence in the Orlando area and more than two dozen roller coasters between them. I asked him who he knew at those companies. He could think of no one. Think again, I said.

Based on the work we had done to revise his résumé, I knew he was a member of the Ohio State alumni chapter in the area. I was aware of his membership in the Tailhook Association, a group of former and current carrier-based naval aviators.

Furthermore, he was a member of the Coasters, a group of like-minded roller-coaster fanatics, and I also knew he was active in his church. I encouraged him to think of each of those four groups as a circle and to consider that he likely knows at least one person in each of those circles who works for one of his two target companies. Those circles are bound to overlap, and every time they do he would be closer to someone who could help him get his foot in the door.

It took a month but it happened. Sure enough, a member of his church had not only graduated from Ohio State but had also been in the navy. George had recently retired from Amusement Parks International (*API*) and had strong ties there. He and Mark met for lunch and hit it off. Mark convinced him to join the Coasters and George made some calls. The next thing you know Mark was sitting across the desk from the VP of park design and development. There was an opening for a project manager—someone to coordinate the installation, testing, evaluation, and launch of both new and enhanced rides, including roller coasters. He received the offer, accepted it, and called me to say, "Hey, Tom. Can you believe it? Wow. It's almost perfect. Somebody else gets to design them, but I get to ride them all I want, as often as I want."

Mark and I continue to stay in touch and you will learn more about his roller-coaster ride later in this book (section VIII).

How about you? What would you really like to do for a living? Before you can answer that question, a little self-analysis is in order. Chapter 2 will get you started.

2. The Education of Self

For most military personnel, the career transition process is as much about education as it is about finding a job. Many people end up working for companies unknown to them when their searches began. Furthermore, they accept positions about which they initially have little or no knowledge. Why does this happen?

One explanation is that most military personnel have little exposure to the private sector prior to joining the service. With a few exceptions (e.g., graduate school, education-with-industry, and defense program management), this lack of exposure continues throughout their time in the military. The resulting insufficient information about employment options creates one of the largest obstacles in the military-to-civilian employment transition. Without knowing the choices, how can one possibly respond to the question, What do you want to do?

Most military personnel base their knowledge of the business world on their experiences as consumers. They are very familiar with companies that brand their products or services. Almost everyone has heard of Intel, Ford, Xerox, Procter & Gamble, AT&T, and UPS. Very few people are familiar with MEMC, Nalco, and Jones Lang LaSalle. All of these companies are world-class and leaders in their fields, but only the first group markets directly to the consumer. On the surface, you might think you will prefer to work for one of the former, but with better information, you might decide that one of the latter is the one for you.

Regarding job categories, there is a certain amount of familiarity with titles like technician, production manager, sales representative, and project engineer. However, business analyst, program manager, consultant, and brand manager might be less familiar. Depending on your educational background, experience, and personality, something in the lesser-known category might be more appropriate for you.

As you get started, I recommend you pay less attention to job titles and focus on job content instead. Start off interviewing for everything for which you are qualified. As you learn more about each of these opportunities, you will also learn more about yourself. Your level of interest in each opportunity will start to clarify and an elimination process will begin. Cross off the ones that do not interest you and focus on those that do. This process works both ways. If you are rejected every time you interview for a particular type of job, then you should reconsider your suitability for that position.

A certain amount of this self-education process occurs before the interviewing phase of the job search begins. Although reading, information interviews, and informal discussions with family members and friends can give you a sense of what is out there, for most people it is the actual job interview that produces the most important information. One way to view this phenomenon is to remember:

A successful job search is an information-gathering process, a by-product of which, if done correctly, is an offer for the job you really want.

Thorough self-education and excellent self-knowledge are critical prerequisites to a successful transition and job search. An important part of knowing yourself is being aware of how you are perceived by others, especially when "others" include potential employers. This perception is explored in the next chapter.

3. Stereotypes

There is a strong demand in the civilian work force for separating military personnel. During my career of recruiting, coaching, and placement, I encountered more than one thousand companies with active hire-the-vet programs. For those of you in military-to-civilian career transition, it is nice to know that the private sector finds you so attractive. However, before your head swells too much, you should examine both sides of that coin.

Interviewers, just like the rest of us, have a tendency to prejudge others based partly on stereotypes. Companies with a history of hiring separating military personnel use the individual interviewing process to reconcile the positive and negative stereotypes associated with that population as a whole. These companies value your:

- **Patriotism and citizenship.** You love your country; have a desire to serve and give back; do not take freedom for granted.
- **Flexibility.** You change duty stations and assignments often; work outside of your academic and/or military specialty; adapt to new circumstances quickly.
- **Work ethic.** You are not afraid of hard work and long hours; do what it takes to get the job done; have a strong mission and goal orientation.
- **Reliability and ethics.** You do what is right; can be counted on to be where you are supposed to be and do what you are supposed to do; your word is your bond.
- **Self-sacrifice.** You can handle deployments, harsh working conditions, and family separation; you consider others before self.
- **Health and fitness.** You are physically fit; well-groomed; never get sick, as measured by the number of sick days you take each year—zero.
- **Demonstrated leadership and management.** You set the example for others; empower your people to succeed; look out for their safety and welfare; are

frequently responsible for thousands of dollars worth of assets and account-
able for it all.

Wow! Put yourself in the shoes of a hiring manager—how could you not want
to hire someone with all of those attributes? But, before you get overconfident,
you should be aware of a mind-set that labels you as:

- **Rigid and formal.** You are uncomfortable outside of your uniform; call everybody sir or ma'am; have trouble relaxing in a business setting.
- **Focused on rank structure.** You are overly attentive to the amount of metal
on the collar or braid on the sleeve; label people as superiors and subordinates.
- **Lacking creativity.** You are used to taking orders; are not an independent
thinker; have pushed any creative streak into the background.
- **Unable to think outside the box.** You rely too much on the plan of the day,
the organizational manual, and the standard operating procedures.
- **Accustomed to guaranteed paychecks.** You are used to compensation based
on *attendance* rather than *performance*. The best and worst performers in a
peer group make the same amount of money.
- **Inflexible.** You are unwilling to take chances; are afraid to make a mistake;
embrace the *if it ain't broke, don't fix it* mentality.
- **Autocratic.** You order people around; they follow you because they might go
to jail if they do not.

Would you hire that person? Taken as a whole, this profile would be unac-
ceptable to any organization. Although this negative stereotype may contain elements of truth, it can in no way be an accurate or fair description of any single
individual in the military. However, the same must be said of all of those positive
attributes listed previously. An individual who could live up to all of those virtues
would be impossible to find. Reality exists somewhere between the extremes.

How can you use this information? Keep in mind that when you walk in the
door for an interview, the interviewer has probably prejudged you to some degree.
Much of this prejudice is based on a combination of positive and negative stereotypes surrounding military personnel. Interviewers, at least the ones who know
what they are doing, will try to get to know you well enough to judge you as an
individual. Your mission is fairly simple:

Reinforce as many of the positive stereotypes as you can, and defeat the negative ones that do not apply to you.

4. Master of Change

Career transition is filled with conflicting emotions. On the one hand, it is exciting to think about starting a new job and a new career. On the other, your anxiety level is high and you are filled with apprehension, mostly because you are about to leave the world of the known and enter the world of the unknown. You are not alone. Change almost always pro-

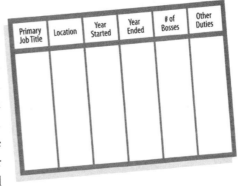

duces anxiety. The best way to deal with this situation is to believe in yourself and do your homework. You should also keep in mind that, when it comes to change, it is what you gain, not what you lose, that matters.

Regarding that homework, here is an assignment for you. Review your career in the military. Think about all the different assignments you have held. Consider all the various duties and responsibilities inherent in each. It might be helpful to use a chart similar to the one above.

Add more rows and columns if need be. For example, number of subordinates, job specifics, or collateral duties assigned could be significant for you. In addition to the variety of assignments, look at how often you transitioned from one to the next. Along with the changes in your functional roles, look at all the times the physical location also changed. How many different bosses have you had? How often have you been asked to perform in a role for which you had no prior training or academic preparation? Consider how varied the backgrounds are of the individuals who have worked for you and for whom you have worked. How well have you handled all of this? More important, what does this say about you?

Transition . . . start-up . . . flexibility . . . new horizons . . . change of station . . . temporary additional duty . . . learning curve . . . turnover . . . guess what? You are already a master of change. Been there, done that, and done it well. Transitioning from a military to a civilian career is just another step in your track record of successful changes. Granted, there are differences in mission, terminology, process, and structure, but you have faced similar differences in the past. Your track record of success, in both performance and change management, is appealing to a civilian employer. In fact, that is one of the major reasons companies like to hire veterans.

Before you start to interview, do some self-analysis. List all the times you have successfully handled change in your career. How did you do it? What did you learn about yourself in the process? Being able to share the answers to these questions with an interviewer will significantly improve your chances of landing a great job, a job that will lead to a continuing set of changes that will come to define your civilian career.

5. The Four Profiles

Many organizations profile their job openings before the recruiting and interviewing process begins. Each opening will have three associated profiles: **education and training, professional,** and **personality.** The first two are often classified as either preferred or required. The third one is almost always required.

There is also a fourth profile and it is arguably the most important one, at least as far as you are concerned—what matters to you? I refer to this fourth profile as **your benchmarks.** Here is a description of the elements of all four.

THE EDUCATION AND TRAINING PROFILE

Most jobs have educational requirements associated with them. Your academic training has to meet certain minimum requirements before you can be considered for the opening. These include high school graduation, courses of study in college, degrees conferred, degree equivalency, technical or trade schools completed, and other classroom- or academic-oriented certifications. Not-so-obvious criteria include academic performance (as reflected in class standing or grade point average) and honors. Additionally, some companies look closely at your non-classroom activities during your academic endeavors.

The circumstances under which you attained your education and training will also receive scrutiny. Did you self-finance your education? Receive academic or athletic scholarships? Work part or full time while completing your education? Were you deployed at the time or on remote assignment? Holding down a job and supporting a family? Serving your country? For college graduates, extracurricular involvement in campus leadership, athletics, service organizations, clubs, and volunteerism are part of your academic profile. Accomplishments and achievements associated with your academic endeavors are important in that they are indicators of your potential for success and growth in the organization. As you can see, there is much more to your academic profile than a framed certificate or diploma.

THE PROFESSIONAL PROFILE

Many organizations ask their staffing personnel and recruiters to keep a specific professional and experience profile in mind for each of their openings. They are able to predict successful candidate profiles through analysis of previous successful employee performance data. By screening résumés, application forms, and performance evaluations, they are able to identify candidates who appear to have the right professional skill set for each position.

What information are they after? There is no single answer. It varies from company to company and from job to job. For example, some companies prefer one branch of service to the others. Some have a preference for junior versus senior personnel, disguising that preference in years of experience or pay grade terminology. Other companies may focus on line or staff assignments. Sometimes a specialization within a service branch is a requirement for the job. Frequently companies look for a particular sequence of assignments or duty stations. Specific designations, military occupational specialties, certifications, or qualifications may be important.

In addition to specific qualifications or experience, the level of performance or degree of success is also scrutinized. An individual with an excellent track record of success will almost always be selected ahead of someone with average performance. Many companies look at it like this:

What you have done is not nearly as important as *how well* you have done it.

Previous success is an excellent indicator of potential success, even if the goals of the new organization differ from those of the former one.

THE PERSONALITY PROFILE

When a candidate appears to match well with the first two profiles of the job, the third profile enters the picture. Unlike the first two, having the right personality for the job is frequently a requirement, not a preference.

The personality profile differs from the others in another significant way—it is almost purely subjective. Academic and professional qualifications can be appraised through an impersonal review of paperwork, but an individual's ability to match up to the personality profile of a particular position can only be determined through face-to-face meetings. Although some companies will utilize telephone interviews or personality testing services during the early stages of the interview process to get a feel for the candidate's interpersonal skills, it is only through direct personal interviewing that they are truly able to determine the personality profile.

Arriving at the personal interview stage is a good sign. You normally only get to this step if you meet or exceed the interviewer's academic and experience requirements for the job. With this prescreening completed, it is the responsibility of the interviewer to see firsthand if the characteristics of your personality match the personality profile of the position. Every company has its own set of standards for each opening. In general, you can count on an appraisal of traits such as communication skills, impact, eye contact, body language, self-confidence, sense of humor, warmth, empathy, energy, integrity, honesty, friendliness, positive attitude, social skills, humility, and work ethic.

Assuming this appraisal is positive, you now match up nicely against the three profiles for this position. Only two things stand between you and an offer. One of these you can control—have you expressed your sincere interest in the job? The second one you cannot—did someone else outperform you in the interview? If the answers are *Yes* and *No*, then congratulations—you get the offer and your search is over, correct? Not necessarily. Just because they have decided to offer you the job does not mean that you will accept it. Your acceptance or rejection depends on the fourth profile.

THE FOURTH PROFILE—YOUR BENCHMARKS

Every job seeker must develop a set of decision criteria (benchmarks) with which he or she will evaluate an opportunity. Once these criteria have been determined and prioritized, the candidate can evaluate how well the opportunity matches up against those benchmarks. Although each individual determines his or her personal criteria, issues such as job satisfaction, growth potential, compensation, location, and quality of life appear on most lists. If the job offer matches up well with your criteria, either initially or potentially, then the fourth profile has been satisfied and you are likely to accept the offer.

Understanding these four profiles gives you insight into the job search process from the perspective of both the company and you, the candidate. In effect, the

job search can be viewed as a balancing act of the first three profiles by the organization and the fourth profile by the individual. When the balance is stabilized, each party appears to be able to satisfy the needs of the other and the stage is set for a mutually beneficial relationship, both initially and in the future. The importance of establishing your benchmarks and using them in your search is covered in section IV.

Once the profiling process is complete, the selection process begins for both job seekers and employers. That selection involves the use of **filters**. The next several chapters will help you learn how to either avoid them or use them, depending on the circumstances.

6. Filters, Part One (Employer's)

Some things are so common in our daily routine that we take them for granted or forget they exist, even though they play an important role in our quality of life. A good example is the filter. When was the last time you thought about the drain

in your sink . . . the spam folder on your e-mail account . . . the noise reduction headset on the airplane . . . the oil filter in your car . . . the paper cone in your coffee pot?

Filters also play a critical role in the success or failure of a job search. Awareness of their existence and their utilization will increase the odds of winning interviews and landing the job you want.

What is the purpose of a filter? Filters are used in any system to eliminate or reduce unwanted particles or impurities, thereby improving the quality of the output of that system. This intended and positive result comes at a price, and that price is measured in two ways. First, there is the direct cost of the filters and their application. Second, there is the indirect cost of the unintended but unavoidable impact of adding resistance to a system. Although the filter is removing the unwanted particles, it is doing so at an additional price—a decrease in the rate of flow. Simply stated:

Filters enhance quality but reduce quantity.

Every employer uses filters throughout the recruiting and candidate selection process. They want to narrow down the field (reduce quantity) and focus on the best fits (enhance quality). Some of these filters are built into the descriptions of the jobs. Others are incorporated into the way the jobs are posted or advertised. Still others are utilized as résumé or telephone screening tools. Many companies utilize automated résumé screening software that searches for keywords.

Most of these techniques come into play before any sort of personal interview occurs. Regardless of how or when they are employed, the goal is the same—to eliminate the less desirable or unqualified candidates as early in the selection process as possible. This not only increases the likelihood of selecting the right person, but also minimizes the amount of money spent on recruiting someone they will not hire.

Here are the most common filters used by employers, followed by a description of their usage. Notice how they can be used in advance of an actual interview.

- **Availability.** In most cases an organization wants to fill its openings as soon as possible. Using the candidate's availability date is an easy way to narrow down the field. The real-time prospects go to the head of the line.
- **Travel.** Civilian employers know that one of the most often cited reasons for leaving military service is family separation. As a result, they will use a job's travel requirements as a way to filter out those candidates unwilling to travel.
- **Education and training.** Most job requirements include some minimal academic standards, and an organization will filter the candidate pool accordingly. Given your standing as a military service member or veteran, you must have at least a high school diploma or GED. Many openings require more education.

Associate's degree? Bachelor's degree? Master's degree? Specific degrees? Professional designations? Additional specialty training? Certifications? Licenses? Some companies will also take a look at performance in an academic setting.

- **Money.** There will always be a wage, hourly rate, or salary associated with any job opening. In most cases it will be stated as a range, such as $18.00 to $22.00 per hour or $58,000 to $67,000 per year, where the spread is based on experience, education, location, and other variables. It does a company no good to pursue someone whose compensation expectations fall outside the range for the job.

- **Geography.** This filter is used to eliminate any candidate who will not or prefers not to live in the town where the job is located. Using this one is difficult when there are multiple locations or when the locations are unknown until the end of a training program. Regardless, it makes sense to eliminate the geographic misfits up front if possible.

- **Relocation.** This filter is frequently used for the same reasons as the travel filter. Military personnel relocate often in the course of their careers. This can have a detrimental impact on their quality of life. Early filtering for a candidate's willingness or unwillingness to relocate initially and at an acceptable frequency helps ensure a better match down the road.

- **Experience.** It is a rare company that hires veterans solely for their potential. One thing that makes a veteran an attractive hire is the built-in experience. Most positions require a certain type and amount of relevant experience, and that filter will be applied to the candidate pool early in the selection process.

- **Working hours.** Some jobs have regular and predictable working hours, while others require a great amount of flexibility. Some companies are only open during normal working hours, Monday to Friday, while others are staffed through the weekend. Many positions require shift work, and sometimes those shifts rotate through a twenty-four-hour cycle. A potential employer will often use an applicant's attitude about working hours as a filter.

You will need a strategy to handle several of those filters. They deserve further explanation and the next five chapters will elaborate.

7. When Can You Start?

This question is one of the most frequently asked in a job search. Throughout the course of the candidate selection process, interviewers will ask it many times. At the end of the process, it is a good indication that they want you and an offer is forthcoming. However, when asked at the beginning of the relationship with a potential employer, it is being used as a filter. To pass through that filter, you can employ an interviewing tactic that uses two availability dates: the *advertised* and the *actual*.

Your advertised date is the one you use at the beginning of your search. It should be the *absolute earliest date* you can start. The key here is that even if it is not your preference, it must at least be possible. For those in civilian employment, this is a straightforward issue—two to four weeks' notice is customary. For military personnel, there are additional considerations. Depending on your branch of service, specialization, and source of commission or enlistment contract, you may be able to exercise some control over when you hang up your uniform.

To determine this advertised availability date, take your final paid day of military service and accelerate it by applying any available terminal or separation leave, job hunting TDY/TAD, and/or early-out options. The resulting date, or rather the month in which it occurs, is your advertised availability date. For example, August 16 becomes simply, *"for the right opportunity, I can start in August."* If you are thinking August 1, see if July 31 is viable. If so, say July. Why? Although it may sound trivial, many organizations apply the availability for employment filter early in the screening process. July might pass through the filter when August would not, and it would be a shame to be eliminated but for one additional day of terminal leave.

The second version of your availability date—actual—comes into play at the end of your search. You have an offer on the table that you choose to accept. You call the company to commit and during that phone call you negotiate your *actual* availability date, i.e., your start date. What was advertised as August a few months or weeks ago is now August 16, or August 1, or July 31, or September 4. At this point, a few days or weeks either way is not important. Why?

> **The big issue has been settled—you and the organization have decided to start a career together. The lesser issues, such as your actual start date, will fall into place.**

Caution: There is one case where this approach does not work. If the organization has a training program that is scheduled to start on August 21 and you went into the interviewing process several months earlier advertising an August availability, you will not be able to negotiate a start date other than August 21. In most cases this requirement would be explained well in advance. To be safe, you can always ask about it in the early stages of the interviewing process.

8. Travel—Are Your Bags Packed?

As military personnel search for civilian careers, many are surprised to learn that travel can be a significant component of certain employment opportunities. Business travel can be exciting and even glamorous; it can also be tedious and disruptive. Time away from home is common in the military and it may have something to do with why many people leave the service. Companies are aware of this and use it as a filter. It is important to decide early in your job search just how much travel you are willing to accept.

First, let's clarify some terminology. There are two types of travel in the corporate sector. Some travel is of a local nature only. You spend a portion of your working day away from your office and your desk, traveling in the local area only. The advantage of this type of travel is that you are home every night. The disadvantage might be a significant amount of time in your car or on public transportation. Regardless, the organization will describe this situation as "little or no travel" since you do not pack a suitcase and you can expect to have dinner at home most nights.

The second type is the overnight variety. The nature of the work and/or the distance from the office makes getting home every night impractical or impossible. You will need a suitcase. You will be staying in hotels and dining out. You will also become very familiar with airports, train stations, or the interior of your car.

Can you accept either of these options? If so, to what extent? In the case of local travel, what portion of the working day or week is acceptable? With respect to the overnight variety, most companies talk in terms of a percentage. However some use nebulous descriptions, such as *occasional, frequent, some, moderate, high, extensive,* or *low.* Ask them to convert this terminology to a percentage and it will be easier for you to understand the requirement. Then again, maybe not. Let's say a company advertises a job that requires moderate travel. You ask for clarification and they give you the figure of 20 percent. What does that actually mean? Assuming limited weekend travel, it means that you will be spending an average of two out of every ten working nights away from home. Notice the word "working." What is a working night? In the basic sense, it is the night before a working day. Given that the average month has twenty working days, then 20 percent travel means you will spend an average of four working nights per month away from home. The word "average" brings up an additional point. Are we talking one night per week, two nights every other week, one four-day trip per month, or some other 20 percent configuration? Do you have a preference? How much does it matter?

Another issue to consider is the type of position. Most manufacturing, operations, engineering, and general management jobs have little or no regular travel requirements. Some off-site functions might require occasional travel, but travel in and of itself is not a function of the job. Other jobs are inherently travel-intensive, such as consulting, sales, vendor quality, tech rep, field engineering, auditing, and recruiting.

How much travel can you and your family accept? You need to be prepared for that question before you start the interviewing process. Consider the options available to you, accept the fact that every job requires some sort of sacrifice, and decide if your sacrifice might come in the form of time away from home. If you are willing to travel, or perhaps even attracted to a position with travel, many additional doors could be open for you.

However, if one of your major reasons for leaving the military is too much time away from home, consider the old adages about *the frying pan and the fire* and *looking before you leap.*

9. Grade Point Average

Frequently a potential employer will use performance in an educational setting as a screening tool. A common evaluator is the academic grade point average (GPA). There are three reasons why a company might focus on your GPA. First, almost everybody has one, and this creates a point of comparison among all candidates. Due to differences in grading systems, academic majors, course difficulty, and extenuating circumstances, this method of comparison is rarely accurate or fair, but it is easy to administer. Second, GPA can be an indicator of potential. Third, there is probably some correlation between GPA and the ability to learn.

Do interviewers really care about GPAs? Most do, but to what degree will vary from company to company. One company in ten will pay little if any attention to it. Another 10 percent will set nonnegotiable GPA minimums. The remaining 80 percent will use it as one of their evaluation points. Additionally, the importance of GPA may diminish for some companies as the amount of time since it was earned increases.

There is much more involved in this issue than simply your class grades. Let's take a look at your high school or college GPA, assuming a 4.0 scale. A GPA of 3.4 or higher will almost always survive this filter. GPAs in the 2.8 to 3.3 range are on the bubble. The odds of rejection increase as the GPA drops below 2.8, but there are ways to improve those odds.

Given a choice, a company will always prefer a bright individual with obvious potential. Fortunately for those individuals with low GPAs, there are other ways to measure both smarts and potential. Here is how to offset a lower GPA and remain competitive for the position.

Should you find yourself in an interview where your GPA is being discussed, it is important to understand why that subject is on the table. Although it is possible the interviewer is using the GPA as a filter to reduce the field of candidates, it is unlikely in this case because the interviewer had an opportunity to apply the GPA filter before meeting you. It is more likely that the interviewer is attempting to gauge your potential and brainpower.

If your GPA is not a good indicator of your potential or intelligence, you must influence the interviewer to use different measuring sticks.

What do you have in your background that will show you are smarter and/or have more potential than your GPA would indicate?

For example, how have you performed in other academic endeavors? Perhaps you have additional coursework with strong academic performance. How well did you do in professional schools or technical training? How about the results on standardized tests? Did your GPA improve significantly between your freshman and senior years? Maybe you can use that information to satisfy the interviewer's concern. If your GPA lets you down, consider using your performance record. Top-notch job performance evaluations, awards, citations, and accolades will not only show a track record of success, but also indicate future potential. A history of stellar performance indicates the likelihood of more of the same.

The possible damage of a lower GPA can often be mitigated by the circumstances under which it was attained. Allowances are sometimes made for people who were employed while they were attending school. Being responsible for dependents or recovering from illness might cause one's academic performance to suffer. Involvement in extracurricular activities, such as campus leadership, varsity athletics, or community activism might also soften the impact. One tactic that rarely works is justifying your low GPA because of the supposed difficulty of the course of study or rigorous academic demands of the school. Maybe you could not maintain a 3.0 in astrophysics at Caltech, but what about those who could?

At the college level, what about your GPA in your major? For some people there is a marked difference between their overall academic performance and their GPA when computed on only those courses in their major. This sword has two edges, however.

For example, you have an overall GPA of 2.49 and a GPA in your major of 3.12. On the upside, consider how well you can do when you are very interested in or have an affinity for the subject matter. The impact can be even more positive if these courses are relevant to the job for which you are being considered. On the downside, getting an A or B in a course that really matters to you while getting a C or D when it does not could send an even worse signal to employers than the one indicated by your overall GPA: that you are unwilling to apply yourself in areas you find dull or difficult.

In summary, keep in mind why GPA matters to some companies. Although it is *one* sign of brainpower and potential, it is not the *only* one. Your goal is to convince the interviewer to consider alternative indicators of these traits, ones that improve your standing and increase your odds of success in the interview.

10. How Much Are You Worth?

One of the hottest issues in changing careers is money, specifically the starting wages or salary offered by a potential employer. Before entering the job market it is important for separating military personnel to understand the differences between a salary in the commercial marketplace and their military paychecks.

Consider the compensation methodology used by the military. Generally, the longer you are in, the more you are paid—time in service, time in grade (TIS/TIG). Although your on-the-job performance influences whether or not you will be promoted to the next pay grade, your base pay has more to do with TIS/TIG than it does with your performance or the value of your contributions.

There are several add-ons to many military paychecks and some are more easily quantified than others. These include basic and variable allowances for quarters (BAQ/VAQ), basic allowance for subsistence (BAS), variable housing allowance (VHA), overseas housing allowance, and overseas cost-of-living adjustments. As with base pay, this is paid independent of performance, based instead on factors such as rank, TIS/TIG, marital status, and geography.

For some personnel, there are additional paycheck components that are independent of TIS/TIG or performance considerations. These include flight pay, airborne pay, dive pay, sea pay, sub pay, combat pay, hazardous duty pay, and retention bonuses offered in communities like aviation and nuclear power. Again, these add-ons are not based on performance. This evaluation gets tricky when we consider indirect compensation, such as the value of medical benefits, the discounts available at base or post retail and recreational facilities, the GI Bill, and the future value of retirement benefits.

Now, let's flip the coin and review paychecks in the private sector. In commercial, for-profit organizations, in most cases:

Employees are paid based on the value they add to the company.

This method of compensation is easily illustrated when the employee is an individual contributor. Consider sales representatives who are paid on commission. Their income is directly tied to personal production and performance since their paycheck is calculated as a percentage of the sales revenue that they generate.

Determining *value added* is not so easy when measuring the contributions from team members and team leaders, in which case the results are often indirect or non-monetary in nature. Regardless, for-profit organizations do their best to measure each individual's productivity and contribution to the mission. Although this measurement or valuation is the major component of the paycheck, there are lesser components. Similar to military compensation, things like longevity, cost of living, and retention incentives do influence a civilian paycheck.

Keep in mind also that many civilian employers offer benefits that may or may not resemble those offered by the military. These include health insurance, life insurance, retirement plans, stock options, and tuition assistance. Those benefits and their value vary significantly from one company to the next and exceed the scope of this discussion. However, you will need to compare the various compensation and benefits packages with each other and with your total military compensation as you evaluate your options.

Now that we have compared the methodology and components of military and commercial paychecks, let's get to the heart of the matter—how much are you worth? What will you be paid? Without knowing you and your background, I cannot answer that question. What I can do however is help you arrive at an estimate.

Take your current gross pay (CGP), subtract out proficiency pay (PROP), retention bonuses (RB), and your AQ (BAQ or VAQ). Add in the tax advantage on your BAS (TABAS) and the result is X, where:

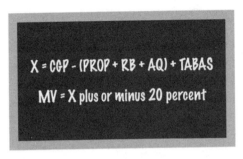

$$X = CGP - (PROP + RB + AQ) + TABAS$$

$$MV = X \text{ plus or minus } 20 \text{ percent}$$

MV equals your market value in the corporate sector, but notice the 20 percent spread on either side. Whether it is plus or minus depends on several factors. How relevant is your military experience to the job? More relevance equals more money. How much will it cost to train you? Training costs might be reflected in your paycheck. Is the proficiency pay you subtracted directly related to the new job? If so, add it back in. If not, forget about it. What is the cost of living at the job location? Are people with your education and/or military specialty in high or low demand? Who pays for the benefits, you or the company? Is the company stable, shrinking, or growing? Most important, are you being hired for your experience or potential or, best of all, a combination of both?

What about those tricky indirect influences mentioned earlier? Depending on the job and the company, there may or may not be a benefits package. If there is one, it will differ from the military version in both content and cost. It may be totally funded by you, totally funded by the company, or, most likely, a blending of the two. Resist the temptation to adjust the value of X until you know the value of the benefits package at your new company.

As to retirement, this is pretty much a nonissue. If you choose to leave the military before you have qualified for retirement, then you are also choosing to leave that benefit behind. You should not expect a civilian employer to add something to your paycheck because of that choice. If this issue is a significant one for you, then you have three choices. One, reconsider your decision to get out. Two, stay in the reserves and continue to accumulate retirement points. Three, focus your search on federal or state government employment where your military TIS will carry over to the new retirement plan.

As you can see, not only are we comparing an apple to an orange, but we must also consider the variety of each in the process. Regardless, keep in mind that there is much more to compensation than just the paycheck.

If you expect your current pay to be reflected in your first civilian paycheck, then you must convince your next employer that you will be just

as valuable to that organization on your first day of employment as you were to the military when you separated.

11. Will You Relocate?

Many résumés include the phrase "willing to relocate" at or near the end of the document. Although it is frequently used to mark the end of the résumé, it is surprising how people often include the phrase without understanding what it actually means. When used appropriately, it can be an asset in your search. Inappropriate usage may create problems.

Military personnel have a reputation for being flexible. Companies that like to hire veterans will mention this flexibility among the reasons they find that group attractive. Included in this label is geographic flexibility. Most military

people change duty stations every two or three years throughout their careers. Many of these moves require a geographic displacement. After four to twenty or more years of this lifestyle, you have obviously learned *how* to relocate. Perhaps you should ask yourself if you *want* to market that skill.

Before we dig any deeper into the meaning of "willing to relocate," consider how relocating in the business world differs from the military version. First, once you are working for a company, the relocation is almost always due to a promotion, i.e., more responsibility and more money. Second, the company usually covers more of the relocation expenses than would the military. Although there will always be emotional pain associated with a relocation, it is nice to know that the financial pain will be lessened. Third, unlike the military, where colonels relocate as often as privates, the frequency of relocation in the civilian sector may decrease as your career advances.

The phrase "willing to relocate" tells the reader that you are prepared to move from the town in which you currently reside and that you would not automatically discount additional relocations to support your career. Depending on the company and the nature of your job, this might mean relocating more or less frequently than you did in the military.

In summary, if both of these conditions apply to you, add the "willing to relocate" phrase to your résumé. This flexibility will make you attractive to many companies and help separate you from the crowd. Otherwise, leave it off. There are better ways to indicate to the reader that he or she has reached the end of your résumé.

The preceding chapters address filters individually, but there are many times when more than one filter is applied to the same system.

Different filters are used to eliminate different kinds of things. In the case of multiple filters, another important factor comes into play—sequence. In most cases in a multi-filtered system, some of the filters are more important than others.

Given that, which filter should be used first and which should be applied furthest downstream in the system? The most important, or critical, or nonnegotiable one always goes in first and the one that is nice to have but not required is used at the end. Here is an example to illustrate.

XYZ Company wants to hire a veteran to work on a security contract in Iraq. An active Top Secret clearance is preferred, but not required. The service branch is somewhat flexible, but there is a strong preference for either Marine Corps or U.S. Army. The company runs an ad for this job in *Stars and Stripes* and posts it on Monster.com. Bob, the company recruiter, ends up with one hundred résumés equally distributed among the service branches. Bob needs to narrow it down to ten before any face-to-face interviews occur. To that end he pushes these résumés through the three filters—service branch, clearance, and location. However, to maximize the odds of ending up with the ten most viable candidates, the filters must be applied in a specific sequence.

Of the three, only one is nonnegotiable—the job is in Iraq, and only in Iraq, so unless the candidate will live in Iraq there is no need to go any further. Although the Iraq requirement was advertised up front and in theory all of those who responded are already open to that, Bob is smart enough to know that in theory is not good enough and that he must verify this nonnegotiable requirement. After a series of e-mails and phone calls, he eliminates half of the résumés. Bob now applies his second most important filter—service branch. Of the fifty remaining résumés, twenty are either Marine Corps or army. Finally, Bob looks at security clearance information on those twenty surviving résumés and finds ten with active TS clearances. Filtering completed and mission accomplished!

How do you use this information? Remember that when recruiters are busy screening résumés, reading cover letters, reviewing application forms, conducting telephone screenings, or interviewing, their mission is to find reasons to say no. They use the aforementioned filters to accomplish this task. Your mission therefore becomes one of survival. Be as flexible as possible and do your best to pass through those filters, but never at the cost of misrepresenting yourself.

Here are two effective techniques:

- Consider using the **FRO** response: **For the right opportunity, I would . . .** For example, your response to a question about your willingness to relocate is "Given the right circumstances, I could most certainly make that work." In the end it is you who gets to define the word "right."

- Answer with a range rather than an absolute whenever possible. For example, if the salary for the job is advertised as $48,000 to $52,000, then your response to the salary question is "I am targeting something in the $51,000 to $54,000 range." That $1000 overlap between the two keeps the door open and minimizes the chances of the salary filter being used against you. Similarly, if your geographic preference is focused on a particular city but you are flexible, then respond to the geography question with "the Southeast region" rather than "Atlanta."

In summary, as you compete for interview opportunities and jobs, remember the importance of filters, both theirs and yours.

Employers look for reasons to say no before they look for reasons to say yes.

Keeping that in mind, you can avoid being eliminated before they have a chance to meet you. They must meet you to discover the reasons they should hire you.

The employer is not the only one who has access to this filtering process. In the next two chapters you will learn how you, the job seeker, can also use them in your search.

12. Filters, Part Two (Yours)

Employers do not have exclusive rights to the use of filters. You should use them also. Your purpose is similar to that of a potential employer—to eliminate as early in the process as possible any opportunities that will not work for you. This allows you to focus your efforts and resources on finding the ones that are compatible.

Candidates tend to use fewer filters, at least in the early stages of their searches. Most focus on the big three, each of which is inherent in the following three questions:

- What kind of a job is it?
- How much does it pay?
- Where is the job located?

For some people there are personal considerations that dictate the use of additional filters. For example, some people refuse to do shift work, or will not take a job with overnight travel, or suffer from a medical condition that precludes a particular working environment.

Knowing your filters in advance will influence your decision about whether or not to interview for a particular opportunity. In theory, if you have specific or minimally acceptable answers to the questions listed above and the opportunity fails to pass through those filters, then there is no need to pursue that job. In reality, you might not have access to some or all of that information in advance and will have to rely on the interview to fill in the blanks. There is nothing wrong with learning as you go, as long as you reveal your nonnegotiable issues as early in the process as possible. The following example illustrates how one job seeker applies multiple filters to his benefit.

Navy Chief Petty Officer Richard Williamson is a machinist mate with experience in HVAC systems stationed in Norfolk, Virginia. His wife is a civilian attorney with a firm in Virginia Beach. They have recently bought a home and their two children attend the local high school. Richard is two months away from retiring, has completed the navy's Transition Assistance classes, and is searching for a job. His search includes three primary criteria: one, he wants to continue his career in the HVAC field; two, because of his wife's job, the new home, and his children and their school, he is unwilling to relocate; three, he wants to match his current compensation.

He registers for a job fair being held in nearby Hampton, Virginia, and is pleased to learn that there will be more than fifty potential employers in attendance. When Richard arrives at the job fair he discovers that among the attending companies, there are ten with openings that target his background, four of which list acceptable salary ranges. He also learns that nine of those ten companies have already reviewed his résumé and requested to see him that day. He attends group presentations for each of those nine and discovers that only two of them (*ABC* Company and *DEF*, Inc.) have openings in the local area known as Tidewater and one of those two, *ABC*, is advertising a salary below his target.

What should Richard do first? Among his three primary criteria, only one is nonnegotiable and that is location—he will not relocate. Given that only two of his target companies can accommodate that requirement, there is no need for him to waste time with the other eight. He first approaches the *DEF* booth and makes his pitch. He then heads over to meet the people at the *ABC* exhibit. Richard interviews well and both companies ask him to follow up with them the next week. Now what? Well, he could call it a day and go home, but he would be better served to talk to the other eight companies on his initial list of ten with the hope that maybe they will have something in the local area in the future.

It is important to identify and apply your filters appropriately, and the subject matter in the next three chapters will assist you in doing so.

13. Quality of Life vs. Quality of Work

One of the reasons for leaving the service most often cited by military personnel is quality of life. If this applies to you, it would be prudent to use it as one of your filters as you search for civilian employment and evaluate job offers.

Although you might hear and use the phrase quality of life (QOL) often, have you ever stopped to consider what it actually means? Start by distinguishing it from its sister phrase, quality of work (QOW).

QOL addresses issues beyond the workplace. Where you live, your commute, personal time for family, schools, hobbies, interests, community service, and cost of living are among those elements that influence most people's QOL.

QOW deals with the internal elements of the job, including working conditions and environment, job satisfaction, corporate culture, coworker relationships, advancement opportunity, etc.

There is a close connection between QOL and QOW. The work you do will have a direct effect on your QOL. Work hours, job pressures, salary, benefits, holiday and vacation policy, out-of-town travel, and job satisfaction have both a direct and indirect impact on your QOL. Conversely, your mental, physical, spiritual, and financial health away from the job will affect your QOW.

In the most basic form, QOL involves two issues—where you live and how much money you make. These are interconnected through geography and cost of living. How does a starting salary of $75,000 in Manhattan sound to you? Well, are we talking about Manhattan, Kansas, or Manhattan, New York City?

For many people, the most significant component of quality of life is where they live, especially when families are involved. Because this is such an emotional and personal issue, it would be foolish to discount location as a job search criterion. Although geographic flexibility is an asset, personal situations dictate whether you can or cannot be flexible. In either case, the geographic filter comes into play.

Telling the interviewer you are open to any location and willing to relocate as often as necessary is an excellent tactic—*as long as it also happens to be true*. No one is truly open. Human beings care where they live, and not all locations are going to be compatible. We fall under subjective influences daily and have little choice but to react to them. For example, you might be open, but does your family also feel that way? Accordingly, you *should* allow geographic location to influence your decision. However, implicit in the word "decision" is choice, and until the offers are on the table, your choices are limited.

Almost everyone allows location to influence a job search. *When* this filter is applied is critical.

Using geographic filters at the beginning of the search will decrease the number of opportunities available. It is to your advantage to use these filters *at the end of your search*, as a final qualifier or tiebreaker. Hopefully it becomes a nonissue—you end up with an A-grade opportunity in an A-grade location. If you are not so fortunate, at least you have increased your odds of having an A-grade opportunity somewhere.

14. Educational Background Check

Should I supplement my existing education before I separate from the service or begin my job search?

I hear that question frequently and I almost always answer it the same way—maybe yes, maybe no. The answer is yes if your current educational profile causes you to be filtered from consideration for a job you really want. The answer is no if you already pass through that filter.

To find out which answer applies to you, you should do an educational background check. This background check addresses two issues: your current educational inventory and your motivations.

An understanding of where you are must precede the question of where you want to go.

EDUCATIONAL INVENTORY

Let's start with what is already in your educational inventory. List high school and post–high school formal and informal academic, professional, and technical training. Indicate whether or not courses were completed, degrees were conferred, certificates were awarded, or requirements were met. Include in this inventory both the basics and specifics of the courses of study and indications of academic success or accolades. Beyond the official curricula and coursework, try to identify what you actually learned.

Most military personnel accumulate an extensive array of specialized training during their time in the service. There are many instances where that training can be converted to civilian educational credits. A useful tool to determine this is the *Guide to the Evaluation of Educational Experiences in the Armed Services*. You can learn more about this online guide at www.militaryguides.acenet.edu.

MOTIVATION

Why are you thinking about enhanced education? There are many reasons to pursue that goal and it is important for you to identify yours. Here are a few to consider:

- Your prospects for promotion during your military career will improve.
- You have a strong interest in a particular field and want to learn more.
- Your academic performance thus far has been poor and this second chance will allow you to redeem yourself.
- You have never really enjoyed any of your academic pursuits and you want to give it one more try.
- Your academic profile is incomplete and now is a good time to fix it.
- You fear that your academic profile is insufficient to get you a good civilian job.
- There is a job or career path that interests you but your current educational profile lacks the credentials to get you there.
- You are not ready to make decisions about your future, and going back to school allows you to delay those decisions for a while without creating a hole in your résumé.
- You have GI Bill education benefits and would hate to waste them.
- You are searching for meaning in your life, and maybe spending more time in an academic environment will help you find it.

Review the list. Which ones apply to you? Which ones are actually relevant to enhancing your professional or career development? Maybe there are additional reasons to consider.

Now that you have completed your inventory and identified your motivators you can better judge the importance of, or need for, additional time in the classroom. Do you have a general or specific employment goal in mind? You may need to do some research to determine the educational and training qualifications necessary for consideration in that field. Look at your educational inventory to see if you are currently qualified.

For example, you want to be an architect. Do you have at least a bachelor's degree in architecture? If you have the requisite academic qualifications in place and they are not outdated, you are all set. If you do not, and if you are focused on and passionate about that field, you really have no choice but to go back to school and get those credentials. The same can be said for other specific positions, such as network engineer, emergency medical technician, corporate financial analyst, etc. However, consider a more general classification, such as inventory manager. Will your existing academic profile and professional experience give you access to that field or will you need additional academic credentials to be competitive?

There are additional factors. Consider the cost of an academic break in your career, both direct (tuition, books, lab fees, living expenses, health care) and indirect (lost income). Are you making selfish decisions or are there dependents to consider? In some cases this will be like starting over. Are you willing and/or able to do that at this point in your life?

Some people offset the cost factor by utilizing programs that are sponsored by the military, the federal government, or the private sector. Although tuition assistance and military funded programs are available, the payback requirements have to be considered. The GI Bill and similar college funds can help. Many companies will pay for college courses and technical training, and there may or may not be payback requirements. Regardless of the funding source, you would be wise to remember:

Many people spend a lot of time and money to supplement their education and training only to find themselves in jobs for which they were already qualified. Do your homework before you go to class. Identify your goals and motivations. Conduct your academic inventory. Com-

pare the two and see if supplemental education or training is necessary at this point in your professional life.

Although it is impossible to provide a simple answer to the opening question in this chapter, conventional wisdom does offer a basic rule of thumb. If your current academic inventory and professional experience give you access to something you want to do, put off any additional academic endeavors for now and go do it. Reevaluate your professional direction after a couple of years and, if necessary, make a course adjustment through modification of your academic profile.

On the other hand, if you are highly focused on a specialty for which you are not currently qualified or competitive and you have the financial resources and support systems in place, go back to school and fix the problem.

If you need to modify your education and training to get the job you want, then maybe there is time to do that before you get out of the military. This may influence the timing of your separation or retirement. Whether or not that is the case, now would be a good time to take a look at your transition timeline—the subject of the next chapter.

15. Transition Timeline

How far in advance of your last day in the military would you like to have your new job lined up? You will probably answer that question in terms of a number of months. Now, take a guess at how much time it takes on average for a civilian company to fill an opening with a civilian employee? Keep in mind that I am talking about the elapsed time from the day that company decides to fill that job until the day that new employee starts work. *Six weeks!*

Does that mean that you will have to wait until your countdown reaches forty-two days before you can even start to interview? Maybe yes, maybe no. The answer is yes if you are targeting a company with little or no history of hiring separating military personnel. The answer is no if you focus instead on companies that have hired people like you before, in which case you can extend that lead time out to three or four months. Four months may work when the economy is robust (plenty of jobs) and the supply of military job seekers (your competition) is low. Three months is better when the economy weakens or the supply increases.

An advertised availability date outside that window is a negative for most companies and you could be rejected solely for that reason. At the three- or four-month point your availability becomes a neutral. Inside of three months they start to smile—your availability has become an asset.

Unlike the uncontrollable factors that influence the outcome of your job search, you may have some control when it comes to your timeline. Although it is hard to wait, doing so might increase your marketability and enhance your chances of success.

However, just because the interviewing phase of the search should not start until the three-month point, it doesn't mean that there is nothing for you to do outside that window. Here are some general guidelines.

To illustrate, let's say that you have eighteen months remaining in the military. Although the three-month interviewing phase (months 3, 2, and 1) is fifteen months away, the preparation and readiness phase begins now. Take that fifteen-month period and divide it into thirds: months 18–14, 13–9, and 8–4.

Dedicate months 18–14 to gathering information. You accomplish this primarily through reading. In fact, reading this book means you have already started and your timing is perfect. You should also read business periodicals, newspapers, and additional self-help books on the subject of transition. I also encourage you to visit websites, research companies, and set up information interviews (discussed in section VII). Talking with friends, relatives, or associates with work experience outside of the military is a great resource, especially if they are knowledgeable about a field in which you have significant interest.

Months 13–9 in the countdown are dedicated to the mechanical, external, or physical preparations that are discussed in section IV. The beauty of these preparations is that, for the most part, they can be done in advance and stored in the closet. When it comes time to interview, you can pull them out, dust them off, tweak them a bit, and you are good to go.

The most important preparations are intentionally saved for last, ensuring that they remain fresh in your mind when the interview phase begins. During months 8–4 in the countdown your focus should be on section V of this book, which is dedicated to those internal or mental preparations and exercises that are the make-or-break factors in a job search. This five-month period is also a great time to press the start button on your self-marketing campaign (section IV) and fine-tune your interviewing skills (section VI).

Please note that my choice of the eighteen-month window is just an example. Although the interviewing phase (three months or less) is more or less fixed, you can commit as much or as little time as you have to the phases leading up to that. You do not need fifteen months to ready yourself and prepare. In fact, you could get it all done in fifteen days if necessary, although I would not recommend it.

SECTION II.
THE SELF-DISCOVERY ZONE

The first section got you started on the important issues dealing with the *Where*, *Why*, and *How* of your transition and job search. Now it is time to focus on the *What*. Depending on your branch of service and specialization, your military experience has made you an expert in something. Included in that expertise is a skill set and a vocabulary that may or may not be appropriate in your new career. You have a lot to learn before your search begins. There is much to think about, and section II will point you in the right direction.

As you read these chapters, you will:

- Take a tasks and skills inventory.
- Learn about the hidden job market.
- Recognize the importance of exploring the unknown.
- Figure out what size organization fits you best.
- Learn how to recognize the best job.
- Become aware of a different bottom line.
- Explore two special situations.

16. From Trees to Toilet Paper

Most job hunting experts recommend that you determine what you want to do before you begin interviewing. Well, I both agree and disagree. For civilians, that advice is likely valid. However, for military personnel without civilian work experience:

A job search is as much about educating yourself as it is about finding a job.

To illustrate, allow me to share with you a personal experience. I was a surface warfare officer and I was trying to figure out what I wanted to do when I got out of the navy. After consulting with friends and family, reading several books, and seeking the guidance of a recruiter, I determined that my division officer assignments had best prepared me for a production management position in the civilian sector. Focusing my search on that type of position, I was fortunate enough to pass a screening interview with a major consumer products company and was invited to a second-level interview at the site.

During the flight from Norfolk, Virginia, to Scranton, Pennsylvania, I had plenty of time to think about the interview and the job. The company I was about to visit called the position "team manager" and it seemed right up my alley: responsibility for twenty-five tradesmen, including training, performance, safety, quality, maintenance, and the management of the associated financial and material resources. Throw in a couple of deployments and "U. S. Navy division officer" would have been an apt title. Before my plane landed, I pretty much knew that this was the job for me.

Early the next morning, a representative from the plant, my sponsor for the day, met me for breakfast. I quickly learned that he was also a former navy surface warfare officer. He was open and friendly and encouraged me to ask questions. The time we spent together at breakfast and during the forty-minute drive to the facility was both helpful and enlightening.

The facility was impressive—more than a mile long, all under one roof. My interview consisted of slowly walking the length of the facility, interviewing with team leaders, department managers, the plant manager, and technicians along the way. What an education I received that day. At one end of the plant, freshly cut timber was being off-loaded from trucks. At the other end of the plant, delivery trucks were loaded with the freshly produced and packaged toilet paper.

If the goal of a second interview is to get an offer, then I had a successful day. Before departing, my sponsor escorted me to the personnel office, where the plant manager offered me the job. After agreeing to respond to the offer within two weeks, I returned to the airport.

Once again, the flight gave me plenty of time to think. As I reviewed my day I realized how educational it had been. I now knew four things that I had not known on the flight up. First, I knew how to turn trees into toilet paper—a fascinating process and much more complex than it sounds. Second, I knew that you should never wear a navy blue suit to a paper mill—I looked like Frosty the Snowman at the end of the day! Additionally, I found out that I was capable of receiving a job offer and that at least one company would have me. And, finally, to my surprise, I knew I did not want to be a production team leader.

I called my recruiter. He was excited to hear that the company had extended an offer, but he was surprised to learn that I would be turning it down. I told him that although I felt highly qualified to be a production manager, once I found out what it really was, I was not all that interested. Parts of the job were great. The team building, the coaching, and the ability to improve processes were appealing. I could see that for the right person, it would be an excellent opportunity with a highly respected company. That person, however, was not me.

Although the similarities between division officer and production team leader pulled me toward production management in the beginning, those same similarities made me realize that being excellent at something will only serve you and the organization in the short run. I also realized that:

You must add passion and job satisfaction to excellent performance to make it last.

Although highly competent in the position, I had not been passionate about being a division officer and I had not been personally satisfied in that role. How could I now possibly commit to what was basically the civilian equivalent?

What happened between my flights up and back? Yes, a successful interview was accomplished. More important, I had received an education. I learned about production management and how impressive a world-class company can be in both its interviewing process and its operations. I also learned more about myself. Being qualified is important, but being qualified *and* interested is even more important.

Sometimes the process is as important as the result. Think of your job search as an information gathering process, a by-product of which, if thorough and successful, will be offers of employment. Some of these offers will be appealing and some will not. At some point, the bells will ring, the lights will flash, and you will know you have found the right job—one for which you are not only qualified, but in which you also have a high level of interest.

I was a bit naive and underprepared. I did not know it at the time, but most of what I learned about myself during that experience was available to me in advance of the interview. I should have done a better job in one particular area—researching myself. The Lifetime Tasks and Skills Inventory in the next chapter would have been a big help.

17. Lifetime Tasks and Skills Inventory

Many people struggle with figuring out what they want to do in their post-military career. What kind of company is best for them? What sort of career path should they target? What civilian job would be the best place to start? These are all important questions, but do not put the cart in front of the horse.

Possibly the single most important element in a successful career change is self-knowledge. Beginning the journey without a thorough understanding of self is a recipe for failure. Before you can answer any of those questions you must be able to answer this one:

Who are you and what makes you tick?

You should begin your preparations with some in-depth soul searching. A thorough personal skills and interests survey will set the stage for a successful search. Gather together some writing materials and follow these steps.

Step One: Think back to your earliest memory of working for either money or to support a charitable cause. Perhaps it was a paper route, selling Girl Scout cookies, mowing lawns, babysitting, selling magazine subscriptions, or fundraising for Little League. Any chore, job, task, or assignment for which you volunteered or were paid belongs on this list. With that earliest memory as a starting point, brainstorm your way forward, through elementary school, middle school, high school, college, full- and part-time civilian work, your military assignments, and post-military experience. Include all primary, secondary, and collateral duties regardless of scope or significance.

Step Two: List all of these items individually under the category of Tasks. How many did you identify? For this exercise to be effective, you need to be thorough. If you do not have at least twenty-five tasks on your list, you are not trying hard enough. Be creative. Think outside the box. Maybe you need some hints: call your parents, look at your school yearbooks, review performance evaluations, or phone a friend.

Step Three: Create a form like the one below.

Step Four: Make as many copies of your form as you have tasks identified. Give each task its own page. Taking one page at a time, put on your thinking cap and fill out the form. It is important to be both thorough and specific. Watch out for all-encompassing words like "management." Such words can imply so much that they result in saying nothing. Although the *how* and the *why* are generally more important than the *who* or the *where*, do not discount the impact of the people with whom you interacted or the physical environment in which the task was being performed.

Step Five: Step away from this exercise for several days. Give your mind a chance to clear. Ride your bike, go for a run, go to the movies, read a book, take a walk, go to the gym. When you return to this exercise you should be able to add substance or detail to your answers.

Task: _____

1. How much enjoyment did I receive from doing this?

    A. What was it about this task that caused me to enjoy it?

    B. What about this task was disagreeable to me?

2. How successful or effective was I at this task?

    A. How or why was I successful in this role?

    B. To what can I attribute any lack of success or effectiveness?

Step Six: Review your forms and highlight any common denominators, trends, or tendencies, using a different color for each. What you end up with is your master set of personal traits, attributes, and characteristics.

Step Seven: Save your work.

Both the tasks and the analysis of each will serve you well, especially when the interviews begin. You will be much closer to articulating your job objective than you were prior to this exercise. After all, what better job is there than one at which you will be effective and from which you attain professional satisfaction?

Let's assume you are about to interview for a position called "project manager" with the *ALPHA OMEGA* Corporation. Having researched the company and with a basic understanding of the role of the project manager, you will be able to answer the interview question: "Why do you want to be a project manager for our company?"

Your answer will sound something like this: "I am very interested in the project manager role because I believe I have much to contribute, for example [fill in as appropriate from your answers to question two]. I also believe that role will be rewarding for me, because [fill in as appropriate from your answers from question one]."

When I finally got around to doing that exercise in my job search, one of the positive common denominators for me was the appeal of a smaller organization. Does size matter to you? The next chapter will help you answer that question.

18. What Size Company Is Best for You?

When you visualize yourself working in a civilian job, does the size of the company enter the picture? Large and small companies each offer both advantages and disadvantages. You should consider these while conducting your job search and again before making a final decision.

Many veterans express an interest in working for a smaller company after they leave the military. The Department of Defense (DOD) is one of the largest organizations in the world, and many people are interested in trying something less bureaucratic and less structured. As a result, those individuals might shy away from the bigger, brand name–associated companies like Procter & Gamble, Ford Motor Company, IBM, General Electric (GE), and others. Depending on their motivation, this could be a mistake.

Much as the navy's submarine service is a relatively small and specialized subsidiary of a parent company, the DOD, major corporations like those mentioned above are often collections of subsidiaries under a corporate umbrella. In the case of GE, these subsidiaries are referred to as business units, and they operate with more autonomy than military service units receive from DOD. On the surface, leaving DOD to work for GE sounds like trading one huge bureaucracy for another. Beneath the surface (pun intended), leaving the submarine service to work for GE Energy could feel much different. You might discover that the corporate culture of the smaller business unit defeats the stereotype of working for great big GE.

The idea of working for a small company can be appealing. Smaller often means less bureaucracy, more decision-making responsibility, and a higher likelihood of making a difference. Although much of that can be true, in some small companies the opposite situation occurs. Smaller sometimes means centralized decision-making at the top of the organization. If the reins are held too tightly, then implementing change and having an impact can be difficult.

Whether or not your big company (*BIGCO*) and small company (*SMALLCO*) stereotypes are accurate or even important to you, there are many other issues to consider, such as:

- **Training and development.** *SMALLCO* might offer you more initial responsibility and, accordingly, have higher expectations of your ability to add value quickly. *BIGCO* is more likely to allow you to incubate for a while, spending money on your training and development before expecting to see results.
- **Benefits.** *BIGCO* has much better bargaining power with insurance companies than does *SMALLCO*, and is more likely to provide a better, cheaper, and/or more flexible benefits package. Similarly, *SMALLCO* is less likely to offer or contribute to a retirement plan.
- **Compensation.** *SMALLCO* will likely be your highest or lowest offer. Expect a higher salary if your learning curve is flat and your current skill set allows

you to contribute immediately; lower if you are brought on board as a high-potential rookie. *BIGCO* is likely to bring you in at the middle of that range— a reasonable starting salary that will grow as you climb the learning curve and your value added increases.

- **Stability.** *BIGCO* has experienced steady growth since its founding more than a hundred years ago. Two years ago, *SMALLCO* was a start-up. Which of the two is more likely to be around five years from now?

- **Growth potential.** *SMALLCO* is growing at 20 percent annually. *BIGCO* has averaged 9 percent growth during its lifetime. You are very good at what you do. At which company will you find better growth? Short-term? Long-term? Do not forget about stability.

- **Span of control.** Look at the classic pyramid organizational structure at *SMALLCO* and *BIGCO*. Find the block on the chart that represents you. Are you the big fish in a small pond or the small fish in a big pond? Which is more appealing?

- **Cross-functional mobility.** *BIGCO* has more divisions, more departments, and, at least on the surface, more options for lateral mobility. However, does the corporate culture accommodate cross-functional transfers? In *SMALLCO*, the marketing department is right next door to the distribution department. Physically, that is an easy move. Realistically, how often does it happen?

- **Level of responsibility.** Accept a job in production at *SMALLCO* and your business card says director of manufacturing. Take the equivalent position at *BIGCO*, and your card says production supervisor. The title alone, however, may not be an accurate reflection of the responsibilities associated with each position.

- **Relocation frequency.** Depending on the type of job and career path, *BIGCO* will require more relocation than *SMALLCO* as you climb the corporate ladder. Additionally, *BIGCO*'s relocation package may be more inclusive and its relocation policies more flexible.

- **Travel.** Assuming travel is an inherent characteristic of the job (sales, consulting, field tech rep), you will probably travel more often with *SMALLCO*.

- **Visibility.** Go to work for *BIGCO* and you might never meet a vice president. At *SMALLCO* the president could know you on a first-name basis.

- **Résumé enhancement value (REV).** Things do not always work out. You might have to go back into the job market. Which option looks better on your revised résumé? *BIGCO* will be the more recognizable of the two, but how marketable is that new skill set? Your depth and range of experience (and title) at *SMALLCO* are impressive, but where else might those things be applicable?

BIGCO or *SMALLCO*? Does size matter? These are simple questions with complicated answers. In the end if you are having trouble deciding, then go *BIGCO*. Why? Should you later decide otherwise, moving from *BIGCO* to *SMALLCO* is easier than the opposite transition. *SMALLCO* likes the fact that *BIGCO* has already dealt with the risks and spent its money on training and development. Start off at *SMALLCO* and many of the reasons that *BIGCO* once found you attractive will have disappeared.

However, as with many of the important issues in life, there is usually enough information present to support your decision regardless of your choice.

The key is to identify the issues that are important to you, weigh them, prioritize them, fill in the blanks as well as you can, make the decision, and go for it!

19. The Classifieds—More Than Meets the Eye

Are you still having trouble figuring out what you want to do? Although this indecision is often due to a lack of knowledge of the options and job titles available, it can also be attributed to an inability to accurately describe the characteristics of a job that would interest you. Recognizing and understanding the significance of those attributes is an important step in being able to add a job objective to a résumé. Here is an exercise that might help in the identification of those attributes.

This exercise involves one of the classic job-hunting techniques—reviewing the employment classifieds. Although it is rarely productive in terms of generating interviews and job offers, there is a benefit to perusing the classifieds on a regular basis. The following exercise will help bring that benefit to light.

Because I believe it to be more effective, these instructions assume an old-school approach. You of course have the option of using the Internet and the cut-and-paste feature of your word processing software as a substitute for the mechanical steps involved.

The first thing you need to do is set aside a part of your Sundays for the next few months. If you are not already receiving a Sunday paper, then consider a subscription. Some of us do not have the discipline to visit the newsstand every Sunday to buy the paper. This exercise also requires a few simple tools that you already have in your home—a highlighter, scissors, and a file folder.

1. Spread the entire employment section of the Sunday classifieds out on your kitchen table. The word "entire" is important because you should not eliminate any of them because of a lack of personal appeal or qualification.

2. Read each ad in its entirety. Should something in the ad grab your attention in any positive sense, circle it with your highlighter. Continue this process until you have reviewed the entire section.

3. Cut out each of the highlighted ads and place them in your file folder.

4. Repeat this drill every Sunday for a few weeks or months, depending on how far in advance of your availability you are doing this exercise.

5. After several weeks, dump all of your clippings on the table and, using your marker, go through each of them and highlight the word or phrase that caused you to save it in the first place.

6. Now it's time for some analysis. As you review all of the highlighted information, look for any trends or commonality. Does anything leap out at you? Perhaps most of what you saved indicates the need for strong analytical skills. Maybe the common denominator is incentive-based income. For many military personnel, leadership is often a central theme. It might also have to do with working environment. If many of the ads you saved reflect working outdoors, then there is probably a message in there somewhere.

This exercise will enhance your ability to discuss many of the elements of the right job for you. That is a critical step in figuring out what you want to do and putting it into words in the form of a job objective. And, who knows—somewhere in that pile of clippings just might be the job of your dreams.

20. What's Behind Curtain Number Three?

I estimate that half of the people who transition from military service to the civilian corporate sector end up working for companies and in jobs that, at the beginning of their search, they did not even know existed. How can this be the case?

In chapter 16 I shared with you part of my own military-to-civilian career transition. In that story I describe how the job I thought I wanted at the beginning of my search quickly fell from my list once I learned more about it through the self-education that accompanies interviewing. Here is another chapter in that story.

My job search was in full swing. The hiring market was strong, my résumé was generating a surprising amount of interest, and many interviewing opportunities came my way. Although most of those interviews resulted in job offers, I was not feeling particularly successful. As comforting as it was to be wanted, my lack of interest in any of those companies left me feeling empty.

After I rejected a series of job offers across a broad range of options, the president of the placement company that was representing me asked me why I was being so picky. I told him that through the process of interviewing I had learned enough about several of my options to know they were just not right for me. Interest level or lifestyle issues allowed me to eliminate manufacturing, operations, engineering, and consulting. Although I found myself focusing on either sales or human resources, none of my offers in those fields excited me.

I liked the independence, self-determination, and scoreboard aspects of sales, but I was not passionate about the products I would be selling. Human resources was appealing due to the helpful nature of the profession, but the starting salaries and career paths were unsatisfactory for me. I told the president I was beginning to think what I wanted did not exist. Is there a job that combines the appeal of both of these options? He smiled and said, "Well, there actually is a job like that—come to work for me."

I was stunned! I had been totally focused on the big-name companies and the traditional job titles. Being a sales rep for DuPont or working in personnel for Procter & Gamble was well within my field of vision, but me—a headhunter? Join a small, privately held company that twelve months ago I had never heard of, in an industry I barely knew existed, and in a job that had never crossed my mind? Was he kidding?

As I thought about it, I realized *that this was my job*. Recruiting is selling—convincing companies to hire military people and convincing military people that I could be of service to them. With respect to human resources, I remembered how much I enjoyed being in charge of my ship's personnel career development program and real-  ized that being a recruiter was similar. Instead of helping young seamen, airmen, and firemen qualify for specialized ratings in the navy, I could help men and women leaving the service learn about their private sector options and help launch their civilian careers.

Although I was not certain I was making the right choice, my confidence level was 90 percent. I felt that the risk of the remaining 10 percent was tolerable. If it turned out not to be the right opportunity for me, then it would still be a great job to have as I looked for something better. I took the plunge and became one of those people who end up working in something totally unexpected.

The moral of the story? You might know exactly what you want to do before your search begins and you go out and find it. However, allow for the possibility that the best job for you might lie behind curtain number three. Perhaps working for a large company with strong name recognition in a classic job title might be just the thing for you, but do not discount the hidden job market. Treat your job search as information-gathering and self-education. Look outside the box. Have faith that you will ultimately discover the best job for you.

21. Experience or Potential?

When you receive a job offer, your potential employer is saying that they want you on their team. They have appraised your qualifications and find you to be a good fit. They have gauged your interest in the job and the company as sincere and at a high level. They have ascertained your needs and expectations and believe they can keep you challenged and satisfied. Finally, they believe you are of a mind to accept.

If they are correct and you are inclined to accept, then you would be wise to first ask yourself this question: why are they hiring me? Knowing the answer will not only influence your decision but will also ensure you are going into your new job with the proper expectations.

Although the complete answer to the question above is complex and will vary from person to person, I will make it simple. That company wants to hire you for one of these reasons:

- They want you because of your experience.
- They want you because of your potential.
- They want you because of a combination of the two.

Which of those would you prefer to be the impetus behind the offer? Let's evaluate each of them.

EXPERIENCE

Being hired because of your experience gives you several advantages. Your learning curve is flat. Because you already know how to do the job, your start-up is less difficult and takes less time. You have relevant expertise, you know the language, and you are comfortable in the environment. You add value quickly. Combining that with the fact that there is little or no cost to train you could result in a higher starting paycheck. The risk for both you and the employer is lower. Neither party has to wonder whether or not you can do the job, because your experience shows that already to be the case. You know exactly what you are getting into, and those unexpected and unpleasant surprises that can occur in a new job are less likely.

POTENTIAL

There are many advantages to being hired for your potential. The employer cares about what *will be*, not what *has been*. Your future matters to the company. They can teach you what you need to know about the products and processes, but they cannot teach motivation—that has to come from within. They will invest a lot of money in your training and development. They expect and will wait for a return on that investment. For you, the chance to try something new and different is exciting. You will expand your mind and broaden your horizons. A new career stretches out before you.

A COMBINATION OF THE TWO

The majority of the companies that hire separating military personnel do so with the intention of getting both experience and potential in the same package. Your experience, whether it is directly relevant to the new job or not, is important because it shows work ethic and a track record of success—the demonstrated ability to get the job done. Your potential is an equally important attribute because most companies do care about both your present and future contributions. You want to be hired for a combination of the two. The learning curve needs to be steep, but not too steep. The paycheck needs to reflect both your ability to add value today and also the employer's willingness to invest in your future.

Caution: A question for those of you who are retiring from the military—are you looking for a new job or a new career? There is a difference between the two. Most civilian employers who hire retirees do so with the expectation that they are looking for a job rather than a career, which is not necessarily a bad thing. In fact, it might be a great thing if that is what you have in mind for yourself. However, some retirees, especially those who are in their late thirties and early forties, really do want to launch a second full career. If that describes you then be prepared to fight your way into being considered by the companies for your potential as a career employee.

22. The Best Job for You?

In the next section of this book we will discuss many of the common civilian jobs that are available and attractive to veterans. Before you read those chapters, take a minute to think about which job is best for you. How will you recognize it when you see it? Do not worry about job titles at this point. Instead, pay attention to the elements or attributes of the job, such as:

- **Enjoyment.** Will the job make you happy? Will you enjoy yourself during most of those long working hours? Will you find yourself itching to get to work and disappointed that the day passed so quickly? Although we never know until we actually get involved in the day-to-day aspects of the job, it is important to look for strong indicators of job satisfaction and enjoyment. Consider also the people with whom you will be working. Will you enjoy their company? Do they share your values and your work ethic? Your coworkers will have a major impact on the enjoyment you obtain from your profession.

- **Learning curve.** How long will it take to get up to speed and start making a contribution? Walking in the door with all the requisite skills and knowledge in place means your learning curve is flat and you are able to contribute immediately. Conversely, if you need a significant amount of training and development before your contributions start to kick in, you are looking at a steep learning curve. Which is the better choice? There is a strong temptation to opt for the flat curve. You already know how to do the job. It feels comfortable and you get up to speed quickly. One problem—boredom can set in just as quickly and the enjoyment factor takes a nosedive. Maybe the steep curve is a better choice. You will have both immediate and continuing challenges. However, if the curve is too steep, your progress will be so slow your employer will start to second-guess the decision to hire you. Your best bet is to find a learning curve in between these extremes—steep enough to provide a challenge but not so steep as to make your progress too slow or too difficult.

- **Value added.** Unlike the military, the business world determines compensation based mostly on value added. The salary you have negotiated reflects the company's prediction of the value you will add during the coming year. Exceed their expectations and get a raise. Fail to measure up and start working on your résumé. Make sure the job allows you to add value relatively quickly. In addition, this value needs to be visible. You could be the most valuable person on the team, but if the value you are adding is invisible, it will be difficult to receive any credit. Ideally, this visible value added will also be measurable—an important issue at your performance and salary review. Try to identify and document your value added so that you can make reference to it at your review.

- **Growth potential.** For growth potential to exist you have to be very good at what you do and your company must be growing. The presence of either one without the other will reduce or eliminate any opportunity for growth. Your best bet is to join a growing company. Is there a high demand for its products or services? Is it gaining market share? Are new products in the pipeline? Is it profitable enough to spend money on research and development? Being able to add value to a growing company will afford you tremendous growth potential.

- **Quality of life.** Will this opportunity give you and your family the quality of life necessary to keep everybody happy? Does the corporate culture seem to support this goal? Will you like where you live? Are the culture and the climate compatible with your needs? Is the compensation adequate to support the cost of living in that locale? Although it is impossible to answer these questions with certainty until you are actually working for the company and living in the community, you can reduce the risk by doing your homework and asking good questions in advance of accepting the offer.

To summarize, what is the best job for you? It is one in which you will **enjoy the work**, where the **learning curve** is neither too steep nor too flat, where you can **add visible, measurable value** in a **growing organization**, and in circumstances which will afford a high **quality of life** for you and your family. When you find one that meets all or most of these five standards, take it—your search is over.

23. Job Hunting from a Remote Location

According to the Defense Manpower Data Center of the Office of the Secretary of Defense, there were approximately 1.43 million service members on active duty as of June 30, 2011. Roughly 30 percent of those people were stationed or deployed outside of the continental United States. In other words, nearly half a million of our military personnel are in what I call remote locations.

As I mentioned in the introduction to this book, 200,000 or so service members leave the military every year. Although I have no way of knowing how many of those 200,000 were assigned to remote locations just before they separated or retired, I am confident in guessing they number in the thousands. For most of them, their military-to-civilian transition process will include a job search. Even under ideal circumstances a successful job search is no easy task, and doing a job search from a remote location is about as far from ideal as you can get.

Are you in that category now or is your next assignment likely to put you there? Have faith. There is hope. During my career, I placed more than three thousand military personnel into their civilian careers, and I estimate a third of them were in remote locations just before they got out. They did it, and so can you. The information in this chapter will enhance your chances when you start your search from a remote location.

Think about your job search as a two-phase operation; phase one is all about preparation and phase two is job searching and interviewing. Although being remote puts a major damper on your ability to interview, it has much less of an impact on the preparation phase. I direct your attention to the chapters in sections IV and V of this book, which focus on the mechanical and mental preparations necessary to support a successful job search. Being in Kabul vs. Ft. Campbell or Diego Garcia vs. San Diego puts you at no disadvantage as far as the information in those sections is concerned. The tempo of remote assignments and deployments typically runs hot and cold, and you can dedicate whatever downtime you have to your preparation phase. By the way, congratulations! The fact that you are reading or listening to this book, perhaps in a remote location, means you are already on board with this concept and have a head start on your competition.

Although the Internet allows you to do some searching while you are remote, it is unlikely this search will produce an actual interview, especially when the company discovers that you are thousands of miles removed from the job site. However, depending on the degree of remoteness, there are occasions when the potential employer comes to your turf. Some of the larger military installations in places like Europe, Asia, and Hawaii will often hold job fairs (see "An Employment Perfect Storm" in section IV) with company interviewers and hiring managers in attendance. Some of the private sector military recruiting firms (see "Headhunters" in section IV) will also host similar events in those locations.

More typically you will need to adjust your expectations and search for job prospects and interviewing opportunities you can pursue once your remote status changes. This is also an excellent time to research any companies that are of particular interest to you. As you will read in "Researching Companies" in section V, one of the most important preparations is learning *how* to do this type of research.

The key to a successful job search from a remote location is to eliminate the biggest obstacle—geographic
separation. Since it is highly unlikely that they will come
to you, you must go to them. This is true whether or
not your résumé has generated any interest in advance.
The only way the soldier in Kabul or the sailor in Diego
Garcia can compete with similarly qualified candidates
in Kentucky or California is to equalize the face time,
the mechanics of the interviewing process, and the costs
associated with interviewing and hiring.

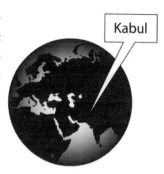

There are three ways to solve this problem, and the best one for you depends
on several factors, namely your timeline, your budget and risk tolerance, and the
attitude or policies of your commander. Here is a brief discussion of the three, all of
which assume the completion of as much of the phase one preparation as possible.

1. Save money, return to the continental United States (CONUS), out-process,
    sell back any unused leave, and then press the start button on phase two: job
    search and interviewing. This approach is the easiest but also creates the most
    risk. You will be conducting your search while unemployed, which means no
    paychecks for a while. This approach could also cost you some money in that
    when you sell back unused leave you do so at the base pay rate only.

2. Four to six weeks prior to your actual return to CONUS to out-process,
    schedule a two- to three-week leave period for the specific purpose of kicking
    off phase two. Check to see if you qualify for any transition leave or permis-
    sive temporary duty (PTDY) orders to support this. Assuming initial inter-
    views generate interest, you will explain to any potential employers that you
    will be back permanently in a few weeks to conduct second-level interviews
    and complete your search. When you return you can use or sell back any re-
    maining leave days and out-process accordingly.

3. Save as much leave as possible, supplement it with any available transition
    leave or PTDY, return to CONUS permanently, and conduct your search
    while on leave. This approach allows you to stay employed while your search
    is in progress. For many people this period of time can last as long as three
    months. You can then out-process just before you start the new job, or per-
    haps even draw two paychecks for a while—the new one and the one you
    draw until your leave runs out.

In section IV, I discuss how placement companies, headhunters, job fairs, and hiring conferences can add value to your job search. For the job seeker stationed in a remote location, those resources add even more value. Returning back to CONUS and getting interviews is not an easy process. It is difficult to generate interest in your résumé, concentrate interviewing activity in a specific location, make this happen in a relatively short period of time, and obtain real-time feedback and status reports from interviewers. Much of that difficulty can be eliminated by using the services of a placement company and/or hiring conference. Earlier in this chapter I mentioned the hundreds of remotely assigned military personnel I placed into their civilian jobs. Most of them first met their new employer at one of my company's hiring conferences.

A final thought on this subject. Remotely assigned job seekers can sometimes be *more* attractive to a potential employer than their CONUS-based competition. There are two reasons for this and both have to do with timing. First, they are typically interviewing with a much closer availability date. Second, they tend to react quickly to job offers and are more likely to say yes when they do.

24. The Geographically Restricted Job Search

Section I emphasized how both job seekers and employers use filters to eliminate mismatches and improve the potential for a good fit. One filter commonly used by job seekers is location—where is the job located and where will you live? Answer those questions and you end up in one of three categories. First, some people do not use this filter at all. For the right opportunity, they will live anywhere. Second, many people are fairly flexible but will admit to preferences. Third, there are those job seekers who for whatever reason can or will live in only one specific location. This third category creates a critical filter, which is the subject of this chapter.

There are many reasons for a geographically restricted job search: the employment of the spouse, special needs of a child, a requirement to care for elderly parents, the inability to sell a home, completion of an academic degree, and health or medical issues, to name a few. No matter why the restriction exists, the bottom line is this: the priority list must be adjusted. Most people put the job and the opportunity at the top, but for the geographically restricted job seeker, location trumps opportunity. There is a bit of good news. Because you are focused on one specific location, there is no need for you to waste time and money looking elsewhere. But the downside is significant.

Your marketability suffers when you cannot offer geographic flexibility. To compensate for this you have three choices:

1. Be more flexible in other areas.
2. Work harder than your competition.
3. Be clever or creative.

I strongly suggest you do all three. Here are some ideas for you. For the sake of discussion, say you have restricted your search to Cincinnati, Ohio.

- **Live there.** Long-distance area codes and unfamiliar zip codes are filters used by potential employers to reduce the stack of résumés. You improve your odds of finding a job in Cincinnati if you have the option of moving there before your interviews begin.
- **Act like you live there.** Should it not be feasible to move to Cincinnati before you have the job, then at least make it look like you live there. Perhaps there is a way for you to use a local address and phone number on your résumé. Check with family or friends to see if this might work. Be careful. Although listing that new cell phone number with the Cincinnati exchange on your résumé increases the odds of getting the phone call, be prepared for the caller's assumption that you could come in for an interview tomorrow.
- **Temporarily live there.** Use some of your separation leave or job-hunting TDY orders and camp out in that town for a week or two. Even if your résumé lists long-distance area and zip codes, your cover letter can inform the reader that you will be in the neighborhood for a specific time period.
- **Get flexible.** You cannot flex on geography so you need to flex elsewhere. Accept a higher amount of travel; work the second or third shift; take a lower starting salary; accept a longer commute; postpone the dream job until later in your career.

- **Read the newspaper.** Focus on the employment section of the classified ads in the major Sunday *Cincinnati Enquirer.* Subscribe to the print edition or read it online. In addition to looking for a job, pay attention to which companies are spending the most money (i.e., buying the most column inches of space) on advertising. Even if it appears that none of the ads apply specifically to you, a large number of ads could mean growth, and a growing company is a better target for you.
- **Consider veterans assistance.** Register with the Cincinnati area local offices of the county, state, and federal veterans assistance programs. Although some of these require you to walk in to register, many of them allow you access to their resources using the Internet and support services online.
- **Look up associations.** Are you a member of any professional or trade associations? Do they have a branch office in Cincinnati? How about a college or trade school alumni group? Many schools offer job-hunting assistance to their alumni. Depending on the size and location of the school, you just might find a Cincinnati-based chapter of your alumni association. Joining the local chapters and participating in their programs and social events is a great way to develop contacts in the area.
- **Join civic groups and volunteer organizations.** Once you are in the local area, consider joining organizations such as the Lions Club, Rotary International, Habitat for Humanity, and the like. Donating your time and talent to help your community will also allow you to expand your job search network.
- **Look at the map.** Just because you are restricted to Cincinnati does not mean you have to live there. Have you ever been to the Cincinnati airport? It is not in Cincinnati. It is not even in Ohio. It's across the river in Kentucky. It would be a mistake to discount a job in Covington, Kentucky.

No job search is easy. The geographically restricted job seeker makes a tough task even tougher. Before you launch this search, take another look to make sure this restriction is not actually a preference in disguise. If that is the case, then do yourself a favor. Do two job searches—the restricted variety as described above along with one that has fewer location restrictions. You might surprise yourself. However, if you must target one specific town, then remember the importance of flexibility in other areas, hard work, and a bit of creativity.

SECTION III.
THE OTHER SIDE OF THE FENCE

It is different out there in the civilian work world. The mission, the vocabulary, and the routine vary significantly from your current situation. Some things make sense; some do not. This section highlights these differences and opens your eyes to new possibilities.

As you read these chapters, you will:

- Explore the options.
- Clarify some terminology.
- Sanitize your vocabulary.
- Open some new doors.
- Figure out the right fit for you.
- Calculate your sales quotient (SQ).

25. What's Out There?

A job search is a stressful time for most people, and this is particularly true for those in transition from the military to civilian status. Although the job search can be difficult for civilians, at least they know the terminology and the titles. Military-to-civilian job seekers, on the other hand, not only have to deal with the stress of the search but also their lack of knowledge about career options and job titles.

What jobs are available? The good news is there are hundreds of companies hiring thousands of people like you into jobs with hundreds of possible job titles. The bad news is there are far too many of them to cover here. However, I can discuss the three general categories of jobs available and in so doing perhaps give you some insight into which category is best for you. Every one of those jobs can be categorized in one of three ways: **individual contributor, team member, and team leader.** Furthermore, every job you have held in the military can be similarly categorized.

- **Individual contributor.** In this case the individual makes a singular and personal contribution to the mission. The work product is his or hers alone. He or she is not directing the efforts of others. The blood, sweat, and tears are those of the individual. Do not confuse individual contributors with loners. Individual contributors can have much interaction with others, both internal and external to the organization. They enjoy autonomy. They do not have to supervise others to be fulfilled. They prefer to see a direct link between their individual effort, their work product, and, perhaps, their compensation. Examples of individual contributors include tradesmen, tech reps, journeymen, accountants, analysts, consultants, sales reps, and recruiters.
- **Team member.** Sometimes individual contributors band together, either formally or informally, and form a team. This leads us to the second category: team member. There are many situations where no one single person can handle all the responsibilities of a project, and it makes sense to assemble a team. Although levels of expertise are often similar, each member has a different area of expertise and is responsible for his or her own contributions to the

team as a whole. Whether or not there is a designated team leader, an informal leader will often emerge. However, it is the collective effort of the entire team that constitutes the contribution to the goals of the organization. An excellent analogy is the athletic team, where individuals playing different positions all share the goal of winning. You can find examples of the team member role in matrix organizations, companies that use self-directed work teams, product development, and brand management.

- **Team leader.** The team leader is assigned personnel, material, and financial resources. The areas and levels of expertise among the team members vary. The team leader sets the standards, builds the team, trains the team, motivates the team, and provides a safe working environment. The collective efforts of the entire team under the direction and control of the team leader become the contribution to the mission. Sound familiar? Most military personnel spend the majority of their time in team leader roles. Many civilian organizations are aware of this experience and focus on hiring veterans because of it. Some typical team leader roles include operations manager, crew leader, shop foreman, production team leader, and manufacturing supervisor.

Which category is best for you? To answer that question, review your time in the military. You have probably held jobs in all three categories. In which ones were you the most effective? Satisfied? Happiest? Answering those questions will give you some clues and the self-knowledge exercises in sections II and V ("Lifetime Tasks and Skills Inventory" and "Tell 'Em What They Want to Hear," respectively) will help. By knowing the role in which you tend to thrive, you will be on your way to finding the best category for you.

26. I Want to Work with People

Not too long ago, at a job fair targeting veterans, a recruiter from a major corporation asked an individual who was about to separate from the military what kind of job he was targeting. He responded, "Well, I would really like a job where I can work with people."

The recruiter frowned, shook her head and replied, "I am very sorry, but all of our openings this month involve working with kangaroos."

Ask most career counselors, recruiters, and interviewers for their pet peeves and you will often hear their disdain for the "work with people" response to the "what would you like to do" question. Unless they have been retained to search for people to work at the zoo, they already know that you want to work with people or you would not have applied for a position with their company. Although the candidate may use the phrase as a way of expressing a personal talent or preference, overuse has caused interviewers to treat it as simplistic, naive, or trite.

Even though the phrase is off-limits, the intended message in the phrase can be relevant and even powerful in an interview. Let's review each of the three words independently.

- **Work.** We know you want to work, but what kind of work interests you? What is your associated skill set? Can you identify the specific tasks at which you excel? Using your hands? Using your mind? In what environment do you thrive—a shop, an office, a factory floor, outdoors, or something else?
- **People.** It is hard to imagine a job that does not have other people in the picture. But what kind of people are you talking about? What type of experience do they have? Is there an educational component that is important to you? How about character and values? Specialists or generalists? Trainees or subject matter experts? Large groups or small teams? Colleagues or customers?
- **With.** I intentionally saved this one for last. In terms of interview content and self-expression, this is the most important of the three. What do you really mean when you say "with"? Define the word in the context that matters to you. Do you want to lead, supervise, or manage? Coordinate as a member of a team? Assist in solving problems? Guide careers? Train? Develop? Influence actions? Sell something? We could go on and on.

As you can see, that three-word phrase when used alone might not get you any points with the interviewer. Touching on one of his or her pet peeves is bad enough, but failing to get your point across is worse. Take the safe route. Decide what you really mean when you use each of those three words. Substitute your meaning and intent for those words and you will not only improve your interview skills but also enhance your chances of ending up in the right job the first time.

27. I Want to Be a Manager

Here is a quiz for you. If you review the text of every performance evaluation in your military record, what word, or form of that word, would appear most often? Give up? With a few exceptions, the answer is the **M** word and all of its various forms—manager, management, managerial, managing, manages, managed, etc. When you think about it, there is nothing earth-shattering in that revelation. Considering what people in the military actually do, everyone from a corporal to a general is paid in part to manage something. Keeping that in mind it should not surprise you to learn that when asked in an interview, "What do you want to do?" or "What type of job do you want?" most military personnel say, "I want to be a manager," or the equivalent.

As convenient as it is to have that word in your skills inventory and documented in your performance evaluations, its usage can cause more harm than good. Because the word "management" says so much, it might also say very little. Using it in any of its forms allows you to avoid saying what you really mean. You end up speaking in generalities and risk never getting specific with respect to your actual skills. This can be a problem in both the verbal and written portions of your search. Here is a drill to illustrate the point.

Assuming you have already written your résumé, go through it and remove the **M** word in all its forms. Now fill in the blanks with words or phrases that convey your intended meaning. What happened?

You will notice two distinct changes. Your résumé grew in length (not a good thing, so you will need to do some editing) and it became much more powerful in conveying your skills and attributes. Instead of "manage," you end up with words like coordinate, plan, control, liaise, lead, create, guide, develop, execute, prioritize, direct, and supervise. This same concept applies to your verbal responses in an interview. Avoiding use of the **M** word will force you to be more specific in both your presentation and in answering the interviewer's questions.

Caution: Do not go overboard. Complete sanitization of the **M** word from your résumé and speech is neither practical nor advised. Moderate usage is fine, especially when the word is being amplified or specified by another word or words. Inventory management, maintenance manager, and managerial economics are good examples. Most military people have much to offer the civilian sector in terms of their leadership and management experience. Just remember to focus more on the experience and less on the management.

28. Operations Management

Bring together a group of people. Make sure they are well trained and well equipped. Give them a clear understanding of the mission. Provide for a safe and ethical working environment. Set the example. Carry out the plan and strive for high-quality accomplishment of the mission. Sound familiar? For many military personnel, that could be a pretty good description of their jobs. It is also a fair description of what civilians call *operations management.*

There are many similarities between team leadership in the military and operations management in the civilian sector. I estimate that more than half of the people leaving the military end up in operational positions when they get out. Although they will have much to learn in the way of systems, methods, technology, vocabulary, and organizational structure, their operations management tools in their toolbox are already well honed and ready to be applied.

Given the similarities, you might strongly consider operations management in the civilian sector. There are, however, some significant ways in which the military and civilian versions differ. Knowing these differences beforehand could make you either more or less interested in that option. Regardless, be assured that the companies that like to hire military personnel into operations management positions are aware of the differences and they will use the interview to make sure you are prepared for the change.

Although the differences are many, here are the three most important issues to consider: ownership of your team, less hierarchy, and the bottom line.

- **Ownership of your team.** In the military, a group leader is never off duty when it comes to his or her people. It is a 24/7 job. Just because the working day is over does not mean the responsibility ends. This level of ownership is not the case in the civilian work force. Your people are only your people when they are on the job. What they do when they are not at work is not the responsibility of their supervisor. The exception, of course, is when what they do off the job has an impact on their performance at work.
- **Hierarchy.** In the military, there are usually many layers in the organizational structure, or many links in the chain of command. For example, in a typical navy division, the machinist's mate works for the work center supervisor who works for the leading petty officer who works for the leading chief who works for the division officer. That means three layers separate the boss from the wrench turner. The civilian version of that division would be much flatter. The mechanic would report directly to the maintenance supervisor, although there might be one additional link (e.g., the shop foreman).
- **The bottom line.** In the military, at least in times of peace, the bottom line is operational readiness. Military leaders care about mission accomplishment, quality, and safety. Civilian operations managers also care about these goals, but they have an additional goal that military leaders can ignore. The bottom line in the corporate sector is profit, i.e., making sure there is more money in the till at the end of the accounting period than there was at the beginning.

If the military version of operations management is one of your strengths, you should consider the civilian version as a way to launch your new career. Keep in mind that in the civilian version you will have little say in the behavior and lives of those you supervise when they are not at work, that you will be much closer to the actual work that gets done, and that you will have to change your bottom line approach from readiness or war-fighting to profit.

Some of these differences might be pleasing and others could be disappointing. You will have to decide if the positives outweigh the negatives. However, if you choose to interview for an operational supervisory, leadership, or management position with a company that has a history of hiring veterans, remember that the interviewers already know what you bring to the table and what you are missing. You are much better off letting them know that you are aware of the differences before they make an issue of them. Better yet, let them know that it is both the similarities and the differences that have you so excited about the work.

29. Engineering

In the two previous chapters you learned how some words have different meanings when applied outside the military. Sometimes these differences will damage a job search because we fail to express ourselves correctly, and other times the damage is done because we avoid or neglect an opportunity due to misinformation. I fell into this trap during my job search.

I was a navy lieutenant on a shore duty assignment in Norfolk, Virginia. I had submitted my resignation paperwork and was three months away from civilian status. A few days before I was to attend a hiring conference I called my headhunter, Ben, to get an overview of my slate of interviews. One of the companies on the list was Ford Motor Company. I chuckled and told Ben that was a long shot because I grew up in a GM family. The only cars my dad ever owned were Chevrolets and Oldsmobiles. I laughed when Ben added that the job would be in Dearborn, Michigan. "Come on, Ben," I said, "don't you remember? Julie [my wife] and I want the mid-Atlantic or Northeast." Ben reminded me I had also professed to be open for opportunities in any location.

"Okay, Ben, tell me about the job."

"It's called product development engineering," he replied.

As I began to laugh I said, "Ben, look at my résumé. I was a management major at the Naval Academy. The only engineering courses I took were the ones I had to take to graduate."

"Not a problem," he replied. "A manager at Ford reviewed your résumé earlier and asked to interview you. Plus," he added, "the pay and benefits are excellent."

"Okay, what the heck, let's go for it," I responded, with a shrug.

I went to the conference and interviewed with several companies. The interviewer from Ford was a former naval officer and a fellow Annapolis grad named Ron. He interviewed me and described product development engineering (PDE).

I doubted my qualifications for the job but Ron was insistent. His educational background and naval career were similar to mine, and he assured me I was qualified for the job. Well, I thought, being qualified was one thing, but how about being interested? Only one way to find out. I accepted Ron's invitation for a second-level interview and site visit in Dearborn.

The job site was not at all what I had expected. I had visions of machines and drafting tables and mechanical gizmos and laboratories. What I found instead was an office building with cubicles and carpet and telephones and a bunch of workers wearing suits, although most of them had their jackets off. A series of briefings and interviews began and I learned much about the job. I was interviewing to be one of the PDEs in the drive train section for a new light truck that Ford would be launching in two years. I was tapped to be the drive shaft PDE and I would work closely with the differential PDE and the transmission PDE. My mission was to make sure that when the plants started to build these trucks in two years my drive shafts would work perfectly and interface correctly with the rest of the drive train assembly.

As I learned more about the job I discovered that I could indeed do this job, but only because it was incorrectly titled. It should have been called PDM—product development manager. There was no engineering. No design, no development, no testing, no evaluation. Yes, all that was being done, but by other people—real engineers. My job was to plan, coordinate, liaise, communicate, expedite, and resolve issues, albeit with technical people and engineers. What I called being a manager in the navy, Ford called being an engineer.

Looking back on it later it all made sense. If Ford really wanted an engineer to do that job, why in the world would they target military personnel? With a few exceptions, that is not what they do; even the ones with hardcore engineering degrees rarely apply that education at the research, design, or development level. Ford liked to see an educational background with good fundamentals in science and math, but what they really wanted was the leadership profile and the demonstrated ability to get things done in a technical or sophisticated environment.

There are two morals to this story. First, do not make your decision on whether or not to interview for a job based on what you think the job title means. Two, given the right qualifications and experience, it is possible that a job title with the word "engineering" in it might just be a good fit for you.

30. Is Consulting Right for You?

Have you ever chatted with someone who makes his or her living as a consultant? It can be fascinating to hear their stories of how they have pinpointed problems, streamlined processes, enhanced morale, increased efficiencies, and put their clients on the path to improved profitability. Variety, changing scenery, and travel can be appealing. There can be an aura of glamour, excitement, and importance associated with the word "consultant" on a business card. However, before committing to this objective, there are two important issues to consider—expertise and lifestyle.

Consultants are experts. Expertise implies both a specific subject matter and a degree of familiarity within that subject matter. Can you be hired as a consultant? Maybe. Here's what you need to do:

- Identify your areas of expertise.
- Measure your level of expertise.
- Find consulting firms that specialize in assisting clients in those areas.
- Generate interviews with those companies.
- Demonstrate sufficient expertise for them to bill your services to a client at an hourly rate high enough to justify hiring you.
- Convince them that you will bill enough hours to cover your salary, expenses, overhead, and profit.

Most consulting firms use a factor called billing ratio to determine whether or not to hire someone. These ratios vary between 2:1 and 4:1, depending on factors such as industry, functional expertise, etc. For this example we will use a 3:1 ratio. Most firms measure the year in billable hours. With fifty working weeks in the year and an expectation of forty billable hours per week, expect an annual goal of two thousand billable hours. Let's say you want a $60,000 annual salary. With a billing ratio of 3:1, the company has to be able to generate $180,000 (3 x $60,000) in your name. Assume one-third of that goes to overhead and expenses, one-third to profit, and the final $60,000 to you. To generate this $180,000 during two thousand hours, the company will have to bill you out at $90 per hour for the entire year. In reality, your rate will have to be higher since generating two thousand billable hours in a year is not easy. So, let's use $100 per hour. Assuming your *area* of expertise is marketable, is your *level* of expertise high enough to get a client to pay your firm $800/day for your services?

What are your areas of expertise? Working with people? Management? National security? Although noteworthy, they are not good enough for most consulting firms. They are too general or vague in nature and are too hard to quantify. Consulting firms look for specific talents. Experience in supply chain management, operations research, weapons systems development, and contracting and procurement will be more attractive to a consulting firm than talents such as troop leadership, flying helicopters, standing bridge watches, or putting ammunition on target.

Of those military personnel who do go into consulting, most work in a specialized field—defense consulting. More midgrade and senior personnel go this route than the junior officer and enlisted service members. This makes sense, when you consider both the area and level of expertise involved.

Assuming you do have the professional and educational profile necessary to be marketable in the field of consulting, there is an additional issue to consider— lifestyle.

Many civilian occupations are customer intensive, i.e., a great amount of time is spent with the customer in his or her environment. Consulting is perhaps the most customer-focused occupation in the business world. A consultant who is not on site with the client is probably not doing his or her job. Although some time must be spent away from the project doing research, analysis, and preparation, the very nature of the job requires being with the client. And, since the client does not come to you, being with the client will impact your lifestyle.

Unless your clients are located in the same town as you, you can expect a significant amount of overnight travel. It is not uncommon for junior consultants to catch a flight late Sunday night or early Monday morning and not return home again until Friday. Being with the client all week, every week for the duration of the project is not uncommon. As you work your way up to senior consultant and manager, you will usually see a decrease in the amount of time away from home, but the travel requirement never goes away completely. Even the partners in consulting firms travel more than their peers in the rest of the business world.

Some consulting firms eliminate the need for out-of-town travel, at least for their junior consultants, by utilizing the concept of the relocating consultant. This type of consultant rarely spends a night away from home, but home changes every time a new project is assigned. A relocating consultant might spend his or her first three or four years with the firm on four or five successive projects in four or five different towns. Sleeping in your own bed every night is comforting, but the location of the bedroom keeps changing. Twelve months in a furnished apartment. Six months in an extended-stay hotel. Eventually this relocation stops. You get promoted to senior consultant and settle down in one town, maybe never having to move again. But now that you are a senior consultant, you will often travel to the locations where the junior consultants on your team or project are both working and living.

For the right person with the right experience in the right circumstances, consulting can be an excellent fit. It offers tremendous exposure to the world of business and industry. Helping people solve problems can be rewarding, travel can be exciting, and variety helps keep things interesting. But for others, the likelihood of high travel and frequent relocation is a deal killer.

How about you? Do those issues ring any bells? If there is something about that lifestyle that is influencing your decision to leave the military, then consulting might not be right for you. Take a look at your list of priorities and decision criteria. Where on that list have you placed family separation and other lifestyle issues? The answer to that question is very important when considering a consulting career.

31. Government Contractors

As they search for new careers, many people leaving the military are attracted to government contractors and consulting firms in the defense industry. Taking relevant expertise to a new job allows for both a higher starting salary and the ability to contribute to the organization quickly. Depending on personal circumstances and individual goals and priorities, this avenue may or may not be a wise choice.

Making a good choice always involves weighing the advantages against the disadvantages. For those considering employment by defense contractors, you may find the following summaries helpful.

ADVANTAGES:

- **Getting the interview is relatively easy.** Most contractors hire according to the requirements of the contract. Whether it is a contract they already have or one they hope to receive, they look for specific, relevant experience. If your experience is a square peg that fits one of the square holes in the contract, then they will call you.
- **The interview is easier.** The necessity of selling your experience is lessened since it is your experience that generates the interview in the first place.
- **Higher starting salaries.** Since your civilian paycheck is supposed to reflect your value added, you will be paid a premium for what you know and who you know. The less money required for your training and development, the more they can give you up front.
- **Familiar turf.** You might be able to hang up the uniform, put on a suit, and move to the office down the hall. It is likely that you will already know some of the people working there, where to park, and the location of the cafeteria.
- **No need to relocate.** Since many contractors key in on your most recent assignment, you might be able to work where you currently live.
- **You can continue to serve your country.** Having been in the business of national defense for most of your professional life, working for a defense contractor will allow you to continue to contribute to that mission.
- **The learning curve is flat.** You can get up to speed quickly. You already know most of the language, the systems, and the mission.

DISADVANTAGES:

- ***What has been* versus *what will be.*** Why is the contractor hiring you? What happens when your special knowledge of people and processes becomes dated? Once they have assimilated your expertise, do they still need you?
- **Growth potential.** Regardless of the level of your personal performance, an organization must be growing before there can be an opportunity for personal growth. Depending on the state of national security, political climate, and the economy, defense may or may not qualify as a growth industry.
- **Risk of being pigeonholed.** Let's say your military service includes four years of weapons systems development and a weapons systems contractor hires you when you leave the service. What does your résumé look like after a few years? Have you expanded or reduced your options?

- **Antiquated technology.** Although the military is state of the art in many areas, it can be one or two generations behind the commercial sector in many others. If your expertise is in an outdated area and you accept an offer from a contractor in that field, then consider how this will look on your résumé.
- **Contract-driven employment.** What happens to your job when the contract expires or the technology or system goes out of favor? Job-hopping. For many people in the defense contracting business, following contracts from company to company is a way of life.
- **Been there, done that.** A shallow learning curve can be a great thing for a while, but it can also lead to boredom and stagnation. Although riskier, some people prefer the excitement and challenge of climbing a steeper curve.

Is working for a contractor the best choice for you? Maybe yes, maybe no. Before you choose, remember that organizations hire people for one of three reasons: experience, potential, or a combination of the two. Most contractors fall into the first category. You will not find many in the second. Fortunately, there are a number of excellent companies that seek a combination of the two. For most people, this combination is your best bet. If you can afford it, you might be better off by trading some immediate gratification for some long-term success.

32. Additional Options

When I decided to write this book, I paid attention to the advice given to most aspiring writers—write what you know. Generally speaking, what I know is military-to-civilian career transition and job hunting, specifically searching for jobs in the for-profit businesses of corporate America. As a result, most of the opportunities I describe and examples I use are focused on that sector of the job market, especially so in this section of the book.

Many veterans will and should pursue careers in fields outside of those with which I am most familiar. Several come to mind: education, medicine, government, not-for-profits, and law. Please do not interpret a lack of information about those fields and others as a lack of endorsement on my part. On the contrary, I encourage job seekers to explore all of their options.

In the course of my career I have discovered several alternatives that might be of interest to you. Here is a description of each as well as a reference for more information:

- **Federal government.** This choice would seem to be a natural second career for many people leaving the military. Not only do you retain your years of service for retirement purposes, but your experience will also often earn you a higher civil service rating. In addition, the Veterans Employment Opportunities Act assures veterans with three or more years of service special consideration in the selection process. Your one-stop shop for this option is www. USAJobs.gov.
- **State government.** Every state participates to some degree in the Veterans Administration's On-the-Job-Training and Apprenticeship Program. Many states assign hiring preference status to veterans. Being a state resident helps, but is not a requirement. To get an idea of how one state looks at veterans as potential state employees, visit www.da.ks.gov/ps/aaa/recruitment/veterans/vetemployinfo.htm.
- **Law enforcement.** I am frequently invited to job fairs to provide interview training to the attendees. I like to walk through the display area to get a feel for the hiring companies in attendance. Recently I have noticed an increasing number of federal, state, and local law enforcement agencies in attendance. This field and career path is a natural fit for many veterans, and not just those with a military police specialty. Here is how one state police agency views hiring veterans: http://oregon.gov/OSP/RECRUIT/military.shtml.
- **Troops to Teachers.** Sponsored by the U.S. Departments of Education and Defense, this program helps eligible military personnel begin new careers as public school teachers. Learn more at www.proudtoserveagain.com.
- **Helmets to Hardhats.** This program gives National Guard, Reserve, and retired and transitioning active-duty military service members a connection to training and career opportunities in the construction industry. Go to this website for details: www.helmetstohardhats.org.

Whether or not you choose to pursue one or several of those options, keep in mind that the information and guidance contained in the rest of this book remain relevant to your preparation and search for a new career.

I am often asked about franchises and other forms of self-employment. Although franchisors were never my clients, I had investigated that possibility when I was getting out and I researched it further so that I could discuss it with those who broached the subject. Many veterans are attracted to the idea of being self-employed. This career choice is indeed a viable option for some, but there is much to consider before you head down that path. The following chapter discusses this option in detail.

33. The Boss of Me

What I would really like to do when I get out of the military is go into business for myself. Be my own boss. Control my own destiny. Sink or swim on my own merits.

That is the response I received from an army master sergeant nearing retirement when I asked him about his employment objective. You may have had similar thoughts during the course of your professional life. Sounds good, right? Is self-employment a good choice for you? Possibly.

Going into business for yourself offers many advantages. You get to call the shots. Decide where you want to live. Wear what you want to wear. Associate with people and products that matter to you. Determine your own working hours. Hire and fire as needed and according to your standards. Reap the rewards of your success. The appeal of self-employment is understandable, but there are additional considerations.

- **Risk.** Military service members are insulated from the volatility of the corporate sector. Market cycles, technological advancements, interest rates, and other variables impact businesses constantly, especially small businesses. According to the Small Business Administration, more than 70 percent of self-employment business ventures fail in the first two years. Can you afford the risk?
- **Accountability.** There will be a big scoreboard up there with your name on it. The numbers next to your name are your numbers. Nobody can take credit for your success and nobody will cover up your failure.

- **Financing/cash flow/credit.** Starting your own business requires seed money. Do you have it? If you have to borrow it, how is your credit rating? Some franchising opportunities require an up-front investment of $5,000 to $100,000. Many business failures can be attributed to running out of cash in the first year.
- **Time off.** How important is it to you? Have you been using those thirty days of annual leave? Being off work on those federal holidays is kind of nice. Guess what? Self-employment often means no vacation, no holidays, and no weekends. This can be true until your business is well established and you can entrust the keys to reliable employees when you are out of town.
- **Working hours.** Twelve- to fourteen-hour days are common in your military experience. Want to cut back a little? Forget it. Being your own boss is 24/7.
- **Employees.** Will you need them? As much as you relish the thought of not having a boss, do you really want to be one? How many employees and what kind of talents will you need? Will you be able to find them? Most business owners will tell you their number one problem is finding and retaining good employees.
- **Preparation.** Although your management expertise may be impressive in the areas of personnel, administration, and materiel resources, you have little or no direct business management experience. You are used to the bottom lines of *readiness* or *war fighting* but you will succeed or fail in business based on one called *profit*. Do you know how to write a business plan, specifically one that will pass muster with a lending officer or a franchisor? Have you taken an accounting course? You may need professional guidance from accountants and lawyers. Are those fees in your budget?
- **Paychecks.** How much will you make? When you work for yourself, you pay yourself last. Once you have covered your overhead, serviced your debt, paid your employees, and given the federal, state, and local government their shares, you can then write yourself a check out of whatever remains.

Considering all of the above, why do some people opt for self-employment? Independence, self-determination, the lifestyle associated with choosing where you want to live or working out of your home, the possibility of earning a living by doing something you are passionate about—these are just a few of the reasons. In addition to weighing these pluses and minuses, you should also consider your current status. Back to the army master sergeant I mentioned earlier.

He will soon retire with twenty-two years of service and receive a monthly pension. He and his wife are empty nesters now that their two children are no longer living at home. She has a degree in accounting and has worked outside the home throughout his career, mostly in retail sales and as an accounts payable/receivable clerk. Other than a small credit card balance and a car loan, they are debt-free. They have been able to save some money and have an excellent credit rating. In addition to being a self-proclaimed motor head, he has spent most of his career in vehicle maintenance. This supports his interest in either opening a truck maintenance facility or becoming a franchisee for Jiffy Lube or Quick Lube.

His situation appears perfect for the self-employment option. How does yours compare? For additional information and guidance on this subject, see:

The Small Business Administration: www.sba.gov

Franchise America: www.franchise-america.com

International Franchise Association: www.franchise.org

USA Home Business: www.usahomebusiness.com

Home Based Business.Com: www.home-based-business.com

Small Time Operator: How to Start Your Own Business, Keep Your Books, Pay Your Taxes, and Stay Out of Trouble by Bernard B. Kamoroff

34. The S Word

A well-respected business magazine surveyed the leaders of the Fortune 500 companies to see what, if any, common denominators of success they share. The survey showed that the most common one was sales experience. More than half spent the majority of their professional lives in sales and marketing assignments. Although that might surprise you, it is easy to understand why: no matter how good its products or services, a company will not succeed if no one buys them.

Starting a new career in a sales capacity might be an excellent choice for many veterans, but most of them shy away from sales. During my career in the counseling and placement of military personnel, I found that only 10 percent of my candidates walked in the door with sales as their first choice. After analyzing their attributes and motivations, I encouraged a third of them to investigate sales as an option. Of those, almost all of them either launched their careers in sales or transferred to sales positions within two years.

What causes this? There is a simple explanation. For most of them "sales" is a four-letter word and something to be avoided. You are likely to feel the same. Where does that attitude come from? Here's my theory—blame it on your parents.

The people who raise us influence many of the values and opinions that we hold on to as adults. Just as they teach us to avoid four-letter words, they instill in us a negative attitude toward sales. From an early age, we are exposed to sales mostly from the perspective of the consumer. We are taught to distrust salespeople. They sell us things we do not need. They charge us more than we should have to pay. When we get it home it does not work as well as it should. When we go back to complain, they are nowhere to be found. With that mind-set, is it any wonder that we have difficulty picturing ourselves in that profession?

There is much truth in that scenario, but the picture is incomplete. The consumer's exposure to sales is only the tip of the iceberg, the visible part. To get the entire picture you must also consider the importance of sales in the free-market system and capitalism. Put aside for a minute your image of the door-to-door salesman or the telemarketer and consider the following:

- Businesses selling to other businesses
- One industrial company using the products of another
- Companies selling products or services that fill existing needs, help other companies solve problems, or make them more efficient
- Hospitals purchasing medical equipment
- Computer manufacturers buying microprocessors
- Delivery companies purchasing trucks
- Oil refineries buying chemicals

The list is endless. Moreover, when it comes to the business world, exceptional service, quality products, and competitive pricing are not enough. What matters is profit. Income must exceed expenses. Without sales, there is no income, and hence, no profit. No profit means no company.

Independent of your current attitude toward the S word, allow for the possibility that you might be among those who should go into sales. It is not my intent to sell you on sales, but rather to expose you to the option. Whether you choose to interview for sales positions or not, I strongly believe that this information is very important for all job seekers.

Interviewing is selling. You may have little interest in the latter, but I know you care about the former or you would not be reading this book.

Sales opportunities come in many shapes and sizes. Let's take a look at several types. Although this list is not all-inclusive, it does represent the varieties most often obtained by service members who lack sales experience.

- **Retail.** Department store clerks and automobile sales personnel are typical examples. They sell directly to the consumer/user of the products. Compensation is paid on a salary plus commission basis or straight commission.
- **Financial.** These products include mutual funds, insurance, annuities, financial planning services, stocks, and bonds. The customer base is either retail (individual consumers), commercial (businesses), or institutional. Income is mostly commission-based, with possibly a small base salary component.
- **Business-to-business (B2B).** One business selling its products or services to another business, which then either utilizes or incorporates what has been purchased for resale to its customers. Compensation is usually a combination of salary and commission.
- **Industrial.** Here an industry is selling its goods to another industry, where those items are incorporated into products for resale. The primary goal is to maintain existing client base. The secondary goal is to develop new customers and/or expand sales within existing customers. Sales reps are paid a salary and bonus.
- **Real estate.** This includes clients in the residential or commercial markets. The product could be raw land, office space, buildings, or houses. Income is highly commission-driven.
- **Consumer products.** Representatives of consumer products companies sell to wholesale or retail outlets, using techniques like shelf-space management, product promotion, and advertising. Being paid a salary with bonus potential is the norm.
- **Technology/engineering.** These sales reps have specific technical expertise or education. They call on a client base that is often highly educated and techni-

cally sophisticated. Products are big-ticket items or capital equipment with high-dollar values, and longer sales cycles are common. Follow-up sales and support is essential. Compensation is salary plus bonus and/or commission.

- **Pharmaceutical.** Sales reps detail (explain and promote) the capabilities of their products to medical professionals. This is indirect selling in that the client (the doctor) is not the user (the patient). Establishing and maintaining relationships is a key component for success. Income is a combination of salary and commission.

- **Medical.** Products include hospital supplies, diagnostic equipment, test kits, surgical instruments, and the like. Some relevant education or experience might be required due to a very knowledgeable and sophisticated clientele. Compensation is commission driven, with the possibility of a base salary and bonus.

- **Manufacturer's reps.** They represent the product lines of several different companies, usually within a specific industry. Many companies use reps as an alternative to having an in-house sales force. These reps are often independent contractors (self-employed). Their income is commission based. Prior sales experience may be required.

- **Recruiting.** Recruiters are the salespeople who work for placement companies, headhunters, and employment agencies. They sell candidates on using their services and employers on hiring those candidates. Commission-based paychecks are the norm.

There are many options when it comes to selling. Several of the above categories overlap and every company has its own compensation structure. Do your homework and you may discover that, for you, sales is actually an eleven-letter word—opportunity.

Even if a job in sales is not right for you, do not discount its importance as part of your job search. Interviewing is selling. Target the potential customer, get your foot in the door, identify the need, and fill it with your product—you.

Speaking of homework, there is some for you to do in the next chapter. The results will indicate your aptitude for selling—and interviewing—and predict your odds of success in both.

35. Your SQ Number

Time for some additional self-analysis, the results of which will indicate whether or not sales is a viable option for you. To get started, let's define three important attributes.

- **Competitive spirit.** The desire to be the best. Ambition to succeed. The competition is the cake and winning is the icing. You prefer them both together, but the cake alone makes it all worthwhile. You are ranked number two of forty, but are disappointed and surprised you are not number one.
- **Likeability.** Easily liked. People enjoy your company. Warm, amicable, friendly, outgoing, genuine, sincere. Others are happy when you walk in the door. A nice person. Fun to be around.
- **Work ethic.** Nose to the grindstone. Get to work early and stay late. Give it everything you have. Focused. Task oriented. Dedicated to getting the job done. No stone left unturned. Dusk to dawn. 24/7. Whatever it takes.

Keeping these descriptions in mind, here is the exercise.

1. Think about all the people in your life, past and present. Using **competitive spirit** as your measuring stick, who among those people stands out as the clear number ten on a ten-point scale, with ten being the highest? Write down that person's name.

2. Keeping that same group of people in mind, which one scores a ten on the **likeability** scale? Write down his or her name.

3. Which person in that group gets the highest marks for **work ethic**? Add that name to the list and give him or her a ten on the work ethic scale.

4. Now, compare yourself to each person in each category and assign yourself a number relative to his or her number. If that person is a ten in that category, then what are you? Be honest with yourself. Most people err on the side of modesty.

5. You now have your three personal numbers for those attributes. Add those three numbers together. The resulting sum will be between zero and thirty.

That is your **sales quotient**, or SQ. This number is an excellent indicator of your potential for success in a sales capacity. An individual with high scores in competitiveness, likeability, and work ethic is prone to succeed in most endeavors; possessing the right combination of these attributes is especially helpful in the field of sales.

Most successful sales reps are as relentless as pit bulls, as friendly as Labs, and as hard working as border collies.

What is your SQ number? For most people, it will be in the 20 to 27 range. Here is a breakdown of all the possible scores and what they indicate.

0 to 5	Hello? Anybody home?
6 to 14	Unlikely numbers for anyone accepted for military service.
15 to 19	You might not be cut out for sales, but maybe you are being too hard on yourself. Modesty is a virtue. False modesty is not.
20 to 26	You can succeed in sales, especially if work ethic is a nine or a ten. Maybe your competition is slightly more likeable or competitive, but you will outwork them.
27 to 29	You need to be in a sales environment. No other occupation can take better advantage of that unique combination of your internal hardworking success motivation and your external amicable personality.
30	I don't think so. No one is perfect. Repeat the exercise and be a bit more realistic in your self-evaluation.

Given an SQ in the range of 20 to 29, does it follow that you should go into sales? Not necessarily. Even with the appropriate attributes for a given occupation, you must also have the desire. However, an SQ in that range means you should at least consider sales as an option.

For reasons that will be discussed in the next chapter, interviewing successfully for a sales position is more difficult than for other types of jobs. Additional preparations are required, and those are covered in section VI.

36. The Audition

Several years ago I was interviewing a slate of candidates in my room at a hotel in Annapolis, Maryland. Unlike my typical recruiting trip, this one was dual-purposed. One of my Naval Academy classmates, a member of the Drum and Bugle Corps when we were midshipmen, had recently retired from the navy, moved to Annapolis, and taken a position as the director of the local symphony orchestra. He was about to turn his lifelong amateur passion into his new profession.

Although we were scheduled to meet for dinner that evening, I unexpectedly ran into him in the hotel restaurant that morning. When I asked him what he was doing there he explained that his first chair tuba player had recently resigned, and he was spending the day at the hotel interviewing potential replacements.

After breakfast we rode the elevator up to our rooms, which happened to be on the same floor but at opposite ends of the hall. Thank goodness for that. Throughout the day every time I opened my door to greet my next candidate I could see a line of tuba players outside my classmate's door. That was fine, but I had to prepare myself and my candidates for the hourly tuba solos coming from the other end of the hall.

We had much to talk about when we met for dinner. After we caught up on each other's lives, I facetiously thanked him for providing the wonderful background music for my interviews that day. I added that I thought he was there to interview. He smiled and replied that the interview was secondary to the audition—if the musicianship was missing, none of the other stuff really mattered, right? A light bulb flashed in my mind.

Most people understand the importance of being well prepared for interviews. Researching the company, doing self-knowledge exercises, and ensuring that your mental and physical preparations are complete will enhance your chances of success. If, however, you are in the process of preparing for a sales interview, then you would be wise to redouble your efforts. Successfully interviewing for a sales position is more difficult, and here is why.

- **Experience.** Simply stated, you have not done it before. This is true for most people separating from the military. Although you may have some experience in sales in your background, you probably have not been in sales as your primary professional occupation. This lack of experience makes the interview more difficult. It is always easier to interview for a job in which you have a significant amount of related experience. The good news is you have sales-like characteristics and traits and you may have some sales-like experience in your background: selling magazine subscriptions for the soccer team or candy bars for the band. Raising money for the Combined Federal Campaign. Convincing your boss to do things your way. Influencing the team to move in the direction you feel is best.

- **Skepticism.** When military personnel walk into a sales interview, the interviewer assumes they are not really interested in sales. The interviewer is skeptical of the commitment to the job and doubts the motives are sincere. Experience shows that most military personnel interview for sales for the wrong reasons. Interviewing successfully is difficult enough when the interviewer believes that sincerity is a given. Think about how much harder it is when the interviewer is predisposed to doubt that sincerity.

- **Competition.** Although a component of successful interviewing is always about beating out other qualified candidates for the job, interviewing for a sales position makes this even more of an issue. It takes a special combination of competitive spirit, likeable personality, and work ethic to be successful in sales. It therefore follows that people interviewing for sales positions will also share these characteristics. Those people are your competition for the job, and they are a formidable group.

- **The audition.** When you interview to be a production manager, the interviewer does not ask you to manage any production during the interview. Interviewing for a human resources position does not require you to perform any personnel actions during the interview. You will not be asked to actually move any material during your interview for a position as a distribution coordinator. But when you walk into a sales interview, you are demonstrating your ability to do the job. In addition to being interviewed, you are being auditioned. The interviewer has the luxury of seeing you demonstrate a significant component of the job during the interview—selling yourself. If you cannot effectively sell yourself—or play the tuba—while in the interview, the interviewer will doubt your ability to succeed in the job.

Bottom line—you have to convince the interviewer that you are right for the job. Without this salesmanship, you are destined to fail the interview. When it comes to sales opportunities, prepare to be both *interviewed* and *auditioned*. Accordingly, preparations above and beyond the norm are critical, and I will address them at the end of section VI.

SECTION IV.
PREPARATIONS (MECHANICAL)

These chapters address getting ready for the job hunting and interviewing process, specifically those physical or overt steps common to all searches for employment. Although largely mechanical in nature, they are important tools. Should they go missing or present themselves inadequately or poorly, the interview is doomed to failure.

Included in those preparations is the construction of your network. That task requires specialized tools, and they are discussed in these chapters.

The information that follows will help you:

- Establish your benchmarks.
- Build a decision-making tool.
- Address the paperwork.
- Try on a new uniform-of-the-day.
- Select and compile references.
- Prepare to market yourself.
- Expand your family tree.
- Maintain control.

37. Your *BENCHMARK* Company and Decision Matrix

Analyze any successful career move and you will always find one important contributing factor—excellent preparation. Think of these preparations as a set of well-honed tools in your transition toolbox. One tool that should be in every toolbox is the decision matrix, which allows you to prioritize your parameters, compare your options, and make a (mostly) rational choice. Before designing this matrix you need to create your *BENCHMARK*.

As you will learn later in this book, there is no such thing as a perfect candidate or a perfect company. However, when a company describes the ideal candidate profile for a position they are attempting to fill, they list all the attributes that would make a person perfect for the job. The company knows it will never find such a candidate but it will use this list of attributes as a benchmarking tool to evaluate all the applicants. The same benchmarking process is available to you. Creating your *BENCHMARK* before your job search begins will add a powerful tool to your toolbox.

Think of *BENCHMARK* as a model that represents everything you could possibly want or need in a career opportunity. Follow this five-step process to design one that will fit your needs:

Step One: Make a list of all of your search criteria. Here are some suggestions.
- Initial position
- Future positions
- Growth potential
- Initial location
- Future location(s)
- Initial salary
- Future salary
- Compensation structure
- Work/life balance
- Benefits and perks
- Working environment

- Corporate culture
- Training and development
- Job satisfaction
- Quality of life
- Cost of living
- Job security
- Coworkers
- Working hours
- Relocation frequency
- Travel
- Résumé value
- Stock/equity
- Financial health

Step Two: List these criteria in order of their priority or importance to you. Certain things are normally more heavily weighted than others. For example, would you give up job satisfaction or growth potential for work/life balance?

Step Three: Assign each attribute a description or value that makes it ideal or perfect for you.

Step Four: Pretend that *BENCHMARK* has made you a job offer for this perfect opportunity. Your first offer—congratulations!

Step Five: With this job offer on the table, it is time to create your decision matrix.

Having created *BENCHMARK* and being rewarded with a job offer, you are ready to design your decision matrix. For the sake of discussion, let's assume that the following items represent the attributes of the perfect opportunity for you, listed in relative order of importance:

1. Growth potential
2. Job satisfaction
3. Quality of life
4. Compensation
5. Initial location
6. Future locations
7. Coworkers
8. Benefits

Attributes:	Weight	Benchmark	CompanyX	CompanyY	CompanyZ
Growth Potential	10	10			
Job Satisfaction	10	10			
Quality of Life	09	09			
Compensation	08	08			
Initial Location	07	07			
Future Locations	07	07			
Co-workers	06	06			
Benefits	05	05			
TOTAL:	62	62			

Now, design a chart in which you list these attributes in the first column and their relative weight in the second column. Use the next three or more columns to list companies as interviews are scheduled. Assign the first of these company columns to *BENCHMARK*. Since the weight column represents the maximum score possible for that attribute and given that the offer from *BENCHMARK* is in theory perfect, assign it the maximum score for each attribute.

This is your decision matrix. You can make effective use of this tool as you go about your job search. As you interview with additional companies, you can fill in the blanks and add up the scores.

You may wonder why I have asked you to create this interview comparison tool when you are still in the preparation phase of your search. The answer, for now, lies more in the process than the product. When you create your *BENCH-MARK* and decision matrix at this stage you add structure and definition to your search. Having already defined your best-case outcome, your goal is clear—find an opportunity that matches up as closely as possible with *BENCHMARK*.

The rest of this book will help you achieve that goal. Although I will not ask you to use these tools again until sections VII and VIII, you should keep them handy in the interim. What you learn between now and then will probably cause you to tweak them a little.

38. The Six Ps

Most people are familiar with the five Ps of task accomplishment: Prior Planning Prevents Poor Performance. When it comes to career changes and job hunting, however, there are six additional Ps to consider.

Career transition can elicit a broad range of emotions. From elation to frustration, from glee to disappointment, from pleasant surprise to disbelief—the typical job seeker will likely experience it all. Keeping the **Six Ps** in mind will help you maintain your perspective during this wild ride and enhance your chances of a successful landing. Let's take a quick look at each of the **Six Ps**: patience, persistence, preparedness, professionalism, presentation, and politeness.

- **Patience.** Things will rarely happen as quickly as you would like. You will need to be patient as you go about your job search. Your priority list will never be the same as that of a potential employer. You have your agenda and potential employers have their own. It is highly likely that the only time in your search when the timeline will be too fast for you is when you get a job offer and the company wants an answer quickly.
- **Persistence.** At first glance, this would seem at odds with being patient. Learning how to balance the two is critical. That tool may start out a little dull, but it will be finely honed by the time your search is over. Do not allow negative feedback or lack of response to derail your pursuit of the job you want. Being persistent does mean not giving up, but it also means riding the fine line between demonstrating your level of interest and becoming a pest.
- **Preparedness.** Going into the job search with a high level of knowledge will eliminate many problems before they have the chance to arise. Knowledge of the organization, knowledge of the position and, most important, a high degree of self-knowledge are the most critical elements of the career search.
- **Professionalism.** Be respectful. Do the right thing. Do what you say you will do. Follow up. Be on time. Make sure your voicemail message is appropriate for potential employers. Check e-mail and voicemail frequently. Return calls. Honor the timelines and deadlines. Get the application form in on time. Write the follow-up letters. Be careful with social networking sites and pay particular attention to profiles and pictures.
- **Presentation.** Look the part. Dress appropriately. Live up to the grooming and appearance standards that are expected of you. First impressions are important, but presentation does not stop there. Speak clearly and with confidence, but maintain your humility. Remember the messages that are conveyed by eye contact and body language.
- **Politeness.** Be courteous. Say thank you. Remember names. Smile. Look people in the eye. Just because someone is sitting in the guard shack or at the reception desk does not mean they are not important. Many organizations go out of their way to see what the administrative and clerical people think about a prospective employee.

Most of this is common sense and common courtesy, but sometimes stressful situations cause us to lose touch with the basics. Remembering the **Six Ps** is a good way to stay grounded.

The chapters that follow are full of practical applications of the **Six Ps**. You will learn how to develop the materials and skills necessary to apply that guidance to your own job search.

39. Documentation

One of the most important steps in mechanical preparation is documentation. This is paperwork—some you have and some that must be developed or obtained. There are seven types and here they are, with a brief discussion of each.

- **The résumé.** This is the most famous and important piece of documentation in your portfolio. One page preferred and never more than two. Every word is true. Makes the reader want to know more. Indicates potential by delineating past accomplishments. There is additional information on this subject in the next chapter.
- **List of references.** It has replaced letters of reference. Lists both personal and professional acquaintances who will be asked to vouch for you. Many companies will call two or three of each category prior to making an offer. You will find further guidance and a sample later in section IV.
- **Performance evaluations.** Gather them together and get them organized. Gaps raise yellow flags. Sometimes used in lieu of reference checks. You might be asked for all of them or perhaps just the most recent three to ten.
- **Academic transcripts.** There is a lot of academic fraud out there. Many companies will require validation of your educational qualifications. Some accept photocopies; others want sealed originals.
- **Certificates of completion/letters of certification or qualification.** If you make reference to certifications or qualifications on your résumé, on an application form, or in an interview, be prepared to produce verifying documentation.

- **A writing sample.** Although most companies will appraise your writing skills through your résumé, cover letter, and post-interview correspondence, some will ask for an additional sample, especially if writing is a large component of the job.
- **Discharge certificate/letter of resignation/retirement paperwork.** Some companies are very sensitive to being perceived as luring people from the military. You might be asked to document that you have separated or that the separation/retirement process has started. This is especially true if the potential employer is a defense contractor.

Assemble this information in a portfolio. Have it with you when you interview. Unless asked for the entire package, do not volunteer it. Most companies do not need to lug around a five-pound notebook with your name on the cover. Instead, produce from the portfolio any information requested. Hopefully, your potential employer will be impressed by both the information and your organizational skills.

Speaking of those organizational skills, there is another way to put them to use at this point in the process. Your search will generate a lot of information, both the digital and paperwork varieties. Here are some examples:

- Copies of application forms
- Website shortcuts or bookmarks
- Contact information
- Travel receipts
- Job-hunting expenses
- A record of telephone calls
- Résumé distribution records
- Reference lists
- Annual reports
- Company research information
- Copies of cover letters
- Copies of follow-up letters
- Résumé variations

- E-mail exchanges
- Addresses and phone numbers

For the hard copies, I suggest hanging file folders in a file drawer or box, organized by company or category of paperwork. For tracking your status with a particular company, you can create a spreadsheet on your computer or maintain a logbook. A calendar, digital or paper, is helpful when it comes to keeping track of interview dates and response times. Many people keep a journal of their preparation, contact, and interview activity with daily entries, updates, ideas, and things to do. Pick a system that works for you, and get organized in the early stages of your job search.

40. Creating Your Résumé

Just the thought of a résumé creates stress for most military personnel, especially those who have never had to use one before. You have to have one, and it has to be good; it is the most important document in your transition toolbox. Physically, it is one or two sheets of paper with three hundred to eight hundred words. Figuratively, it is also a bridge, one that connects your past to your future.

Do you have one? Is it on your things-to-do list? Having trouble getting started? Try this approach. Read several *how to write a résumé* books. Do a draft to the best of your ability. Gather together one hundred résumé experts. Give each of them a copy. Wait a few days and collect all of the revisions. What do you have? One hundred distinctly different versions of your résumé. Hmmm, so much for that idea. Now what? Keep reading.

There is no such thing as one size fits all when it comes to a résumé for separating military personnel. That group includes: enlisted personnel and officers; two years of service through thirty-year careers; combat arms and staff corps; hundreds of different military occupational specialties; varying degrees of success and levels of training, education, and competency. Given the variety within that segment of the population, no single template is appropriate and no two careers are ever the same.

I encourage you to write your own résumé. At a minimum, be sure you are the primary author. Getting professional guidance in some form is highly recommended. Sometimes you will pay for that expertise and other times it will come to you gratis. However, under no circumstances should you allow your résumé to become someone's attempt to force your unique experience into a prepackaged template.

I have written, reviewed, edited, or tweaked more than four thousand résumés during my career and have experienced firsthand what works and what does not. When it comes to developing an effective résumé I keep four primary goals in mind:

A résumé should:
- Be easy to read.
- Present experience to indicate potential.
- Entice the reader to want to know more.
- Do no harm.

Although much of the conventional wisdom regarding résumés is so full of holes and exceptions that neither convention nor wisdom seems particularly appropriate, I do recommend the following general guidelines as you set out to accomplish these four goals.

STRUCTURE

Seven Seconds Test. When someone reads your résumé for the first time, he or she will pay close attention for seven seconds. If this quick scan generates interest then he or she will keep reading or go back and read more thoroughly from the beginning. Sometimes a résumé fails this test even before it is read. The reader picks it up and thinks, "There is no way I can digest this one quickly, so I'll skip to the next one in the pile." Much of what follows will help your résumé pass this test.

Length. You get one page for every ten years since high school or college graduation, but not more than two pages. One exception—applying for government jobs will frequently require more information than will fit on two pages. Otherwise, if you must go to a third page, consider the use of an addendum. Always make sure the important information is on the first page or the reader may never see page two. Also, the second page should repeat your contact information and be clearly labeled as Page 2 of 2.

Addendum, supplement, or amplification. This standalone document amplifies the information on your one- or two-page résumé. Its use allows the reader to get into your résumé, become interested, and, if necessary or appropriate, find additional information.

Paper quality and color. There was a time when expensive, colored paper with off-set printing and fancy graphics would separate a résumé from the competition in a good way. Technology changed all that. Scanners and fax machines hate textured paper, high rag content paper, raised ink, and unusual graphics. Go back to the basics—plain white copy paper and black ink. Paper is becoming less of an issue given the increasing requirement for digital submission of documents.

FORMAT

Chronological résumé. This is the classic approach. The information is organized in sections and in chronological or reverse chronological order within those sections. The common section titles are Contact Information, Objective, Summary, Education (and/or Training and/or Certifications), Experience (or Military Experience and/or Civilian Experience), Accomplishments, Additional (or Personal or Other) Information. Some résumés include all of those sections; others will have only three or four.

Functional résumé. This type of résumé abandons chronology and instead focuses on functional expertise. The experience section is replaced with functional headings that consolidate and summarize similar responsibilities and accomplishments, independent of the timeframe in which they occurred. Here are some typical functional headings: Project Management, Command and Control, Operational Leadership, Customer Service, Quality Control, Training and Development, Systems Engineering, and Process Improvement.

Caution: Functional résumés raise yellow flags. This is due to their ability to hide information. Employers know this and are suspicious. Since there are no references to dates and timelines, it is easy to disguise unemployment, job-hopping, career stagnancy, educational staleness, and age. Unfortunately, a functional résumé often leads to a guilty until proven innocent mentality for the interviewer.

Chrono-functional résumé. Although most military personnel are well served by the classic reverse chronological approach, some find the functional version attractive. This is especially true for individuals with more than ten years of military service. There are two reasons for this. One, listing every single assignment during a ten- to thirty-year military career reads like job-hopping to a civilian employer, especially one with little or no history of hiring military personnel. Two, it is difficult to stick to the two-page limit. Keep in mind that when faced with the yellow flag of a functional résumé, many employers want to see the entire career path laid out in timeline format. This is where the chrono-functional hybrid comes into play. Take the functional format and add an abbreviated reverse chronological experience section, listing only the primary job titles and the years in which these assignments were held.

CONTENT

What vs. how well? Most employers care as much, or perhaps even more, about your potential as they do your experience. For that reason, as you write your résumé keep in mind that in most cases *what* you have done is not nearly as important as *how well* you have done those things.

Keywords. Many companies use résumé scanning software to screen résumés. This process is keyword driven, and your résumé has to hit those hot buttons. Which ones? If you have a specific job in mind, then make sure your résumé contains position-specific and industry-specific terms. Your best bet is to take them directly from an employment ad, job posting, or job description. If your target is a company rather than a specific job, then visit the company's website or read its annual report and look for keywords in the mission statement or core values of the company. If you have no particular company or job in mind, then choose keywords that best reflect what makes you tick and what matters to you in your job. Once you have selected your keywords, position them prominently and repeat each one if possible.

Military terminology. Before you release your résumé for public consumption it needs to be sanitized. Make sure it is free of acronyms and phraseology that has little meaning outside of the military. Have it reviewed by someone who has never served and modify your verbiage accordingly. When I did so I changed "CMS custodian" to "controller of classified material." Do not go overboard here. That résumé also indicated that I had been the "director of communications" and the "human resource manager" on my ship. The navy terms "communications officer" and "administrative department head" would have been just fine.

Personal information (PI). Other than the obvious need to include your name and contact information, there is much debate on the subject of including any additional PI on a résumé. I am in favor of it, within limits. In terms of space and placement, it goes last—the bottom of either page one or two. If PI is the only thing on page two, then eliminate it. There is no reason to include vital statistics, health, religion, or political information. Any reference to marital status and children on a résumé is a gray area. Some companies prefer to hire married people, and some jobs put a severe strain on families. If you do not know or are not sure, omit it.

On the other hand, including things like community service, volunteer work, second language fluency, travel, hobbies, and interests might pay dividends for two reasons: this adds an extra dimension and a human element to an otherwise inanimate document, and it gives the interviewer icebreaker material. Over the years my résumé included such things as running, sailing, membership in Rotary International, and my Chesapeake Bay retriever, Maggie. Many was the time when these tidbits served as conversation generators.

EDITING

White space. To pass the seven seconds test your résumé must send the signal that it will be an easy and quick read. The key to this is white space—that part of your résumé where there is no ink. This is a balancing act. You need the ink to convey your message but too much ink makes the reader less likely to read it. Here is the drill. Find all the unnecessary or superfluous ink and get it off the page. For example, why say:

I improved the damage control qualification rates in my division by 20 percent over the previous fiscal year through the increased use of shipboard practical drills and additional shore-based training, and my commanding officer awarded me a letter of commendation.

When you can say:

Commended for a 20 percent increase in damage control qualification rates.

You have conveyed the important information—the improvement and the recognition—with less than half the ink. Yes, the interviewer might want to know *how* you did it, but if you are asked that question, then the résumé has done its job—you are being interviewed.

Bullets. Another white space management technique is the use of bullets. Bulletized information stands out and does not require the use of full sentences or complete punctuation. Ink is flying off the page. Brevity counts—a bullet that takes up more than one line is either *too* wordy or *two* bullets:

- *Increased damage control qualification rates by 20 percent*
- *Awarded the Navy Commendation Medal*

Too much information? At the beginning of this chapter I mentioned the importance of your résumé enticing the reader to want to know more. The only way to know more is to talk to you, and talking to you manifests itself in the form of an interview—your goal. Putting too much information on the résumé is a mistake, even if you can do so and stay within the length guidelines. If in the process of reading your résumé the interviewer learns everything about you, then what is the point in meeting you? Tease or tempt the reader into wanting to know more.

Writing sample. Although not the norm, some interviews will require a writing sample. Whether or not one is requested, you will automatically be providing every interviewer with a writing sample.

Your résumé is a de facto writing sample.

It is a direct reflection of not only your writing skills but also your preparation, attention to detail, and accuracy. It must be letter perfect. No misspelled or misused words. No typos. No grammatical errors. You should take the time to proofread it several times, frontwards and backwards, and ask others to do the same. Use spelling and grammar verification software, but due not rely it alone. Oops—see what I mean?

OBJECTIVE

Does a résumé need a stated objective? That question comes up frequently in any discussion of résumé-writing. Several of the how-to books state that a résumé should always begin with a description of the type of position the writer is seeking. Still others say that including an objective might make the résumé too limiting. So what should you do? Well, like most career transition issues, it depends.

Skip to the end of this chapter and review the sample résumés of Michael Ortiz. Notice that neither one includes an *OBJECTIVE*. Depending on Mike's circumstances, his choice to omit it is either a wise or a foolish one. If Mike is focusing his search on a specific position, then stating his desire for that position in the form of a job objective on his résumé can be a powerful tool. Consider this example:

OBJECTIVE   *Service department manager for TIDEWATER BMW*

Upon reading this, the HR manager at the BMW dealership will have no question about Mike's objective. Assuming that position is available and the employer feels he is qualified, Mike's résumé has done its job. However, what if that position is not open or Mike's experience is inadequate? Since his objective was clearly stated and that option is not available, his résumé goes in the round file.

Some people try to get around that potential problem by stating their objective in general terms. Consider this:

OBJECTIVE   *Leadership position in an automobile dealership*

Mike will not be pigeonholed as a result of that objective, but he has created another problem. Since he gives no indication what he really wants to do, his résumé may join its cousin in the trash can.

Why not just leave the objective off of the résumé? That technique will only work in either of two special situations:

- Mike just happens to have an inside connection who will shepherd his résumé along its way and verbalize his objective to any interested parties.
- Mike includes a well-written cover letter with his résumé. This document includes a statement of his objective and amplification of his experience most relevant to the position. The next chapter addresses cover letters in detail.

In the end, you may have two versions of your résumé. You can use the one without an objective when you know there is someone hand-carrying it through the system and advocating for you along the way. In the alternative, take advantage of the powerful signal that can be sent with a specifically worded objective on your résumé, assuming of course that it is what you really want to do and that the targeted organization is likely to have that position available.

COMMON RÉSUMÉ MISTAKES

In addition to improper use of an objective statement, there are additional common résumé mistakes. Here are several for your consideration.

- The line "References available upon request" at the end of the résumé is a waste of space.
- Your résumé should not include a list of references. Most companies will check personal and professional references before making an offer. That decision is so far downstream from the résumé review stage that providing references with the résumé is premature and possibly even presumptuous. At some point you will need a **list of references** and that is covered in a later chapter.
- Including your date of availability for employment is almost always a bad idea. Availability is one of the most commonly used filters so why give them that before they have even met you? If they meet you and like you they might wait two or three months to hire you, but if your résumé says you cannot start for two or three months they will move on to the next one. One exception—if you are available immediately then go ahead and list that fact.
- Expressing a willingness to travel and/or relocate is fine, as long as it also happens to be completely true. Otherwise you are at best wasting space; at worst being deceitful.
- Do not include your military rank or rating when you put your name on the résumé. Doing so reinforces the negative stereotype associated with rank that was discussed in section I. If appropriate, you can list it in the experience section.
- Personal pronouns are problematic for two reasons. One, using words like *I* and *me* and *my* can give a résumé an unintentionally egocentric flavor, causing the reader to question your ability or willingness to be a team player. Two, they create unnecessary ink as they are rarely needed to convey meaning. For example, in the paragraph on bullets, earlier in this chapter, notice how the missing personal pronoun *I* has no impact on the meaning.

EXAMPLES

For an illustration of many of those guidelines and some of those errors, take a look at the before and after versions of the résumé of Petty Officer Third Class Mike Ortiz, USN.

As you know by now, creating an effective résumé requires a great deal of effort. You will invest a significant amount of time and perhaps some money in

(Before)

MM3 MICHAEL S. ORTIZ, USN

22 Bay Court, Apt 32   Norfolk, Virginia   22222
(727) 555-1991   motorhead@squidnet.com

EXPERIENCE

FMSU, Little Creek, VA (December 2002—present)

POIC of Fleet Maintenance Support Unit. I was responsible for managing my team of 12 sailors tasked with providing emergency power plant maintenance assistance to forward deployed Fleet units. I managed tool shop and spare parts inventory. I was responsible for creating an environment that would enhance the reenlistment rate of the assigned sailors. I managed the budget and petty cash accounts. I was in charge of TQL and 3M systems.

USS LANCASTER (AOE 72), Camden, NJ (November 1999—November 2002)

POIC of M Division. I managed continuous operation of the engines, compressors and gears, refrigeration, air-conditioning, gas-operated equipment, and other types of machinery. Stood EOOW watches. Responsible for a ship's steam propulsion and auxiliary equipment and the outside (deck) machinery. I effectively educated a numerous amount of my subordinates by conducting classes and mandatory training of military common tasks (CTT) and survival skills which were required to be updated yearly. I stood watches in the engineering spaces and managed MMs, BTs, and EEs while underway. Managed the "Sailors for Kids" program.

Autobahn Motor Sports, Cherry Hill, NJ (June 1997—August 1998)

I was responsible for performing engine diagnostics and maintenance on high performance automobiles. I was promoted to shop manager after six months. Managed the pit crew for the Rally Team.

TRAINING & EDUCATION

AS Technology Management 2003, Chesapeake Community College, Chesapeake, VA; completed courses toward BA degree; Machinist Mate A School; Marine Diesel Maintenance Course; 3M School; TQL Training

ADDITIONAL INFORMATION

Traveled throughout Europe and Central America; fluent in Spanish; computer literate; hobbies include motorcycles, historical fiction, and personal fitness.

(After)

Michael S. "Mike" Ortiz

(757) 555-1991 (cell)   motorhead@squidnet.com   22 Bay Court, Apt 32
(804) 444 0001 (work)   ortizm@fmsu.navy.mil   Norfolk, VA   22222

TRAINING & EDUCATION

Bachelor of Arts (in progress), Old Dominion University, Norfolk, VA
- Human Resource Management Major
- GPA: 3.6/4.0
- Veterans Club, vice president
- 50 percent complete; graduation target December, 2010

Associate of Science 2007, Chesapeake Community College, Chesapeake, VA
- Technology Management Major
- GPA: 3.5/4.0

U. S. Navy Training & Schools
- Mechanical Maintenance School (Honor Graduate)
- Marine Diesel Maintenance Course
- Planned Maintenance School (Finished first in a class of 27)
- Total Quality Leadership Training

MILITARY EXPERIENCE   *Machinist's Mate, U. S. Navy (2004—2010)*

Fleet Maintenance Support Unit, Little Creek, VA (2007—2010)
Selected as Team Leader of a 12 person rapid deployment team, responsible for providing emergency power plant maintenance assistance to deployed Navy ships.
- Improved response time by 25 percent; received Commendation Medal
- Nominated for advanced professional training
- Received Commendation for improving personnel retention by 30 percent
- Reduced spare parts procurement costs by 10 percent
- Recognized for leadership and conflict resolution skills
- Promoted to next pay grade one year earlier than normal

USS Lancaster (AOE 72), Camden, NJ (2004—2007)
Served as Work Center Supervisor for a 25 person maintenance shop responsible for ship's primary and auxiliary mechanical systems.
- Unit awarded the "Blue D" for having the fewest of generator failures in the Atlantic Fleet
- Qualified as Engineering Room Supervisor
- Received Surface Warfare Certification
- Commended for starting "Sailors for Kids" service program
- Recognized for effectiveness in training and development of subordinates

CIVILIAN EXPERIENCE   *Autobahn Motor Sports (AMS) (2003—2004)*

High Performance Mechanic
- Promoted to lead shop mechanic after six months
- Commended for engine maintenance and diagnostic skills
- Selected to lead the AMS Rally Team Pit Crew

ADDITIONAL INFORMATION
- Traveled throughout Europe and Central America
- Fluent in Spanish
- Familiar with most software applications in a Windows environment
- Hobbies include motorcycles, historical fiction, and personal fitness

pursuit of that goal. In the end it is worth it, and, if you stop and think about it, you really have no choice. Stick with it. You will feel such relief when you have finished writing it and even more when you have finished using it. But remember:

Your résumé is never really finished. It is a living document. It may morph during your job search as circumstances dictate, and it will grow as your career grows.

41. Cover Letters

The cover letter is a powerful tool that is often underutilized or overlooked in a job search. A well-written cover letter will fine-tune the connection between your résumé and the targeted opportunity.

A résumé should never travel alone. It needs an escort. In an ideal world, this escort is a person—someone who knows you, knows your objective, and makes sure your résumé receives the appropriate attention. In some cases this individual is someone within the organization with whom you have some personal history. In other cases, this person has come to know you through that organization's interviewing process. Regardless, your résumé will receive some level of personal attention and the need for a cover letter is eliminated.

But what about those times when your résumé starts off on its own? Perhaps you are responding to an advertisement or submitting your résumé to an organization unsolicited. Considering there is no person to shepherd your résumé at this point, an accompanying cover letter becomes very important.

An effective cover letter can never be a form letter. If you create a standard letter and simply modify the address and salutation each time it is used, you will diminish its power and effectiveness. Since no two companies are the same and there are always variances among the different jobs, each cover letter must be unique. Although the actual content varies, the themes are standard. Here are the four parts of a well-written cover letter and a brief discussion of each.

- **Impetus.** Why are you submitting the résumé to this company for this position? What caused you to do so? Perhaps it was an article in a business magazine or a catchy television commercial. Maybe a classmate or neighbor works

Jeffrey A. Jones

1322 East Nittany Street
State College, PA 18745

(814) 676-1633
jjones@psu.mba.edu

July 15, 2011

Mr. Robert Pearson
Vice President, Quality Assurance
HEMCO
1800 Main Street, Suite 1976
Downingtown, PA 19388-1488

Dear Mr. Pearson:

Last week you addressed my operations management class during your visit to the graduate school of business at the Pennsylvania State University. During your remarks you stressed the importance of both planned and corrective maintenance programs as elements of a productive quality assurance program. I found this information insightful and have incorporated much of it in my operations research thesis. I am writing to thank you for your remarks and to ask you to consider me for the position of Manager of Quality Assurance, as advertised on your website.

On my resume you will see that I served five years in the Navy before enrolling at Penn State for my MBA. Two of those five years were spent as the Main Propulsion Assistant and Quality Assurance Officer on my ship. A major part of my duties included management of the ship's planned and corrective maintenance programs, for which I received a Navy Achievement Medal. My resume also includes an overview of the internship I held last summer at the J. I. Case Corporation, where I helped institute a new statistical process quality control program.

Although not mentioned on my resume, I successfully completed the Navy's schools for material maintenance and quality assurance. Additionally, having grown up on the family farm, I am very familiar with the operation and maintenance of farm and construction equipment.

Please review my resume and contact me if you have any questions. It is a short drive from State College to Downingtown and I would very much appreciate the opportunity to meet with you and interview for the Manager of Quality Assurance position. I will call your office next week to ensure that you received this letter. Thank you very much for your time and consideration.

Sincerely,

Jeff Jones

there. An employment advertisement in the newspaper or on the Internet caught your attention. Simply, what caused you to sit down at the computer to compose the cover letter and address the envelope?

- **Focus.** Draw the attention of the reader to the section of the résumé that shows the most relevance to the position for which you are applying. This could be your education, some specific work experience, a certification, or even your physical location. Again, look for relevance and connection.

- **Amplification.** You can use the cover letter to amplify certain sections of your résumé to make you look even more qualified for the job. This paragraph allows you to add more detail or provide additional information or both.

- **Action.** What is the next step? What are your expectations? What would you like to happen next? What will you do in terms of follow-up? In many cases you will have little choice other than waiting for a reply. Sometimes you need to take action to determine the status of your résumé and the company's level of interest, such as offering to visit, calling in a few days, or following up with an e-mail.

Consider the example on the opposite page.

Let's review. For the most part, Jeff's letter is well written. It is a little wordy, but appears to be correct with respect to spelling, punctuation, grammar, and syntax.

Regarding content, Jeff has covered the four critical elements effectively. In his first paragraph, the **impetus** behind his letter is clear. Jeff enjoyed Mr. Pearson's presentation, visited the company's website, and found a position of interest. In his second paragraph, Jeff asks Mr. Pearson to **focus** on the most appropriate portion of the résumé—his experience in quality and maintenance. The third paragraph gives Jeff the opportunity to **amplify** his profile beyond what is included on the résumé. In the final paragraph Jeff clearly states his follow-up **action**.

A few additional thoughts. First, brevity is important. It is hard enough to get a potential employer to read your résumé without diluting your chances even more by attaching a long and wordy cover letter. Rule of thumb—never more than one page. Second, much like your résumé, a cover letter is a de facto writing sample. It needs to be well written, grammatically correct, and without errors. Third, a cover letter can be a powerful substitute for stating an objective on your résumé.

The cover letter is an important tool in your transition toolbox. It does not take much time to write an effective one and even less time to make sure that it reflects well on your writing abilities. From helping open the door to making sure it gets to the proper destination, a well-written cover letter can be a valuable escort for your résumé.

42. Your Reference List

Many organizations will complete a reference check before extending a job offer. They do this for three reasons: it helps verify some of the information you have provided; hearing what previous employers and acquaintances have to say about you can be an effective screening technique; and protection—a positive reference check in your file is a great defense for the personnel department should a problem arise regarding your character or performance after you have been hired.

Years ago, a letter of recommendation was a standard document in the paperwork supporting a job search. Job seekers would ask their references to write open-ended *to whom it may concern* letters, and these endorsements would be given to potential employers as needed. This practice has all but disappeared, having been replaced by the reference list. This is simply a one-page summary of information prepared by the job seeker that identifies those individuals he or she has chosen as personal and professional references.

Notice the two categories—**Personal** and **Professional**. The former are people who know you for reasons other than the military. They will be asked to comment on your personality, citizenship, and character. Consider people such as family friends, neighbors, clergymen, coaches, academic advisers, and teachers. Your professional references will be asked to comment on your professionalism, work ethic, and performance. For this category, target current or former direct or indirect supervisors, not peers. In both cases, select individuals who are easy to contact. Although your former commanding officer would give you a great endorsement, a potential employer might not be willing to track him or her down in Iraq or Afghanistan or wait for him to return from a deployment under the polar ice cap.

A surprisingly frequent mistake in compiling a reference list is including people without clearing it with them in advance. If someone agrees to serve as a reference, then obtain permission to release his or her contact information. Not only is this courteous, but it also reduces the chances that one of your references receives a totally unexpected phone call late one evening from *XYZ* Corporation regarding a reference check. Under those circumstances, the information provided by your reference might be much different than you expected.

Let's take a look at the format and physical presentation. It should be one page in length and on the same type of paper as your résumé. The top should look like the top of your résumé—name and contact information. Title the page **REFERENCES** and include two subheadings: **Personal** and **Professional**. Under each subheading list three individuals. In addition to the name, include the mailing address, phone numbers, email address, and the nature and duration of the relationship. Above is a sample.

A few notes:

- Obtain permission from your references before you put them on your list.
- Provide your references with a copy of your résumé. This helps them help you.
- Understand that companies will not check all six. They typically contact three or four. Listing more is recommended because not all of them will be easily reachable all the time.

- Ask your references to let you know when they receive a call. That is a strong signal that an offer is forthcoming.
- Notify your references if you know that reference checks are about to begin.
- Do not panic if your references are not called. Some companies never check references, relying instead on a review of your performance evaluations.
- Be sure to call or write your references to say *thank you* when your search is over. Your gratitude and professionalism will be remembered when you ask for their assistance again in the future.

43. Application Forms—Thank Goodness I Made a Copy

I was just about to call it a day and go home when the phone rang. I was tempted to ignore it, but that's just not me. I picked up and barely had time to say hello when I heard the panicked voice at the other end of the line say, "Tom, thank goodness you are still in the office. I screwed up. I sure hope you can help me."

I did not need to ask who it was. Command Sergeant Major Bobby Boudreaux's Cajun accent is very distinctive and we had spent an hour on the phone earlier that day in preparation for a follow-up interview. He was scheduled to fly to Houston early the next morning to interview with a big paper and packaging company. I replied, "Bobby, calm down. Whatever the problem is, I'm sure we can fix it. What's going on?"

He explained to me that he messed up the application that he was to take with him to the interview the next day. The instructions on the front page of the ten-page form included this statement: "It is critical that you read this form in its entirety before proceeding."

Anxious to get it done so that he could pack his suitcase, Bobby ignored that instruction and just started filling it out. It was page seven that got him into trouble. Right there in the middle of the page were the words: "Now that you have reached this point, there is no need to read any further. Simply skip to the last page, sign and date in the indicated spaces, and place the blank form in the envelope provided."

I asked if he had made a copy and his reply confirmed my suspicion. Bobby was lucky. I had that application form on my computer and could e-mail a replacement.

Interviewing and job hunting require a tremendous amount of paperwork, including résumés, cover letters, follow-up/thank-you letters, writing samples, and application forms. Like all mechanical preparations, paperwork only becomes an issue when done improperly or left undone. Our subject here is the application form, which many companies treat as a formality, but you would be ill advised to do the same.

Proper completion of the application form ensures that it will not be a cause of rejection. There are ten issues to consider:

- **Make copies.** The first step is to make copies of the uncompleted form. Why? Well, it is nice to have a working copy to play around with before you go final. In addition, you might make an error, and a clean copy is preferable to correction fluid. This can be problematic when completing an online form, but many of them offer a save prior to submission feature. If not, you can always refresh or exit and start over.
- **Attention to detail.** Read it. More specifically, read it cover-to-cover before any ink hits the page. Why? Sometimes there are instructions later in the document that affect what you may have already written. The extreme example is the story of Bobby Boudreaux above. Unlike Bobby, follow the instructions. Otherwise, thank goodness for those copies you made.
- **The proper materials?** Now you are ready to begin, maybe. Do you have the proper materials? Did the instructions specify black or blue ink or number two pencil? Do you have access to the information requested? Previous addresses? Contact information for references?
- **Be thorough.** Unless instructed otherwise, you should leave nothing blank. You do not want to be interpreted as lazy or lacking attention to detail. Never use the phrase "See résumé." That is code for "I am too lazy to restate what is already on my résumé." Be careful with phrases like "open" or "flexible" because some companies treat those responses the same way they would a blank space. Your goal is to appear flexible and keep open as many doors as possible. You can accomplish this goal and still fill in the blanks by being a little creative. For example, if the opening is in Atlanta, put *Southeast* in the geographic preference box. Rather than listing a specific salary, put down a salary range. For example, if you are targeting $60,000, then you could indicate a range

of $55,000 to $65,000. Under objective, two things are important. First, make sure your response indicates something you are both interested in and also qualified to do for that company; second, make sure that position is available.

- **Accuracy.** There are two parts to this one. First, make sure that everything you put on the form is truthful, accurate, verifiable, and documented. No guessing. If you use estimates or approximations, make sure you qualify that information accordingly. Second, there is no excuse for typographical errors, spelling errors, poor grammar, or other mistakes that would reflect badly on you.

- **Military service?** Many application forms are not designed to take into account the number of different assignments typical service members have during their time in the military. Some application forms have a special section for military service and it is usually a relatively small space. What to do? Consider the space available and summarize your total military history in the space allotted—do not overflow to an attachment unless the instructions give you that option. Ignore the "See résumé" temptation.

- **Make more copies.** Assuming you have your final product in your hands, what now? Make copies. There are several reasons for this. One, potential employers have been known to lose application forms and your foresight will be rewarded. Two, once you have completed one company's form you will have much of the same information requested for another's. And, three, you might need to recall exactly what you put on the form when you submitted it months or weeks ago. If you are completing the form online, print it before you submit and exit the application function.

- **Timeliness matters.** For some companies, the application form is the first step in the evaluation process. For others, you are only asked to complete one as the final step before receiving an offer. Still others wait until your first day in the new job to have you complete one. Whenever you receive it, treat it like a time bomb. You need to return it before it explodes. Unless the company representative specifically states otherwise, you should complete and return it immediately. Although timeliness is important, do not sacrifice accuracy, neatness, and completeness in your desire to return it promptly. Consider using an express delivery service. This can both make up for lost time and also send a strong "I am interested" signal.

- **Do you need assistance?** If you are completing the application form at the beginning of the process with a company, you are probably on your own. The exception would be the availability of a personal advocate in that company. For instance, the Uncle Harry or Aunt Mary you will learn about in chapter 45. If a recruiting firm sponsored you to this company, then one of its counselors can help. A career coach is another option. If you are filling out the forms at the end of the recruiting process and you either have an offer or one is highly likely, then take advantage of the fact that you now have allies in the company—people who want you on the team.
- **Prepare a cheat sheet.** All of the previous guidance assumes that you will have the time and ability to complete the application form in advance of the interview. What if that is not the case? Although unusual, you might find yourself filling out the forms while you are on site with the company. Take the time to prepare a cheat sheet. Include a summary of the information that is typically requested on an application form and a list of references.

Successful use of the application form is not difficult. Just keep in mind accuracy, neatness, attention to detail, and a back-up plan—personal attributes already in place due to your military service.

44. Uniform of the Day

How does it feel to be out of uniform and not in violation of military regulations? Now that you are about to finish your time in the service, you are probably looking forward to putting your uniforms in the closet and relishing the prospect of wearing them a lot less (reserve commitment) or never again. Not so fast. Many civilian jobs have uniform clothing requirements associated with them. Even for those that do not, there will be at least one more uniform of the day in your wardrobe.

Pretend you have an interview tomorrow. Go to your closet and select what you are going to wear. If you are like most military personnel, what you select is probably going to be inappropriate. There could be two reasons for this. First, you might not be aware of what is appropriate interviewing attire. And, even if you know what is appropriate, you might not have it in your closet at this time. Regardless, you probably need some guidance and a trip to the mall.

One of the first issues to resolve is what the company expects when it comes to interviewing attire. It is often possible to find out this information in advance. Go to the source. How was this interview arranged? Contact the person who set it up for you and seek guidance. This is relatively easy if the arrangements were made through a third party, such as a relative, friend, or a placement company. If however the interview resulted from a website application or a mail campaign, obtaining this information could be more difficult. One option is to simply ask the representative of the company what interviewing attire would be appropriate. This can be a little awkward, since you want to avoid coming across as naive or high-maintenance. When in doubt, take the safe approach—think conservative.

Dressing for an interview in a traditional or conservative manner will never be held against you. The reverse may not be true.

Realizing that you are overdressed for the interview is unlikely to cause any damage, but walking into the room to discover you are the only one not wearing a suit will be difficult to overcome. You may be able to adjust your interviewing attire for subsequent interviews, if you are invited to return.

If the interview is a second-level or follow-up event that takes place at the job site, and if the job site is heavy industrial or manufacturing or construction re-lated, then the dress code will often reflect that setting. Under those circumstances you might be advised to wear more casual attire.

One of the key elements of a successful interview is being memorable. How-ever, that memory should have nothing to do with what you wore to the interview. If it does, rest assured it was the inappropriateness of your attire that stuck in the interviewer's mind. The reward for dressing appropriately is no recollection on the part of the interviewer regarding what you were wearing.

Here are some general guidelines regarding interviewing attire:

- **The suit.** Men: conservative, two-piece, wool or wool blend; solid or pin-stripe or very subtle pattern; navy blue or charcoal gray; pants and jacket of the same material; belt or suspenders (not both). Women: similar to men's, with additional colors of black or maroon; traditional skirt length; pantsuit is acceptable.
- **The shirt.** Men: starched long-sleeve solid white or pale blue cotton; spread, tab, or button-down collar. Women: solid-color blouse of cotton, silk, rayon, or blend; conservative neckline or moderate collar.

- **Neckwear.** Men: silk tie, conservative color, solid or subtle stripes or pattern. Women: none, or simple gold chain, strand of pearls, or silk scarf.
- **Shoes.** Men: conservative, black or cordovan leather with laces; well polished and scuff-free. Women: conservative closed toe, closed heel pump or flat; black or color coordinated with suit.
- **Jewelry.** Men: minimal; not more than one ring per hand; no visible body piercings. Women: understated; not more than one ring per hand; simple studs or small hoops or no earrings.
- **Accessories.** Keep to a minimum; simple portfolio or notebook; cell phone (turned off or silenced); if a pocketbook is necessary, smaller is better; simple wristwatch.
- **Grooming.** Men: recent haircut; clean-shaven or well-groomed facial hair. Women: recently cut and styled hair; pulled back or worn up if appropriate.
- **Common errors.** Droopy socks; overpowering perfume or cologne; sport coats or blazers; visible body art; *statement* or *message* ties; logos; poorly laundered shirt; ill-fitting clothing; no undershirt; multi-function, multi-timezone dive watches; poorly maintained shoes; audible e-mail or text notifications.

As you have figured out by now, the information provided above reflects a conservative approach to dressing for an interview. The reason for this tactic is simple—better safe than sorry. It is highly unlikely that overly conservative or traditional attire would ever be held against you. Conversely, it will be difficult to recover from an interview situation in which you were dressed inappropriately.

Being memorable is very important, but make sure that memory is not based on what you were wearing.

45. Finding Uncle Harry or Aunt Mary

Before you can interview with a company you must figure out a way to get your foot in the door.

Turning a piece of paper (your résumé) into a chance to compete for the opportunity (the interview) is much easier when you have help.

Where do you get this assistance? Take a look into the future. Your search has ended and you are about to accept an offer—congratulations!  Now look in your rearview mirror at your relationship and interview history with that company and you will find that one individual who deserves most of the credit for helping you get your foot in the door. Who is that person? Uncle Harry or Aunt Mary.

Uncle Harry? Aunt Mary? Who are these people? They are a critical part of any successful search. Before you can interview with and go to work for any organization, you must first find someone there who is willing to go to bat for you. He or she will help you open the door, help you keep it open, shepherd your résumé, and coach you through the process. Meet your Uncle Harry or Aunt Mary.

He or she might be an actual relative or simply a pseudonym for someone else, known or unknown to you at the beginning of your search. Either way, you have to source an Uncle Harry or Aunt Mary inside the company in order to have any chance of an interview. You need connections to make this work, the more the better. Combine all of those connections and you have a network, where every node on that network is personified as an Uncle Harry or Aunt Mary.

The concept behind networking is simple—whom do you know and whom do they know? You may be familiar with a party game called The Six Degrees of Kevin Bacon. Here is the concept. Pick anyone on the planet and you can connect him or her to the actor Kevin Bacon through a maximum of four other personal connections in a sequence. Hence, the six degrees.

You do not have to know a Hollywood actor to make this work. In theory, any two people can be connected by tracking the relationships between four or fewer other people. The same theory explains why networking can be such a powerful job-hunting tool. Given the power of the Internet and the advent of social and professional networking sites, the number of degrees necessary to make the connection is falling rapidly.

Expand the network enough and eventually you will find Uncle Harry or Aunt Mary.

Caution: As effective as networking can be, it has a downside. A tremendous amount of work is required to make it pay off. You must ask people for help, make phone calls to people that do not know you, and overcome the feeling that perhaps you are imposing. You may also find yourself bumping up against closed doors, while running the risk of being rejected or ignored. Try not to take it personally and stay the course. In the end, the results will more than offset the effort and frustration.

There are seven ways to develop your network, and here is an overview of each.

Inside connections. Although for most people Uncle Harry is a euphemism for the inside contact they are attempting to develop, some of us have an actual Uncle Harry we can utilize. Make a list of family members or friends who hold influential positions in companies that are of interest to you. Although having the vice president of operations looking out for you is altogether different from your cousin Vincent who handles security at the front gate, keep in mind that Vincent also has connections at that company.

Assuming there are positions available for which you are qualified, your Uncle Harry will get you the interview. Depending on your relationship, in addition to making the right connections, he will give you insights on both the opening and also the person, or people, who will be interviewing you. Do not worry about nepotism. Although his influence got you the interview, successful performance in the interview process is required to get the job. Remember, however, Uncle Harry is doing you a favor. Make sure you are well prepared for the interview. Your performance will reflect back on him.

The Internet. A resource that barely existed not that long ago has become one of the most powerful tools available to the job seeker. Just think of all the potential Aunt Marys out there in cyberspace. All that potential must be tempered with caution, however. Just as very few classified ads are actually of interest to you, most Internet job postings will be similarly inappropriate. The key to successful use of the Internet as an interview-generating tool is selectivity.

Although services like Careerbuilder.com and Monster.com are well known resources, are the organizations using those sites trying to find people like you? Utilize a service that specifically targets your skill set or specialty. Employers who are predisposed to hire the military profile will utilize these sites and will be much more receptive to your posting or inquiry. According to a recent study by Vet-eransToday.com, here are the most effective job boards for veterans (listed alpha-betically):

- CivilianJobs.com
- DefenseTalent.com
- HireVeterans.com
- MilitaryHire.com
- RecruitMilitary.com
- Taonline.com
- VetJobs.com

Social and professional networking sites such as Facebook, MySpace, and LinkedIn have also developed as legitimate job search and career development platforms, but caution is advised with respect to content and your postings. Make sure the accessible information presents you to a potential employer in a positive way. Remember, pictures are forever!

Additionally, exercise control over the dissemination of your résumé. Without proper controls, your résumé distribution could get out of hand. Although you hope to generate a new Aunt Mary, being ill-prepared for her unexpected phone call is unlikely to produce the desired results. More about this later in "The Run-away Résumé."

Recruitment advertising. Also known as the help wanted ads and classifieds, this is the most traditional and also least effective method of finding your Uncle Harry. Those who use this approach do so because it is relatively easy even though it can be tedious. Frequently by the time an opening shows up in the classifieds, it is filled or a viable candidate has already been identified. The company is running the ad for either public relations purposes or U.S. Equal Employment Opportu-nity Commission (EEOC) requirements.

One great reason to use the classifieds is to support a location-focused job search. If you must live in Chicago, then pay attention to the classified ads in the Sunday *Chicago Tribune*. In addition to the specific ads, see which companies are buying the most column inches of recruitment advertising. Whether or not you are qualified for the positions listed, a lot of advertising indicates growth, and growth means opportunity. Perhaps there are appropriate opportunities available beyond the ones being advertised.

Your odds of success are very low. Consider yourself fortunate if 10 percent of your inquiries generate a response, and that response might not be a call from your new Uncle Harry. A postcard or e-mail acknowledging receipt of your résumé may be as good as it gets. So why even bother with this avenue? Again, it is relatively easy and inexpensive, it can help the geographically challenged, and you might get lucky.

Alumni associations. Most trade schools, colleges, and universities offer their graduates some sort of post-graduation career guidance and counseling. Some schools offer sophisticated web-based and national career guidance. Other schools use much less formal or geographically specific programs. Contact your school or alumni association to see what programs are available.

At some schools, these programs are sponsored by the Office of Alumni Affairs or the equivalent. At others, the alumni association administers the service. Depending on the extent of programs offered, these services will either be free or a subscription will be required. In any event, consider joining the association and start participating in alumni events in your city or the cities in which you would like to live.

Attend those networking breakfasts and cocktail parties. Look for links to social networking sites. Whether it's through a formal assistance program or an informal chat over coffee, perhaps you could run into your Aunt Mary and discover she also attended your school.

Veterans service organizations (VSOs). These and other military-focused professional groups offer an approach similar to that of alumni associations. Organizations such as the Military Officers Association, the Retired Enlisted Association, the Non-Commissioned Officers Association, the Navy League, the Association of the U. S. Army, Veterans of Modern Warfare, Iraq and Afghanistan Veterans of America, Vietnam Veterans of America, and AMVETS can be valuable resources. This value is three-fold:

- They might offer a career transition program.
- They probably sponsor conferences, fairs, meetings, or social events.
- Their membership shares a common bond with you.

Already a member? Give them a call or visit the website to see what type of services they offer. Not a member? Now is the time to join. Remember, there is a strong likelihood that Uncle Harry is already a member in good standing. For a complete list, visit http://www1.va.gov/vso.

Transition Assistance Program (TAP). This program was established to address the needs of separating service members as they move into civilian life. TAP is a partnership among the Departments of Defense, Veterans Affairs, Transportation, and the Department of Labor's Veterans Employment and Training Service (VETS). One of the missions of TAP is career transition assistance for service members and their spouses. This assistance comes in several forms, including interview workshops, résumé guidance, and seminars on job search techniques. There are TAP offices at most military installations, and the individuals who staff these offices are not only transition professionals but also likely to qualify for Aunt Mary status.

Although TAP applies to all services, each branch has modified or expanded the content and services to meet the needs of its service members. For example, the U.S. Army offers TAP in the form of the Army Career and Alumni Program, or ACAP.

To learn more about TAP, VETS, ACAP, and similar resources, visit www.turbotap.org, a site for all military personnel, regardless of branch. When you complete the online registration form you are directed to the programs most appropriate for your individual situation.

Placement companies. Also known as employment agencies, headhunters, or search firms, these organizations can be a very powerful tool. A professional, experienced recruiter or counselor at a placement firm can be your Aunt Mary connection in a company where you do not already have one.

Placement firms maintain relationships with hundreds of companies. They are aware of available positions in their client companies and can strongly influence interview activity there. The client companies value these services and pay the fees. If the **ABC** Company has a strong relationship with a placement firm and you have no personal Aunt Mary at **ABC**, the placement firm has a much better chance of getting your foot in the door than do you.

Caution: When using a placement firm, remember that they are not all created equal. Check them out carefully and remember—they are best when used as a supplement to, not a replacement for, your overall plan. Watch out for placement companies that place restrictions on your search. Do not work with one that requires you to sign a contract or forces you to use them exclusively. The next chapter provides additional information on this topic.

46. Headhunters

As the previous chapter indicated, a placement company (aka headhunter) can be an excellent resource. However, make sure you select the right one.

The word "headhunter" is used to describe someone who works in the executive search industry. Executive search companies are hired by organizations to go out and find executive-level talent for them. Other than a few well-placed generals and admirals, few military personnel will ever find themselves the targets of an executive search. The headhunters that target military personnel are more accurately described as placement companies. Although technically inaccurate, the term "headhunter" is convenient for the sake of this discussion.

Getting interviews is all about having contacts, and a headhunter can be your contact at a potential employer where you do not already have one.

Headhunters establish and maintain relationships with their client companies. They get to know you, your search criteria, and your motivators. They help you get your foot in the door. More important, they know where the doors are, who has the keys, and what is behind each of them.

A good headhunter will be more than just a doorman. He or she can also be an excellent talent scout, coach, mentor, and matchmaker. Most military personnel do not really know what they want to do in the civilian sector. Once they get beyond "work with people" and "management" (see chapters 26 and 27, respectively), they have a difficult time expressing their job objectives. A good headhunter will evaluate a candidate's marketability, identify areas of interest, and assist in preparing for interviews. Given the significant amount of value added, how much should you expect to pay?

Nothing. That is correct—nothing. How can this be? Headhunters are not charities. They have expenses. They work for profit. What is the source of their revenue? Their client companies value their services and pay for them. These fees can be substantial—a $20,000 fee on a $60,000 salary, for example. What is the economic justification? When using a headhunter, a company can decrease or eliminate many recruiting expenses, such as the costs associated with screening, evaluation, testing, and travel. Although those costs can be substantial, the real savings occur in the management of risk. Using a headhunter can increase the odds of both an offer and an acceptance, thereby reducing risk. Reducing risk saves money, significantly so.

Although a good headhunter is a powerful resource, identifying the good ones and determining which one is right for you are not easy tasks. Consider this list of **DOs** and **DON'Ts**:

DO keep in mind that some headhunters take offense at that term, preferring to be called counselors, recruiters, or placement specialists.

DON'T assume they are all created equal. Most of them will profess or confess to some expertise or specialization.

DO seek out one that meshes well with your background and/or priorities. Some specialize in a particular geography or a specific industry or a target segment of the military population. Visit www.rileyguide.com and www.military.com for information about headhunting companies that focus on veterans.

DON'T sign anything. Reputable headhunters will not ask you to sign any contracts or letters of understanding. Even if they do not require you to sign, the fact they even have such a contract is a danger signal.

DO be selective. Yes, they will screen and interview you prior to taking you on as a candidate, but you should also interview them and ask for references.

DON'T pay any placement fees at any time. Make sure they are fully fee-paid by their client companies.

DO ask for a list of clients. Reputable headhunters are proud of their client lists and use them as a marketing tool. An unwillingness to disclose this information is a danger signal.

DON'T allow them to market you to companies without your approval in advance. Duplication of effort can lead to sponsorship conflicts, the resolution of which will diminish your chances of receiving an interview.

DO remain proactive in your self-sponsored job search beyond the activities of the headhunter. Be open with them about your independent activity.

DON'T work with headhunters who require you to cease all job search activity beyond what they control, regardless of how they attempt to justify such a restriction. A request for an exclusive relationship is great for them, but whose job search is it anyway?

DO ask them for their appraisal of your marketability and their ability to assist you in getting what you want.

DON'T register with more than two headhunters. If you pick the right one, one is all you need. Having a fallback position may be a good idea, but keep in mind that if you reduce their odds of placing you too much, then their incentive to assist you will also be reduced.

DO be upfront with your headhunter(s) about your overall plan. Let them know the companies where you have inside connections. Tell them of your plans to use other headhunters, but remember—very few people like playing second fiddle.

DON'T self-sponsor to a company that the headhunter has proposed to you as a potential employer—being upfront and ethical flows both ways.

DO keep in mind that a headhunter can be an excellent supplement to, but never a total replacement for, your overall search plan.

DON'T work with one who has little experience in the business. It is their experience, knowledge, contacts, and savvy that gives you value. If you are assigned a rookie make sure he or she has the backing of an experienced team.

DO work with a headhunter with whom you feel some sort of a connection. Look for a feeling of trust, empathy, honesty, ethical behavior, and maybe even some background commonality. Personal one-on-one contact is always preferred.

DON'T work with a company where your file is continuously handed off to someone new. Look for continuity and closure. The good headhunters know that your long-term value to them as a representative of a client company in the future far exceeds the short-term value of placing you.

Military-to-civilian placement companies have been around since 1970. I was a partner in one of the best for almost thirty years. I am a believer. How about you—should you go this route? Use this list of **DO**s and **DON'T**s and the information in the next chapter to determine if a headhunter would be a valuable addition to your job search team.

47. An Employment Perfect Storm

Picture this: gathered together and separated by a curtain are two distinct groups of people. On one side of the curtain are dozens of job seekers. On the other side are company representatives with hundreds of jobs to fill. The job seekers are there because a large group of hungry employers are in attendance and the recruiters are there because they have openings and expect to find an impressive talent pool—an *employment perfect storm.*

Depending on the two guest lists and the number of controls that are in place, what you are witnessing when the curtain comes up is either a **job fair** or a **hiring conference.** Regardless of the label, these events can have a positive impact on your job search.

Job fairs. These events may be hosted by private sector or not-for-profit organizations or agencies, such as college alumni associations, professional societies, TAP/ACAP offices, and veterans groups. A job fair is set up like a trade show. There is a central exhibition area with booths, tables, signage, and static displays. Dozens of companies are in attendance and representatives from each are staffing their own bit of turf. Each company may have paid an attendance fee and they will pay nothing more, whether they hire ten people or no one.

The job seekers attend free of charge, or there might be a nominal registration fee. When the doors open, the candidates enter the exhibition area and begin to roam. The line in front of one company's table may be long and there may be no one in line at the booth next door. A candidate gradually works his or her way to the front of the line, hands the company recruiter a résumé, and has thirty seconds to land a follow-up interview later that day.

Although highly productive, job fairs are not without flaws. They are usually open houses, i.e., there is little control on who can or cannot participate, and there is no guarantee that the advertised companies will actually attend. There is no way of knowing in advance if the job seekers will match the openings. There could be much standing in line, or perhaps no one stands in the line. Even with these risks, the job fair has strong potential to add value to a job search. Most of that value comes from the fact that highly motivated and mutually interested parties are coming together in a central location.

Now let's take the job fair concept and refine it. By adding some controls, eliminating the open house, and personalizing the matchmaking process, a job fair morphs into something a bit different.

Hiring conferences. Keeping job fairs in mind for a moment, consider the following questions. What if attendance for both candidates and companies was by invitation only? What if the employer paid a fee only when a hire was actually made? What if the candidates were screened in advance, based on both qualifications and interests? What if the organization sponsoring the event knew enough about the needs of both the candidates and the companies that they have pre-scheduled one-on-one interviews, eliminating the need for both the central exhibition area and standing in line? What if both parties knew in advance what was in store for them? The candidates have an indication of which companies are on their schedules, and the companies have screened résumés and approved their slates of interviews.

Answer these *what ifs* in the affirmative and you end up with a hiring conference instead of a job fair. One more difference—unlike job fairs, hiring conferences are almost exclusively sponsored by private companies, most of which are in the career placement industry.

Be it a hiring conference or a job fair, there is value to be found in each, the obvious being the efficient use of the time and money of both parties. Although job seekers may incur travel costs (transportation, hotel, food, etc.), they pay nothing or little to attend. The key to finding additional value is in being selective. Find events that target either your professional/academic profile or a particular segment of the job market that holds strong interest for you. Prior to attending a job fair, try to obtain a list of the companies that are expected to attend and a list of the positions to be filled.

Due to the pre-scheduled nature of a hiring conference, there can be additional value added. A day or two in advance, the organization hosting it may be able to give you a preview of your interview schedule with both the names of the companies and the types of positions. This is important for two reasons: you will have time to do your homework and you will know in advance whether or not you should attend. A well-established and professional placement company will provide you with this courtesy as a standard procedure.

Bottom line—incorporating one or both of these events into your overall search plan will increase the odds of finding the right opportunity for you.

48. The Runaway Résumé

"I am sorry, but we will not be able to interview you after all. Your résumé is in our applicant tracking database several times. Normally that would not be a problem, but because you are being tracked under three different source codes, we will have to reject all copies. . . . Yes, I know that seems unfair, but to pursue you would lead to a conflict over sponsorship. . . . Well, let's see. We have you in the system three times. Once as an internal employee referral, again under your own Internet application on our website, and a third time on the letterhead of one of our placement companies. . . . Again, I am truly sorry. I know it seems unfair, but it is corporate policy to resolve potential conflicts like these before they become real, and sadly for you, this is the easiest way for us to control the problem."

Now, that is one update that you never expected to receive. What went wrong? Everything you hear says to use a multi-pronged approach and this is your reward for being thorough? Unfortunately in many cases it is. As important as it is to be thorough, it is equally important to maintain control of the distribution of your résumé. This is a classic example of the double-edged sword. It is certainly true that the more avenues you pursue, the more options you utilize, the more contacts you develop, the more likely you will find the right job. However it is equally true that all of this prospecting will also increase the odds of conflicts. Although these conflicts will not always kill the deal, they do raise the possibility of rejection and should be avoided if possible.

What can you do to de-conflict your job search? Although there is no foolproof methodology, there are several steps you can take to minimize the odds and reduce the possibility of conflict.

- **Use the Internet selectively.** Although it is a powerful tool, you must be careful. This is especially important when you submit your résumé to an Internet-based service that then makes it available to a list of clients. Before utilizing that type of service, learn their rules of distribution. What sort of controls can you exercise? Do you grant permission or, at a minimum, receive advance notification before a subscriber gets your résumé? Does the service sell or make your résumé available to other services? Discuss these issues with the service and share with them your expectations of how your résumé will be handled.
- **Network.** Whom you know and whom they know comprise one of your most powerful search tools—your network. But, like an Internet search, your net-

work can overlap and get out of control. As you develop your contacts and accept offers of assistance, you should also ask them to inform you when they pass your résumé along to someone else. This allows you to keep track of your résumé and eliminate the possibility of overlap before it happens. Social networking via sites such as LinkedIn and Facebook is a powerful way to extend your network and market yourself, but balance that benefit to prevent an uncontrolled viral distribution of your résumé.

- **Communicate with placement companies.** As beneficial as they are as a supplement to your overall search plan, they can also be a root cause of conflict. Make sure that your headhunter is aware of your desire to maintain control of your résumé distribution. Let him or her know that you do not want your résumé distributed to a company without your permission. Any high-end, reputable placement firm will extend you that courtesy as a matter of course. Should they balk at that request or refuse to represent you under those conditions, find a more professional firm that will do as you ask.

- **Keep a log.** Most of us do not have the brainpower to mentally track all of the different avenues our résumé is traveling and all of the stops it is making along the way. Keep a written record of your résumé distribution. Note the date it was distributed, the destination, the sponsor, and any subsequent communication trail. List not only the company name, but also the division, subsidiary, location, and point of contact. Although many companies use centralized résumé tracking systems, others empower each of their business units or locations to recruit independently. Just because the distribution center of *XYZ* Company in Atlanta has your résumé on file does not mean the purchasing department in Denver has access to it, or then again maybe it does.

As you can see, thoroughness has its price. That price—mostly in the form of caution and record keeping—will produce dividends in the end. Minimizing conflicts will enhance both the quality and quantity of your employment opportunities.

SECTION V.
PREPARATIONS (MENTAL)

Unlike the physical or external nature of mechanical preparations, mental preparations occur internally. Assuring your mental readiness for the search is the mission of this section.

What is in your head? What is in your heart? What is in your gut? What comes out of your mouth? Knowing the answers to those questions enhances your self-knowledge, which is critical to interview success.

As you go through this section, you will:

- Gain insight through self-knowledge exercises.
- Learn how to use the most powerful tool in your transition toolbox.
- Discover your hidden talents.
- Become familiar with the message you want to convey.
- Figure out what really matters.
- Learn how to turn weakness into strength.

49. The Power of Questions

The questions you ask throughout the job-hunting process have a major impact on its outcome. To understand why questions are important, let's start by asking one:

Why do we ask questions?

There are two answers; one is fairly obvious and one is somewhat obscure, but both are important.

The obvious reason we ask questions is to get answers. There is much to learn about a potential position and a new organization before we can commit to a new career. What are the responsibilities of the job? What is the potential for career growth? How is individual performance measured? What is the corporate culture? Will the compensation, benefits, and location support quality-of-life goals? The answers to these and other questions will help the job seeker decide if the opportunity is right for him or her. However, implicit in the word "decision" is a choice, and unless you have an offer to work for the organization, do you really have a choice?

Before making an offer, a company has to believe you have strong and sincere interest in the job. You must, of course, tell the company you are interested—they need to hear those words. But hearing the words is not enough. The company also has to feel what's behind those words, which leads us to the second and less obvious answer:

Asking questions is the single most powerful tool available to you to express your interest in the company and the opportunity.

Given that a lack of sufficient and/or appropriate questions is one of the most often cited reasons for rejection in the interviewing process, this topic deserves special attention. What questions will you ask in an interview? Now is the time to compile your list. As you do so, remember the dual-purpose nature of asking questions. The right ones will either help you gather information, convey interest, or both. There are additional factors to consider—scope, timing, and content. We can address these factors by taking a look at some sample interview questions, specifically these ten:

1. Why is this position available?
2. When would be the first opportunity for promotion?
3. Who would be my supervisor?
4. Is tuition reimbursement part of the benefits package?
5. What is the biggest challenge of this position?
6. How much will the company spend on research and development (R&D) next year?
7. Is there anything absent in my experience that is important in this job?
8. When will I be eligible to participate in the 401(k) plan?
9. What is the next step in the interviewing process?
10. Are there exercise and child daycare facilities available onsite?

For the sake of this discussion, assume you are interviewing for a position called distribution manager, you are in the early stages of the interviewing process, and the interviewer, Richard, is in charge of distribution operations for the company.

- **Scope.** When asking questions it is important to consider the perspective of the individual with whom you are interviewing. This is part of interviewing empathy, the importance of which cannot be overemphasized. What is important to Richard, and what falls under his span of control? Look at question six. Even if he knows the answer, is this subject within the scope of the interview? If Richard just happens to also be the director of R&D, then perhaps yes; otherwise, no.
- **Timing.** Look at questions four, eight, and ten. Are these questions appropriate during the job-hunting process? Everyone cares about benefits. But consider the timing. In the early stages of the process, the answers to these questions are irrelevant. Unless you work for the company, what difference does it make what perks are available? When should you ask these and similar questions? Wait until the job offer is on the table. With the offer in hand, the answers to the self-interested questions will influence your decision whether or not to accept.
- **Content.** Look at the odd-numbered questions. See how powerful they can be? Asking them gives you information that you need and sends a strong *I am interested* signal to the interviewer. They are appropriate for both the scope of the interviewer and the timing of the interview.

Question two was saved for last because it deserves special analysis. Since both you and your potential employer care about your career path and growth potential, this question needs to be asked. Be careful of your phraseology, timing, and frequency, however. Bringing it up too early or too often might send a signal of disinterest or impatience.

Questions are powerful tools in your transition toolbox. Like the skilled craftsman about to begin an important project, you need to decide which ones to use, gather them together, sharpen them, practice a little, and time their usage appropriately. Applying the right tools at the right time will help you build a successful career. The critical nature of questions is amplified further in "All of My Questions Have Been Answered" in section VI.

Many of the questions you will ask in an interview will stem from the research you do on that company before the interview. Asking questions based on research shows the company that you care enough to have done your homework. The next chapter will help you develop your research skills.

50. Researching Companies

It is very important to research a company before the interview. Not only will you learn much about the organization, its people, its products, and its culture, but you will also improve your odds of a successful interview. It will be apparent to the interviewer that you care and that you worked hard to prepare. This research also gives you the background to enhance the quality and quantity of your questions.

Although researching a company takes time and can be tedious, it is not difficult. What is difficult is learning *how* to research a company.

Given that, you would be wise to master the art of company research well in advance of your first interview. Once you are aware of the resources and how to use them, the process is fairly simple. What will take you three or four hours to do the first time will be accomplished in less than an hour when you are preparing for an actual interview.

I suggest that you develop and practice this skill by selecting a real company as the subject of this exercise and go about your research as though the interview is coming up soon. Make sure you do not waste all of this hard work and valuable information. By selecting a company with which you know you will be interviewing or one where you hope to do so, you may be able to actually use the results of this practice.

Let's get started. It is not that hard to research a company that is incorporated in the United States and publicly traded on a stock exchange. Privately held companies, companies headquartered overseas, and start-ups are more difficult. Although the Internet has simplified the process, it has also created an issue. Yes, doing the research is easier, but with that ease comes higher expectations of thoroughness and accuracy. Speaking of accuracy, resist the temptation to believe everything you read on the Internet, especially when it comes to blogs and open sources like Wikipedia. When Internet research was not an option, an interviewer might forgive an inadequate effort, especially if the company was in the difficult-to-research category. That forgiveness is now much less likely to occur.

There are three angles of attack to keep in mind as you do your research:

- What does the company want you to know?
- What do the business analysts have to say?
- What information is available in the public media?

To answer the first, visit the company's website. Here you will find information about products, sales, profitability, corporate officers, subsidiaries, locations, and press releases. You should also read the company's annual report, especially the cover letter from the president or CEO.

The answer to the second is easy to find if the company is publicly traded. There are dozens of investment-oriented websites at your disposal. Perhaps you use an investment advisor who would share with you his or her research or steer you in the right direction.

The answer to the last exists in the archives of magazines and newspapers. The popular search engines are a good place to start. For more targeted information you might use private sources. One excellent resource is the online research tool available through the *Wall Street Journal*. Although this is a paid subscription, the fee is modest when you consider the wealth of accessible information. You would be hard-pressed to find any company, foreign or domestic, public or private, start-up or Fortune 500, which the *Wall Street Journal* has not researched or profiled to some degree. Publications such as *BusinessWeek*, *Fortune*, and *Forbes* are helpful, as are web-based magazines like *Slate*.

Researching a company in advance of your interview will pay double dividends. Not only will you get a sense of whether or not it is the right kind of company for you, but you will also enter the interview armed with valuable information necessary to demonstrate your level of interest in that company—a critical element of interview success.

Caution: As powerful and important as the Internet is when it comes to company research, it can also make you lazy. Everyone has equal access to that resource and everyone will utilize it, at least in theory. Accordingly, it would be a mistake to stop there. To separate yourself from the crowd, you must do more. Develop an inside connection. Visit retail outlets. Talk to customers or suppliers. Be creative.

51. Knowledge Is Power

Most of us are familiar with that axiom. It applies to many aspects of our everyday lives. Whether shopping for a new car, picking stocks, or choosing a course of action in our career, having as much subject matter knowledge as possible will maximize the likelihood of a positive outcome.

As you have discovered, you must do a significant amount of preparation, both mechanical and mental. Mechanical preparations require physical activity (for example, *writing* a résumé and *buying* an interview suit), while mental preparations require thought (what are my strengths and weaknesses?). Knowledge is so important it crosses the borders and is an integral part of both categories.

There are three types of knowledge critical to interviewing success: knowledge of the **position** for which you are interviewing, knowledge of the **company**, and knowledge of **self**. Attaining the appropriate level of knowledge in each category requires a combination of both mental and physical preparations. Let's take a look at each of the three.

- **Company knowledge.** What do you know about the company? Have you done your homework? This was discussed thoroughly in the previous chapter, "Researching Companies."
- **Position knowledge.** For what opening are you being considered? What does the job entail? Knowing as much as possible about the job will allow you to present yourself in an appropriate way. Whether it is a generic job title or a specific position description, this advanced knowledge will assist you in sending the appropriate signals to the interviewer.
- **Self-knowledge.** Who are you and what makes you tick? What are your attributes, skills, traits, and personality characteristics? More important, which of these are the most appropriate for your target opportunity? Having a thorough knowledge of self is a critical element of interview preparation. In addition to your inventory of skills and traits, you must be ready to discuss specific examples of each. Saying you possess a particular talent is not good enough. You have to be able to prove it is true, and the best proof is an actual anecdote or example from your life that illustrates that talent.

Just as the amount of power can vary depending on the source, the three types of knowledge discussed here are not created equal. Take a minute to study this pie chart.

Slices A, B, and C represent each of the knowledge categories mentioned above, and the size of each slice indicates relative importance. Which is which? The answer

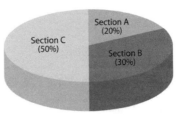

The Knowledge Pie

Section A (20%)
Section B (30%)
Section C (50%)

might surprise you. Here is a clue. Consider the relationship between the accessibility of a resource and its value. Think about a grain of sand and a diamond. Which of the two is easier to obtain? Which one has more value?

- Slice A represents the relative importance of **knowledge of the company.** This section is the smallest of the three because it is the easiest to obtain. The Internet has made it even easier still. You and your competition have equal access to this information and it becomes a common denominator, unless of course you fail to obtain it.

- Slice B, **knowledge of the position**, is slightly larger than Slice A and therefore slightly more important. Why? Again, the answer relates to increased difficulty in learning about the position and the increased possibility that you or your competition will show up for the interview with insufficient information.
- That leaves Slice C, which is as important as A and B combined. **Self-knowledge** can never become a common denominator. Every individual is unique and what he or she brings to the table is also unique. Exceptional self-knowledge can sometimes offset deficiencies in Slices A and B, but the converse will not be the case.

With a high level of self-knowledge and an understanding of both the company and the position, you can present yourself to your potential employer in such a way that he or she cannot help but see you in the job, doing it well, with a smile on your face.

Sometimes your research and knowledge will produce an unexpected result. What if you discover that you are interested in the company but you feel unqualified for the job? You could certainly walk away, but it might be time for a preemptive strike. Joanne Kelly, an aircraft maintenance officer stationed at Dover Air Force Base, was facing just such a dilemma and here is how she handled it.

She is scheduled for an interview in a few days and she has strong interest in the organization but feels unqualified for the position. The only thing stopping her from canceling the interview is that her mentor, a former squadron commander, arranged it for her as a favor and she does not want to appear ungrateful or embarrass him. What should she do?

Let's take a look. On the plus side, Joanne knows much about the organization. She did her research and it seems to be an excellent fit with respect to corporate culture, location, and growth potential. Her mentor is familiar with the company, knows several people there, thinks Joanne would be a good fit, and has set the stage for her. On the minus side, Joanne read the job description, knows she lacks some key qualifications, and does not want to waste the company's time. However, she also does not want to damage her relationship with her mentor by declining the interview. Her mentor has encouraged her to meet with this organization and interview for the position.

Everyone walks into an interview missing something that would make him or her ideal for the job. Nobody is perfect. Sometimes the missing qualifications are deal-breakers. Sometimes they are not. One way to minimize the damage is to launch a preemptive strike.

The *preemptive strike*—put your shortcomings on the table before the interviewer makes an issue of them.

This approach gives you several advantages. It takes away some of the interviewer's power. It also shows you have both an understanding of the position and excellent self-knowledge. Finally, it allows you to emphasize personal attributes that could offset your lack of qualifications. These may include having a strong interest in the field, being well read in the subject matter, having demonstrated success in a similar environment, being a quick study, having a propensity for the discipline, and exhibiting a high level of self-motivation. These and similar traits can often overcome missing qualifications. Although this tactic does not always work, one thing is certain. If you are rejected, the reasons will not include *weak self-knowledge, poor attitude, naiveté,* or *apparent lack of interest in the position.*

By the way, Joanne went forward with her interview. She put her cards on the table early in the process, admitted her missing qualifications, and emphasized her level of interest and trainability. The next day her mentor called to say she had been well received. One week later she received a letter of rejection. A week after that the organization invited her back to interview for a different position, one for which she was much better suited. Offered and accepted. Another successful mission completed.

52. Wallflowers and Cheerleaders

Ever notice how some people walk into a room and energize it by their mere presence? I call those people cheerleaders. How about an individual who is so low key that he or she sort of disappears within the décor? I call that person a wallflower. Allow me to introduce you to Capt. John Wilson, USMC.

I met John on a recruiting trip to Newport, Rhode Island. He was assigned to the Naval Academy Prep School as a staff officer and assistant football coach. He was separating from the Marine Corps in about nine months and we were meeting to discuss his plans.

Before our appointment I reviewed a draft of his résumé and his credentials were impressive. He attended Villanova University on an ROTC scholarship, played varsity football, majored in economics, and made the dean's list six out of eight semesters. After commissioning, he completed The Basic School at Quantico and was deployed to Afghanistan twice before his assignment in Newport. His performance evaluations were excellent and he had been awarded a Bronze Star. I thought of a dozen companies that would love to hire that profile. My expectations were growing and there was a knock on the door, right on schedule.

I opened the door and John came in. He made an excellent first impression. Tall and athletic in stature, he looked great in his Marine Corps uniform. We shook hands, introduced ourselves, took our seats, and started our session. My mission was to evaluate whether or not I could represent John in his job search and his mission was to determine whether or not to accept my assistance, if offered.

Forty-five minutes later I told John I could not help him and that I suspected his job search was doomed to failure. The disbelief on his face was the only emotion I had witnessed on his part since he had walked into the room, and that was the problem.

His credentials were excellent and his job search parameters and requirements were reasonable, but where was the personality? There was no energy, no passion, and no inquisitiveness. One-word responses, and it was like pulling teeth to get even that. I explained to John that on paper he was a winner; in person he was a dud.

That lit his fuse. He came out of his shell. He was energized. He leaned forward in his chair and looked me in the eye and let me have it. He admitted that he was shy and a bit reserved, but that he had lived his life believing that actions speak louder than words. He pointed to his success in college and the Marine Corps as proof of the validity of that belief. He went on for fifteen minutes, citing several examples of the effectiveness of his quiet leadership style. More important, he did all of this without becoming defensive or argumentative. He delivered the information in a positive way, with just the right mix of self-confidence and humility. What a transformation. The winner was back. At that point I told him that maybe I was wrong about him.

"John," I said, "I have known you now for an hour and you made a believer out of me. But here's the problem. If it takes that long for you to show an interviewer who you really are and what makes you tick, you will fail."

He looked confused and asked why.

"Because you do not get an hour! You get five to ten minutes to make the interviewer believe that you are as good as your résumé. The good news is this is fixable and I know you are coachable. We can work together to fix this, so let's get started!"

He agreed and we met several additional times over the next couple of months, preparing him for what turned out to be a very successful job search.

Interviewing successfully is a challenge, and it is even more difficult for the introverts, or wallflowers, of the world. It is harder for them to show interest and build empathy. They can do those things but they take too long. It is much easier for the extrovert, or cheerleader, who appears interested even if that is not the case. Consider the above diagram: this is the **Wallflower: Cheerleader** scale.

John and I agreed that he was coming across as a wallflower, and it was time to make some adjustments to his approach. Since the primary issue was getting him to open up to the interviewer as early as possible, I encouraged him to launch a preemptive strike. He would share with the interviewer that he knew his reserved, quiet style was sometimes misinterpreted as disinterest. He would assure the interviewer that was not the case. Although John might still be rejected, it would likely be for some other reason.

There is an additional consideration. What if you are an extrovert—interviewing is easier, and you have it made, right? Not so fast. Cheerleaders have their own set of problems, namely sincerity and staying power. The extrovert may send an immediate and automatic message of interest and enthusiasm, but will the interviewer believe it is real? Will there be enough there to sustain this overt enthusiasm throughout the entire interviewing process, or will the energy fade and in the process reveal a person who does not live up to the initial impression? Experienced interviewers are aware of this and tend to hold cheerleaders to a higher standard, which is fine as long as they live up to it.

Are you a cheerleader? A wallflower? A bit of both, depending on the situation? Guess what? It is not about the label. What matters is substance and delivery; self-knowledge and presentation; sincerity and staying power. Do not take too long to get warmed up, and remember: a great smile can only take you so far.

53. Weaknesses—Use Them to Your Benefit

What is your biggest weakness? Tell me about a time in your life when you failed. Are there any big disappointments in your life? Tell me about your flaws. What would you change about yourself if you could? What's wrong with you? Tell me why I should not hire you for this job?

Those questions and their cousins may be among the most difficult ones you encounter during the interviewing process. Assuming you have enough self-awareness to acknowledge flaws and enough self-confidence to put them on the table, to do so is counterintuitive. What is to be gained by giving an interviewer reasons to reject you?

Look at it this way—what alternative do you have? Pretend you have no weaknesses? Claim you have never failed? There have been no big disappointments in your life? You are not aware of any flaws? Nothing needs to be changed? You cannot think of a single reason you should not be hired? You could certainly try that approach and in the process you would be presenting your potential employer with a truly unique asset—the perfect candidate for the job.

Ahh, and there is the rub. As you will learn at the end of section VII, there are no perfect candidates, and that is a good thing. You are a human being and you are by nature flawed. Those flaws, or weaknesses, come with the package. An acknowledged weakness or failure will rarely be used as the sole cause of rejection. It is more likely that you will be rejected because of your inability to discuss the issue or a lack of any action on your part to correct the flaw or mitigate its impact.

Your ability to discuss weaknesses and failures, to talk about lessons learned in the process, and to address how you are compensating for or correcting the contributing factors will cause the interviewer to view these flaws in a positive light.

Do not confuse weakness with a lack of qualification. If the job requires a Spanish speaker, then any inability to do so is a qualification issue, not a weakness. Weaknesses are typically personality or character driven. Here is a personal example.

As I was preparing for my job search, I was advised to get ready for the "What are your weaknesses?" question. I wrestled with that for a day or two, and, knowing full well I was about to go down a slippery slope, I asked my wife for help. She took it easy on me, only pointing out half a dozen or so weaknesses. There was one in particular that I ended up using quite frequently in the course of my job search—I had a tendency to not adequately consider the input of others when formulating a course of action. I shared this with the interviewer but would also immediately add that because I was aware of my tendency to do this, I would compensate accordingly and try to be less committed to my own ideas and more receptive to alternative points of view. By answering the question this way, I was able to turn my weakness into multiple strengths—self-knowledge, consensus building, and leadership.

As you prepare for the weakness question you should consider a similar approach. Be honest with yourself and with the interviewer, but also be clever. There is no danger in letting the interviewer know that you have a tendency to try to do too much yourself, or that you sometimes have a hard time delegating, or that you are often irked to discover that others are not as committed to the task as are you, or that . . . , well, you get my drift. Of course, it is a good idea to add to that confession that your self-awareness allows you to make this weakness less of an issue or perhaps correct it completely.

Notice how I mentioned honesty and cleverness in the same sentence. You have to be careful with how honest you choose to be in any discussion of your flaws. There is a limit. Do not be like the candidate I worked with several years ago who, when asked the weaknesses question, replied by saying, "Well, I have to admit that sometimes I just don't feel like working all that hard."

54. Camaraderie and the Power of People

Several years ago one of my clients asked me if he should expect the same level of camaraderie in a civilian job as he had in the military. My answer was no, and yes.

There is little in the civilian workforce that can approximate the bonding that occurs in the wardroom, ready room, or foxhole. Military personnel in those environments put up with much hardship—long hours, stressful working conditions, danger to personal safety, separation from loved ones, and more. However, because they are all in it together, they get through it. This mutual self-sacrifice, teamwork, and unity of purpose contribute to individual bonding, unit cohesion, and, ultimately, the camaraderie in question.

With perhaps the exception of law enforcement, firefighting, and emergency medicine (notice the common denominator), it would be difficult to find a civilian occupation that approximates the conditions of the foxhole. It follows therefore that finding the military version of camaraderie in a civilian occupation is almost impossible. Some people do get close, but often it is simply a matter of time.

Hail and Farewell parties, personal sponsors, turnover periods, contact reliefs—these are examples of the military's effort to ease the move from one duty station to another. Because of the high frequency of duty station rotation in the service, the system must accommodate these moves. Getting on board and up to speed quickly contributes to the automatic welcome-to-the-club experience that awaits most military personnel when they report to a new duty station. Civilians do not do it this way.

Many military-to-civilian career changers will tell you that initially the camaraderie and esprit de corps was absent from their civilian jobs, but it began to develop gradually during the first twelve to eighteen months of employment. This delay is due in part to the fact that unlike in the military where acceptance comes quickly, in the civilian sector you have to earn this membership over time. You might also have to take the initiative. Do not expect a welcoming committee to pull up in front of your house your first week on the job (if ever), nor should you line up a babysitter in anticipation of your Welcome Aboard party. Those things or their equivalents will come, but it takes time and you have to earn them.

The kind of people with whom you work and the corporate culture of the organization will influence the feeling of camaraderie.

Similar feelings can come from relationships you develop with neighbors, church congregations, and through volunteer activity. Take a look at the people in those military foxholes. They share much in the way of values, ethics, commitment, sacrifice, training, reliability, citizenship, and courage. Can the same be said of the civilian workplace? Maybe yes, maybe no.

Is there a lesson here? How about this: as you transition from the military to civilian sector and as you evaluate opportunities and offers, in addition to things like money, location, benefits, growth potential, and job satisfaction, perhaps there is one more issue to consider—are these my kind of people? If not, do you really want to work there? If, on the other hand, they are, then do not discount their importance in the big picture. Here is another chapter in my personal transition story.

During my job search, I had a routine I would go through after every second-level interview. The market for military personnel in the business world was strong and I was fortunate enough to visit several companies during my search. On my way home from those interviews I would collect my thoughts, review the events of the day, and consider the opportunity. I was getting pretty good at briefing my wife on what I had seen and she had become accustomed to my reports. Her reaction to what turned out to be the last of these briefings caught me by surprise.

She picked me up at the airport and we went out to dinner on the way home. We took some time to catch up and she asked me about my interviews that day. After going on for a while, I noticed she was shaking her head and smiling. I stopped and asked her what was so amusing. She laughed and said, "Well, if you get an offer, that's where you are going to work."

This reaction surprised me. She had never responded like that in any of our previous discussions of this sort. When I asked her to explain, she said that for thirty minutes I had not said one thing about the job, the company, the office, the benefits, the working environment, the potential compensation, or the location. She knew nothing about those issues, but she knew much about Neil, Terry, Ben, Linda, and Mike.

All I had talked about were the people. How nice they were. How much they seemed to like what they were doing. How friendly and upbeat they appeared. How most of them had backgrounds similar to mine. How they seemed to be *my kind of people.* My wife pointed out to me that in all of my previous reports, I had not spent nearly as much time, if any, talking about my potential coworkers. This time, she said, even without knowing much about the job, she could tell by the sparkle in my eye, by the tone of my voice, and by my enthusiasm that I had found my niche.

Fortunately for us, she was right. I received an offer the next day and a week later we were flown to the headquarters in D.C. for the company holiday party. Both of us had a great time—she loved the people also—and I accepted the offer before the evening was over. We continued to attend those company holiday parties for the next thirty years.

Is there a moral to this story? Perhaps. In addition to your other search criteria, do not overlook the power of people. There are very few jobs that operate without coworkers or interpersonal relationships of some sort. The importance of these relationships when it comes to your quality of life, quality of work, and job satisfaction should not be overlooked. As you go about your job search, I hope that you are fortunate enough to find yourself thinking,

These are my kind of people.

55. Tell 'Em What They Want to Hear

Interviewing successfully requires thorough preparation, including an understanding of interviewing empathy, an awareness of the position for which you are interviewing, and, most important, a high degree of self-knowledge. A successful combination of those three requirements forces an interviewer to visualize you in the job, and that is a critical component of a successful interview. The following exercise, Circles Within a Circle, and the application of the results will enhance your chances of making that happen.

Draw a large circle on a piece of paper. Using a quarter as a template, fill that large circle with at least twenty smaller circles. Inside each circle write down a word or a phrase that describes you in a positive way, e.g., your attributes, talents, skills, strengths, and traits. Do not restrict your selections to only professional attributes. Consider also those in your scholastic, athletic, social, intellectual, and interpersonal inventories. Solicit input from people who know you well. Having trouble coming up with twenty or more? Think outside the box. Here are some you may have skipped:

Good cook . . . soccer player . . . restores antique cars . . . good sense of direction . . . Spanish language fluency . . . juggling . . . poker player . . . good at completing Sudoku puzzles . . . distance runner . . . good listener . . .

Now take a look at each one and see if it could stand alone in a professional sense or if it would be better to break it down into components that have professional relevance. For example, the circle labeled "soccer player" is replaced with circles labeled "team worker," "physically fit," "excellent spatial awareness," "competitiveness," and "goal setting"; "good cook" is replaced with "creativity," "attention to detail," "organizational skills," and "time management skills."

Also look for those labels that are accurate but too broad in nature to be helpful. For example, "leadership" and "manager" are likely two of your circles. They should not be. Break them down into their components. What is your leadership style? What makes you a good manager? How about "fairness," "example-setting," "empathy," "ethical behavior," "time management skills," "decisive," and "plans ahead"?

That big circle is you and all of those smaller circles are what make you tick. But simply saying something is true does not make it true. You need proof. Take a separate sheet of paper for each of the small circles. At the top of each page write down the word or phrase that appears in that circle. Think long and hard about that word or phrase and then write down an example from your life when that particular talent or attribute played a significant role in what you were doing or what you achieved. Be detailed and specific, and make sure that the application of that word or phrase is obvious. Again, it may be helpful to seek input from others.

Sometimes more than one example is necessary, particularly when you are interviewing for more than one type of position. For example, if "competitive" is one of your small circles, you could use it to interview for both supervisory and individual contributor roles, but the example you cite would be different in each case. You may also discover a circle for which you cannot come up with a good example. If that is the case, discard it. If you cannot prove its existence by way of an example, then it cannot be useful, even if it is true.

Now that you have completed the exercise, you can employ the results in an interview for any job for which you are basically qualified. Here is how that works. You are interviewing with the *ABC* Company for a position called Job X. You share with the interviewer every single one of those small circles and all of the examples to back them up. Mission accomplished, right? No, you blew it.

Yes, you have excellent self-knowledge and all the proof in the world, but when you give the interviewer everything on the list, you are actually hurting your chances. Why? Chalk it up to TMI (too much information). As good as they are, not every item on your list is relevant to Job X.

Here is another way to look at it. Consider that big circle called *you* to be the master set. To interview effectively for Job X you must choose the proper subset. Review the description and requirements of Job X. Now peruse your master set and select only those attributes that relate to Job X. Those characteristics and the examples that back them up become your X subset. When you interview for Job X you present yourself only in terms of X. In essence:

Every question you ask, every answer you give, every story you tell, and every attribute you highlight is intentionally X-flavored.

This tactic forces the interviewer to view you favorably for the position. The beauty of this technique is that you can turn right around the next day and interview for Job Y, or Job Z, or any job for which you can present an appropriate subset of relevant attributes. This can even work if you find yourself interviewing for a position about which you know nothing. You have no job title or job description upon which to base your pitch. Now what subset should you use? Consider this scenario. You are asked,

"What kind of job would you like?" And you respond, "Well, I am not sure what you would call it, but the best job for me would be one in which I could employ these skills and strengths . . ." You complete the sentence by filling in the blank with the subset that consists of your best attributes and examples from the master list. Hopefully you hit enough of the interviewer's hot buttons to receive further consideration for at least one of the available positions.

During a recent interview preparation session, I was describing this Circles Within a Circle exercise to the group. My intent was to emphasize the importance of presenting oneself in such a way as to be appealing to the interviewer. In mid-sentence one of the attendees interrupted me to say, "Tom, it sounds like you are advising us to just tell the interviewer what he or she wants to hear." Resisting the knee-jerk reaction of saying "no way," I thought about that statement for a moment and replied that, well, yes—in essence that is *exactly* what I am recommending, albeit with one important prerequisite.

One of the most important tools in a successful job search is *interviewing empathy*. It is natural to identify and focus on what is important to you, but for an interview to be successful, you must also remember what is important to the interviewer. Hitting as many of those hot buttons as possible will contribute to your success. With prior knowledge of the particulars of the job, the company, the location, and the interviewer, you should be able to hit those buttons. As just noted, it is important to flavor your presentation so that the interviewer develops a strong sense of you in the position he or she is attempting to fill. Simply stated:

To interview successfully, you must master the art of telling the interviewer exactly what he or she wants to hear, *as long as it also happens to be the truth.*

Consider the reverse. What if you fail to emphasize information about yourself that is both true and relevant to the position? That might have been the very piece of information the interviewer needed to designate you as the right person for the job. As you keep truth and relevance in mind you should also remember the importance of interviewing empathy. Empathy is rarely automatic. It has to be built and you must do your part. How? Be a good listener. Pay attention to what the interviewer is saying, both the words and the message behind those words. When you respond, incorporate some of those words and show that the message is received, understood, and in sync with your talents and motivation.

Here is another way to view this issue. Fast-forward to the end of an interview and look inside the interviewer's mind. You will see one of four possible pictures:

- An image that has remained blank, distorted, or out of focus.
- A clear and detailed picture of you in a job much different from the one he or she is trying to fill.
- An image of you in the job he or she is trying to fill, but you appear to be unhappy, dissatisfied, ineffective, or bored.
- There you are, in the job, doing it well, with a big smile on your face!

Obviously option four is your goal, unless you are not interested in the job. Successful interviewing is relatively simple. You must present yourself in such a way that, when you leave the room, the interviewer has a clear, accurate, and truthful vision of you, happy and productive in that job.

SECTION VI.
INTERVIEWS—TIPS AND TECHNIQUES

It is time to come face-to-face, literally, with the challenge: interviews. In section VII you will learn about the actual physical event called an *interview*, but first we will address the interpersonal dynamics that occur during the interview, i.e., *interviewing*.

In the following chapters you will:

- Master a new language.
- Gain insight into interviewers.
- Find out about the negative interview.
- Polish your delivery.
- Send the right signals.
- Prepare for the unexpected.
- Learn how to make a memorable impression.
- Go the extra mile.

56. Body Language

Language is a critical component of any successful interview. I am referring primarily to the words that come out of your mouth. Whether you are answering questions, asking questions, or talking about yourself, words are critical. There is, however, an additional language of a nonverbal nature that also has a major influence on the success of an interview.

Body language plays a large role in any interview. Just as an interviewer will look for meaning in the words you use, he or she will also interpret much from your mannerisms. Remember that:

Your body language influences the interviewer's impression of you, especially in the areas of self-confidence, honesty, and level of interest.

Body language has many components and they each deserve discussion.

Eye contact. This is the first type of body language that comes into play in the interview. Even before the handshake, the candidate and the interviewer establish face-to-face contact. What would you think of the interviewer if he or she failed to look you in the eye? Poor eye contact will cause the interviewer to feel the same about you.

This visual contact continues throughout the interviewing process. Your eye contact says much about you. If you have difficulty looking the interviewer in the eye, not only do you risk being labeled as indifferent toward the position but you may also show a lack of self-confidence. Although poor eye contact can occur at any time during an interview, it is especially damaging when it occurs while the interviewer is speaking.

Many people do better with their eye contact when they have the floor than they do while they are listening. What message is being sent in that situation? What *you* are saying is so important that you look the listener right in the eye to make sure he or she is paying attention. But when the other party has something to say you seem distracted, looking out the window or examining your nails. To interview successfully you must be a good listener, and good eye contact is one way to demonstrate that skill.

The goal is not 100 percent eye contact. That never happens. Scientists have determined that the average person blinks twenty thousand times per day. We have to blink to keep our eyes moist and everyone looks around a little during conversation. The key is to make sure the breaks in eye contact are minimal in both occurrence and duration. Under those conditions they will go unnoticed.

Many people who suffer from poor eye contact do not even know it. Do yourself a favor—ask a friend or acquaintance to appraise yours over a period of time. What do they say? Ask them to be deadly honest with you. If you do have an eye contact problem it can be fixed before you start interviewing. Practice it in low-stress situations. Focus on what the individual is saying. If you find it hard to look someone directly in the eye, here is a trick. Pick a spot on the person's face near the eyes and look at that instead. The temple, the bridge of the nose, or a freckle are possibilities. Since most eye contact problems improve as you settle in to the interview and relax, you can gradually shift your focal point to the interviewer's eyes.

Handshake. Soon after making initial eye contact with an interviewer, there is a high likelihood that you will shake hands. A brief, firm handshake is a normal and expected way to both initiate and close an interview. Neither your gender nor the gender of the interviewer should have any impact on the handshake—do not change the handshake because the interviewer is a woman.

The handshake is a unique form of body language because it is the only interview activity that involves touching. Many scholars believe that the handshake originated in the early development of mankind when if two strangers came in contact it was assumed that both parties were armed. There was likely to be a weapon in the right hands of both individuals. In peaceful situations it was therefore common for each person to extend an open, empty hand to show they were unarmed. In Western cultures, this exchange has evolved into the contemporary handshake and has become an expected and common practice in social and business situations.

An appropriate handshake is critical to the interviewing process in that it both opens and closes most interviews. For that reason, here is a brief discussion of several issues surrounding the handshake.

- **Initiation.** Normally each party extends the right hand simultaneously. If this does not happen, wait for the interviewer to initiate. The handshake at the beginning of the interview includes introductions and the one at the end is accompanied by a statement of gratitude for the interviewer's time and attention.

- **Gender equity.** Many men will modify their handshake if the other party is a woman, shifting to a lightweight grip when shaking a woman's hand. Some men do not even attempt to shake a woman's hand and will only do so if the woman initiates the gesture. Many men use the Queen Mary variety of handshake when shaking a woman's hand. In that version the man grips the woman's fingers only, rotates her hand parallel to the ground, and gives it a little dip. Men in the military are notorious for these faux pas, especially with women in the business world. If you are a woman, be sure to offer your entire hand, not just your fingers, when you shake hands.

- **Grip strength.** How firm of a grip should you use? You need to balance the need for a firm, self-confident grip against the risk of damaging someone's hand. One rule of thumb is the doorknob test. The amount of wrist and grip strength necessary to turn the typical doorknob is also appropriate for the handshake. And remember, no adjustments based on gender.

- **Limp wrist/cold fish/sweaty palms.** If your handshake suffers from any of these symptoms, your interview is at risk. The handshake sends an immediate signal regarding your self-confidence. Ideally you can privately either warm up your hand or wipe it down just before the interview.

- **Duration.** How long should it last? The length of the handshake depends on several factors, including familiarity, social situation, etc. For an interview, the contact should be minimal—a second or less.

- **Arm-pumping.** Some people feel the need to combine arm-pumping with a handshake. This vigorous up and down movement of clasped hands may come off as overly familiar and is not appropriate in business situations.

- **Eye contact.** It is important to establish and maintain eye contact during the handshake. These two pieces of body language together do much to signal both your self-confidence and level of interest.

The handshake is so much more than meets the eye. Although it is a common form of personal and professional introduction or greeting, it also sends important messages between the participants. I suggest you practice yours with friends or family members—people close enough to you to provide honest feedback.

Mannerisms/gestures. Most people have and use them, consciously or otherwise. They can have both a positive and negative impact. Many of us cannot communicate without hand gestures. That is fine, as long as talking with your hands does not become distracting. Some people are naturally fidgety—they just cannot sit still. They squirm in their seats. They constantly cross and uncross their legs or reposition their hands. Although you should not sit ramrod straight and unmoving in the chair, neither should you allow overuse of gestures or mannerisms to interfere with your presentation.

Posture. Your physical bearing and posture sends an immediate signal to the interviewer when you walk into the room. So does the way you sit in your chair. The message you hope to convey is one of being relaxed and confident without coming across as timid, overconfident, or cavalier. How should you sit in the chair? Well, it depends on the chair. It is easy to sit on the front half of a rigid, straight-backed chair and lean in to the conversation, but try to do that in a down-filled easy chair. Should you mimic the body language of the interviewer? Lean forward when she does? Cross and uncross your legs when he does? Yes, if you are doing so naturally. If you are overemphasizing or focusing on this issue, it will come across as forced or rehearsed. An excellent exercise is to put on your interviewing suit and practice sitting in every chair in your house.

Facial expression. People with a warm, natural smile have an advantage in any interpersonal situation. This is especially true in an interview. Not only does it convey self-confidence, it also makes the interviewer feel good. You come across as a nice person who appears to be very interested in the opportunity. On the other hand, some people have difficulty smiling, especially on demand. What should you do? Do not force it. You will run the risk of projecting insincerity. Rehearsing with a friend or in front of a mirror is good preparation.

Caution: The information presented above assumes the setting is one of Western cultural norms, specifically western European and North American common business practices. If it is likely that your job search will bring you in contact with other cultures, you would be wise to familiarize yourself with the differences before you begin the interviewing process. One excellent resource is *Kiss, Bow, or Shake Hands: How to Do Business in Sixty Countries* (by Terri Morrison et al., Adams Media, 2nd edition, 2006).

57. Interviewers: The Good, the Bad, and the Ugly

Interviewers are like weed killers. They come in many different packages, but they all have the same purpose—improve the quality of the field. While it is an interviewer's ultimate goal to find the right person for the job, frequently they cannot get to the selection stage without first reducing the pool of qualified candidates. Understanding the way an interviewer's mind works will enhance your chances of surviving the cut.

The most important thing to remember about interviewers is that they are human. Although they try to remain objective, subjectivity creeps into the process. An interviewer will frequently make up his or her mind about a candidate in the first five minutes and could have formed an opinion even earlier than that. Preconception, stereotyping, and prejudice will often influence the interview before it begins. This influence can have either a positive or negative impact. All interviewers are prone to predisposition, whether they realize it or not. Self-awareness and personal acknowledgement of this fact separates the good interviewers from the bad ones.

Assuming the interviewer has reviewed your résumé in advance, he or she will have formed an opinion of you before you walk in the door. Maybe the interviewer favors your branch of service or dislikes your military specialty. You share the same college experience or you graduated from a rival institution. You wrote a functional résumé and he or she prefers chronological. The good interviewer recognizes the likelihood of this preconception and will give you the entire interview to change his or her mind. The bad interviewer lacks this self-knowledge and nothing you do in the interview will change his or her opinion.

Notice how this can work both ways. With the good interviewer, you can turn around a negative preconception by interviewing well, but failing to validate a positive preconception could result in a Dear John letter. With the bad interviewer, a positive impression stays that way (good news), but you are powerless to overcome an initial negative one.

How can you use this insight? Since you cannot read the interviewer's mind before he or she meets you, do your best to influence the decision once the interview begins. Be courteous, be positive, sell yourself for the position, validate the positives, defeat the negatives, and make a friend.

So much for the *good* and the *bad*—how about the *ugly*? Although there are no ugly interviewers, many of them do use ugly tactics in the interview process. For more on this subject, turn to the next chapter.

58. What's with That Tie?

One of the tools used by some interviewers to narrow down the field is the negative interview. Negative interviews come in three basic shapes. This chapter will help you recognize and deal with this tactic if it happens to you. Consider the experience of Capt. Kevin Single-ton, U.S. Army.

Kevin was stationed at Fort Drum, New York, when we met. He attended a hiring conference at my invitation, did well, and received several invitations for site visits. The first one on his calendar was a trip to the headquarters of an international mining company to interview for a sales opening. We spent several hours preparing. I wished him luck and asked him to call me at the end of the visit. Here is the gist of what he told me.

He arrived at the site a few minutes early, was met in the lobby by the same person with whom he had interviewed at the hiring conference, and was given his agenda for the day. He looked it over and saw a series of one-on-one interviews with three of the company's regional managers, followed by lunch and a tour of the facility.

At the appropriate time, he knocked on the first door and the interviewer invited him in. The interviewer perused his résumé, shook his head, and said, "Why am I interviewing you? You are not qualified for this job. Your résumé indicates a lack of challenging assignments. Couldn't cut it in a line unit, right? I see that you graduated from Midwestern A&M University. I have yet to meet someone from that school who I would hire. Your grade point average shows either a lack of mental acuity or laziness while you were in college. What's with that tie? I bet your mother gave it to you. It is the ugliest tie I have ever seen. You must be from Chicago. The only people who wear brown shoes with a blue suit are from Chicago. You can leave now."

Kevin killed some time, walked down the hall, knocked on the next door, and was invited to come in and take a seat. After some chitchat, the interviewer commented on how impressed she was with his credentials. She marveled at his breadth of experience and how well he had done in all of his assignments. She noted that he had recently held a high-visibility position on a general's staff. Then she frowned, shook her head, and remarked, "This job is not a good fit for you. You are obviously overqualified. With your experience, you would find the work much too mundane. It is just not right for you. The hours are long, the sacrifices are great, and the rewards are small."

She showed him the door and wished him well. Kevin took the elevator to the next floor and knocked on his third door of the day. He received no answer. He knocked a little louder. Still no answer. Just as he was about to knock one last time, the door opened and a disheveled man invited him in and offered him a seat. As he sat in the wobbly chair, Kevin noticed that the room was very hot, maybe 100 degrees. His wool suit was becoming more and more uncomfortable, especially when he saw that the interviewer was wearing shorts and a polo shirt. His chair was facing the window and the sun was blazing, making eye contact with the interviewer difficult.

Kevin shifted in his chair only to discover that the interviewer was watching a televised tennis match and eating a sandwich. The sandwich was half-eaten when the phone rang. Ten minutes into that phone call, there was a knock on the door. The interviewer signaled for Kevin to answer it. Kevin opened the door and was greeted by a crew of painters who had come to finish the trim. As the crew entered the room with their ladders and buckets of paint, the interviewer looked over at Kevin and asked, "Would you like to finish my sandwich?"

Kevin declined but one of the painters took it. The phone rang again. The interviewer answered it, listened briefly, hung up and, on his way out the door, looked back over his shoulder at Kevin and said, "Keep an eye on that match for me. I'll be back in a couple of minutes."

One of the painters handed Kevin a brush. That was it for him. He left the building, hopped in his rental car, and headed to the airport with hopes of catching an earlier flight. Hard to blame him, right? How about you—what would you do under similar circumstances? Hmmm, not so fast.

Why would a company utilize such tactics? Why would you ever want to work for a company that would treat you that way? Here's why. It's only a test.

The interviewer needs to narrow down the field and only those who pass the test remain under consideration. Many people, when subjected to any of the above examples, will remove themselves from consideration. That is exactly what the interviewer hopes will happen.

Kevin was not only the victim of the intentional negative interview, but was unlucky enough to experience all three varieties—personal, job, and situational. In his first interview Kevin was the negative focal point. In the second one the job was presented in a negative light. In the third, the interview situation was purposely structured to make him uncomfortable.

What should you do if you find yourself in a negative interview? Assuming you recognize it for what it is and you are interested in the position, the fix is relatively simple. Stay positive. Do not get defensive. Maintain your sense of humor. Keep smiling. Kevin would have saved himself with something like, "This tie? Yes, it's pretty bad, but you should have seen the one I wanted to wear! Compared to the hours I am used to, what you are describing is a piece of cake. Would you mind if I take off my jacket, turn down the thermostat, and adjust my chair? Sure, I haven't eaten all day and I love tennis."

Of course it would be over the top to actually eat the sandwich or paint the room; the important thing is to maintain composure. Once the interviewer sees that you will not take the bait, things change rapidly. You have passed the test. He or she will now move on to other, perhaps more subtle, ways of evaluating you for the opportunity.

Do not be overly concerned about this issue. Negative interviews are not all that common. This approach is most likely used when the job itself contains strong confrontational elements. For example, many positions require a great deal of customer or client contact. Sales, consulting, and customer service are good examples. Customers can often be difficult, to the point of being rude, impolite, and unprofessional. But, they are the customers and the customer is always right. The negative interview allows the interviewer to assume the role of the customer and expose the candidate to some of the realities of the job. If a candidate cannot take the heat in the interview, he or she is likely to fail in the job.

It is more likely that you will encounter elements of a negative interview, such as an occasional barb, a negative comment about the job, or an awkward situation. Now that you know what to expect, you will be prepared to handle it with confidence, grace, and good humor. There is gamesmanship in the interviewing process. Understanding the rules and tactics of the game in advance will enhance your chances of success.

59. From Adversary to Advocate

It was my *Dr. Jekyll and Mr. Hyde* interview. I was a lieutenant with two months left in the navy, attending a hiring conference and in an interview with Dave, the personnel director of an international computer hardware manufacturing and marketing company. It did not take long for Dave to turn into Mr. Hyde. Nothing I could do was right. No matter what example I used, or what questions I asked, or how hard I tried, I could not connect with him. He nitpicked my résumé, challenged or ignored my responses, and questioned my sincerity and level of interest. He went from being in my face to glancing frequently at his watch.

Since I was interviewing for a sales position, I was prepared for the possibility of a negative interview, but this was over the top. I got to the point where I felt I had nothing to lose, so I took the plunge. During one of his distracted moments I said, "Dave, tell me please, if you find an acceptable candidate today, what's the next step for that lucky person?"

His response indicated that the successful candidate would be flown to corporate headquarters for a series of interviews, testing, and a tour of the facilities. I said, "Dave, I am very interested in this job with your company and I want you to reserve me a seat on that plane." At that point we both stood up and shook hands. As Dave showed me the door, I noticed a new expression on his face. A smirk? A smile? I could not tell, but what difference did it make considering I would never see him again? Good-bye, Mr. Hyde.

Imagine my surprise the next day when I answered the phone and Dave was on the line. He told me that I had done well in the interview and that he had recommended me for the headquarters visit. I was dumbfounded but did my best to hide it. We compared calendars and I committed to a date. Dave said he would take care of all of the travel arrangements and get back to me. He also said he would be sending me some information that would help me prepare for the interviews and the testing and he suggested some additional reading. He ended the conversation by saying that he was looking forward to introducing me to the corporate interviewing team and that he would do all he could to help me do well. Hello, Dr. Jekyll.

To gain insight into the interviewing process, let's examine the role of the initial interviewer. Most often your first personal contact with a potential employer occurs when you meet a representative of that company in a neutral setting for a screening interview. Do not be fooled by the word "neutral." Although the setting might be neutral—not your living room and not the company's boardroom—the balance of power is not. The interviewer's power to accept or reject you occurs much earlier in the process than your power to accept or reject an offer.

A company will typically want to meet several qualified candidates for each opening. To identify this pool of talent, the company will screen dozens of résumés and conduct numerous telephone interviews. Once the final contenders are identified, a company representative will be tasked to meet with them and conduct the initial interview. The interviewer desires to narrow down the field even further, possibly looking for only one or two finalists. This "narrow down the field" mission portrays the relationship between the interviewer and the candidate as adversarial, at least in the beginning—the interviewer is looking for reasons to say no.

Some candidates make that task an easy one for the interviewer. They eliminate themselves from contention. How? They are late for the interview. They are inappropriately attired. Their body language is poor. Interviewers love it when the candidates are so cooperative. Many candidates avoid these obvious mistakes and make the interviewers dig a little deeper, where they may discover insincerity, a low interest level in the position, overconfidence, or insufficient company research. Any candidate who is still in the running at this stage starts to notice a change in the attitude of the interviewer. Instead of looking for reasons to say no, the interviewer is looking for reasons to say yes. Once the interviewer decides to recommend the candidate for the job, this *adversary* becomes an *advocate*.

The interviewer will go back to the company and lobby for the candidate, recommending him or her to one or more hiring managers for their openings. The candidate is then invited to the job site for a round of interviews.

At this point the interviewer often becomes a coach and a mentor. He or she wants the candidate to do well. A well-received candidate reflects favorably on the interviewer. Conversely, a candidate who does not do well damages the interviewer's credibility.

When Dave went back to headquarters and recommended me for the position, he was stamping his seal of approval on my forehead. I had his endorsement, and my success in the interview process would reflect well on both of us. My adversary—Mr. Hyde—had become my advocate—Dr. Jekyll.

Keep in mind that as you prepare for an initial interview you may know little about the interviewer. One thing you can count on is meeting an adversary who, with proper preparation on your part and a little bit of positive interpersonal chemistry, can become your advocate and mentor throughout the interviewing process.

60. All of My Questions Have Been Answered

Hydroelectric. Geothermal. Solar. Nuclear. Fossil fuel. Wind. These power sources have a major influence on our daily lives. When it comes to a job search, however, it is the *power of questions* that drives the turbine from the initial interview through the offer and decision.

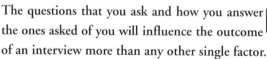

The questions that you ask and how you answer the ones asked of you will influence the outcome of an interview more than any other single factor.

Much like the damage that can be done due to an outage of electrical power, an outage of questions during the interview can have a devastating effect on the results. To illustrate this, here is the tale of Lt. Mike Gonzales, USN.

I met Mike several years ago in Annapolis, Maryland, where he taught mechanical engineering at the U.S. Naval Academy. Mike had decided to leave the navy, and I was assisting him with his preparations. Unlike many junior officers in his situation, he had a well-defined objective in mind with respect to the type of company and position he was targeting.

Mike's goal was to work for an international company in power generation where his fluency in Spanish would be an asset. In addition to his master's degree in mechanical engineering and his shipboard engineering tours, Mike was bilingual. The grandson of Cuban emigrants, he grew up in Miami in a household where English and Spanish were used interchangeably. Being single and with no geographic restrictions, Mike expressed an interest in working for a company that would allow him to travel to Spanish-speaking countries or even be assigned to one as a base of operations. I told him that although something that specific would not be easy to find, he was indeed qualified for it and we would try.

As luck would have it, I received a call from *HEMCO*, an international heavy equipment manufacturer, a few weeks later, during which Dennis, the manager of human resources, described a special opportunity. He e-mailed the specifications and I could not believe my eyes. It was as if Mike himself had written the job description. *HEMCO* wanted to hire a junior military officer with a mechanical engineering education, experience in power generation, fluency in Spanish, and a willingness to live in Buenos Aries and travel throughout South America as *HEMCO*'s resident expert on emergency diesel power backup systems.

I submitted Mike's résumé and set up a phone interview for him. He did well and was invited to fly to *HEMCO*'s corporate headquarters in Chicago, Illinois, for a series of interviews. Understanding how lucky he was to have this opportunity and how important it was to interview well, Mike redoubled his interview preparations. He did extensive research into both *HEMCO* and its competitors, learned all he could about emergency diesel power, brushed up on the questions he was expecting, and reviewed the list of questions he intended to ask. He even managed to locate a Spanish language textbook on thermodynamics and some Spanish language technical manuals on *HEMCO* emergency generators. We met the day before his trip and reviewed his preparations. I asked him to call me from the airport in Chicago before he boarded the airplane to fly home.

Mike called me the next evening and I could tell by the tone of his voice that the interviews had gone well. He had discussions with several managers, one of which was conducted entirely in Spanish. He felt that he had done well answering their questions and selling himself for the job. I asked him to predict the outcome and he felt fairly confident that he would receive an offer. In fact, as a last-minute addition to his schedule, he was taken to meet the president of *HEMCO*'s international division. We both felt that was a very good sign. As we were hanging up the phone, I told Mike I would call Dennis the next morning to get the results of his interview.

I reached Dennis and shared with him Mike's feedback. He was not surprised to hear how enthusiastic Mike was about the position. Mike had done a great job of selling himself and expressing his high level of interest. Dennis told me that the interviewing team was quite impressed with Mike's questions. I asked if he had done well enough to receive an offer and Dennis replied that, yes, all of the feedback so far had been extremely positive and that all of the managers were recommending an offer. There was, however, one more step. Dennis had not yet discussed Mike with the division president. Although the division president was not a part of the interviewing team and the team was empowered to make the offer without presidential approval, Dennis would not finalize an offer without first checking with him. Dennis was to meet with the president later and he promised to call me after the meeting.

I hung up the phone and called Mike. I told him it was not in the bag, but all indications were positive for an offer. We were just awaiting the president's input, which the HR manager felt was simply a formality. Almost as an afterthought, I asked Mike to tell me about the session he had with the president. Mike thought it had gone well. They had spent fifteen minutes together, with Mike mostly responding to the president's questions about Mike's time in the navy. The president shared with Mike that he, too, had been in the navy. Mike also mentioned that the president asked him if he had any questions. Mike replied that no, all of his questions had been thoroughly answered by the interviewing team. I told Mike I would call him later that day, as soon as I heard from the HR manager.

When five o'clock rolled around and I had not heard anything, I called Dennis. He then told me that he had almost dialed my number several times, but was finding the call difficult to make. Mike was not going to get the offer. Although the division president told his managers that he would defer to them, he would recommend against an offer. Why? The division president was disappointed that Mike did not ask him a single question, even when he purposely gave him the opportunity to do so. He told Dennis,

"Here I am, the president of the international division of one of the largest companies in the world, with over twenty years of experience in the industry, and this candidate does not have even one question for me? I am not sure what disappoints me the most—his apparent lack of interest or a lack of judgment. Regardless, I cannot endorse him."

I disconnected, took a deep breath, and made myself dial Mike's number. He picked it up on the first ring. I delivered the bad news. I could tell he was completely surprised. The irony is that his questions *had* been answered by the time he met the president and he felt he was exercising *good* judgment by not taking up too much of the president's time.

The moral of the story?

NEVER run out of questions! Never decline to ask them when given that option. Make them kick you out the door with questions on your lips.

Mike could have saved himself with one simple question: "Well, sir, although your team did an excellent job of answering my questions throughout the day, I do have one for you. If you don't mind, would you share with me some of your thoughts about your career with *HEMCO*?"

Like other forms of power, the power of questions can be stored, but the only benefits come from their actual usage. Fortunately, they are a renewable resource and can be effectively recycled. Any questions? Wait, I almost forgot to ask you one. Would you like to know how things turned out for Mike?

The day after he received the bad news he called me to say that although he disagreed with the president's assessment, he understood that a person's perception is their reality. Realizing that he, Mike, was responsible for that perception, he wanted to correct it. We discussed several approaches and, although I let him know that the odds were against him, he decided to try.

He overnight-mailed a very well-worded letter to the president, reemphasizing his interest in the company and expressing regret that he had not taken advantage of the opportunity to pick the brain of someone with so much experience in the industry. Mike also called Dennis, the HR manager who had set up his trip, to express his gratitude for having had the opportunity to interview and to apologize for not doing well with the president. He also asked for another chance. Mike told Dennis that he was prepared to travel back to Chicago at his own expense for the opportunity to get just fifteen minutes on the president's schedule. The HR manager told Mike that although he felt the matter was dead, he was willing to propose it. He promised Mike a call the next day.

Early the next morning Mike's phone rang. Hoping for the best but prepared for the worst, he picked up the phone expecting Dennis. It was the president, saying:

"Mike, I just finished your letter when Dennis came in to deliver your proposal. Let's save us both some time and money—do you have any questions for me?"

Mike got the job. The last time I heard from him he had relocated from Buenos Aires to Caracas and was enjoying his job and the life of an expatriate. He had just finished a big emergency power project with the largest hospital in Venezuela and was planning to take some time off to visit his family in Miami. He had recently gotten engaged, and his bride-to-be, who had never been outside of Venezuela, was very much looking forward to spending some time in Los Estados Unidos.

As we were about to hang up he added, "Hey Tom, it looks like I finally figured out this question thing after all—she said yes!"

61. Please Leave a Message at the Beep

What phone number are you using in your job search? Home? Office? Cell? More than one? You should select the number or numbers that are both convenient for you and also ones that make you easily accessible. That phone number will show up in many places: on your résumé, application forms, cover letters, follow-up letters, and below your e-mail signature, to name a few. Including your phone number on these documents grants the reader permission to use it. Since it is impossible to always answer your phone, you need to arrange for a message service, either digital or personal, when you are unable to answer.

Most military personnel include an office phone number in their contact information. This is rarely the case with civilians. When civilians do a job search they usually do not want their employer to know about it. Including the work number could put the individual's job at risk. Due to the contract nature of enlistment and the notification requirements to resign or retire, the military almost always knows when someone is job hunting while still on the federal payroll. Since you have nothing to hide, you can include the office phone number. This assumes, of course, that your office environment and supervisor's attitude will support you receiving calls at work. Is your line private? Does it roll into a voicemail system? If not, who will answer your phone when you are not there?

In most cases the home number is preferred. In addition to offering the greatest degree of privacy, it also affords a comfortable setting in which to talk. However, you are least likely to be near that phone at the times it is most likely for a potential employer to call you—normal working hours. Who will answer that

phone during the working day when you are not there? Do you have an answering machine or voice-mail option?

Cell phones are fast becoming the norm. Most people are carrying them and use them every day. Some people have disconnected their landlines and use only their cell phone. As convenient as the cell phone can be, it does pose problems. It is unrealistic to assume it will only ring at convenient times. We often have to ignore the call or turn off the phone. What if your next employer is using your cell phone number without success because your voicemail is full or inactive?

As you can see, regardless of the location or type of phone, you will need some sort of reliable voicemail feature or answering machine. Although technology gives us many options, there are two things that are not optional—the system must be user-friendly to the caller and the greeting must be succinct and professional. Verify your name and the number reached and give the caller quick access to the beep. Opt for a remote access feature and return all calls promptly.

When returning or initiating a call you may reach an automated attendant. If so, be sure to identify yourself, reference the person whose call you are returning, and leave your number. You should also ask for a return call and offer to try again later. The telephone is a critical tool in any successful search. Do not let a failure to communicate stand in the way of success.

62. Be Memorable

When it comes to winning an interview, one of the toughest obstacles to overcome is the fact that the numbers are against you. A typical company will sift through hundreds of résumés to find a dozen or so qualified contenders for one position. By the time the company narrows it down to a few finalists, the common de-nominator effect kicks in. All of the finalists are qualified for the job. They all have shown interest in the opportunity. Nice suits, excellent references, and polished interviewing skills are the norm. Everyone, including you, is starting to look the same. What can you do to change this? To answer that question, consider this one:

At the end of the day, which candidate will be the most memorable?

To illustrate the importance of this, I will share with you the circumstances under which two of my former clients, Bill and Dan, first got to know each other.

Several years ago at the conclusion of a hiring conference, Bill, the corporate recruiter for an international telecommunications company, shared with me his feedback on the candidates he had interviewed that day. The conversation went something like this:

"Well, Bill, how were your interviews today?"

"Great day, Tom, as usual. There were several excellent candidates on my schedule."

"Thanks, Bill—that's good to hear. I am especially interested in the results of your interview with Dan. How did he do?"

"Dan? Dan? Help me out here. Which one was he?"

"You know, tall, thin, from Jersey, Air Force captain stationed in . . . ."

"Oh, right, Dan. Sorry, seems like a nice guy, but he is not a fit."

"Really? That surprises me. I think he is a great guy. He thought he did well with you today and he ranked your opportunity as his number one choice. What was he missing?"

"Well, Dan reminds me of my dad's old Buick."

"Old Buick?"

"You know, well made, comfortable, solid as a rock, dependable, starts every day, but will never pass anybody."

Dan called the next day to get the results of the hiring conference. He had done well on several of his interviews but was very disappointed to hear that Bill's company was not one of them. He handled the feedback well and with some introspection and interviewing empathy was able to see both the humor and the truth in the comments. He realized the importance of perception, enthusiasm, selling himself, and that *being* interested is worthless without the ability to *demonstrate* that interest. Taking this to heart, Dan refined his approach and his interview style and continued his search.

About six weeks later Dan attended another hiring conference, one at which Bill also happened to be in attendance. Recognizing this opportunity, Dan realized that, contrary to conventional wisdom, he just might have a second opportunity to make a first impression. He went out of his way to make sure that he and Bill just happened to be on the same elevator that day. After the door closed, Dan stuck out his hand to a somewhat surprised Bill and said,

"Hi Bill. Remember me? I'm your dad's old Buick."

Two weeks later Bill offered Dan the job, he accepted, and both of them are now friends and regional vice presidents at that telecommunications company.

Although you can be remembered for the wrong reasons (lack of enthusiasm, inappropriate questions, poor choice of attire, or poor body language), being remembered in a positive sense adds significantly to your odds of success. Here are a few pointers that will help you be memorable for the right reasons.

- **Smile.** Be pleasant, attentive, and empathetic. Set the stage to be likeable. It is hard to forget someone you like. Keep a sense of humor—respond to that of the interviewer and show your own. Inject the room with positive energy.
- **Tell your story.** Illustrate it with examples, especially those that might elicit some emotion. For example, talk about a time you overcame adversity, set yourself on the right course, came to the aid of others, or improved someone's quality of life. Use personal anecdotes, especially those with a human-interest component.
- **Ask good questions.** They are powerful tools. Their usage provides you with information, displays your interest, and contributes to your being remembered.
- **Pay attention.** This applies not only to what the interviewer is saying, but also to the physical environment. If you are in the interviewer's office, look for clues to his or her identity. Pictures? Personal items? Certificates? Awards? Building empathy will make you memorable.
- **Be solicitous.** Ask interviewers to tell you about their careers. Get them to talk about themselves. When they do so they tend to get happy, and happy interviewers will associate that feeling with you and remember you for it.
- **Ask for feedback.** Will you recommend me for the position? Is there any additional information I can provide? As you can probably tell, I am new at this—do you have any pointers for me?

- **State your interest level.** Do not make the interviewer guess how you feel. Be bold. He or she will remember you for being direct and sticking your neck out.

Unlike many factors that influence the outcome of an interview, *being memorable* is within your power to control. Use what you have learned about the importance of interviewing empathy. Pay attention to the interviewer's signals and respond accordingly. It all boils down to building an amicable and mutually beneficial relationship with the interviewer.

When selecting candidates, companies use several techniques. Résumé screening, application forms, interviewing, testing, and reference checks are some of the more common ones. When all is said and done, however, it is often "the airplane test" that determines the final outcome.

The *ILC* Corporation, an international operations and logistics consulting firm, has been hiring people with military backgrounds for more than twenty years. *ILC* uses one of the most thorough candidate screening processes in the country. For a recruiting firm, dealing with *ILC* can be a frustrating experience. Because their standards are so high, finding the right people for them is difficult. However, knowing in advance that *ILC* will consider only those candidates with exceptional academic and professional profiles, my nominees were always top-notch.

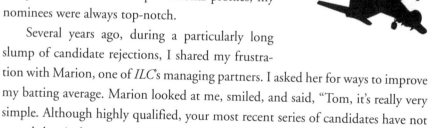

Several years ago, during a particularly long slump of candidate rejections, I shared my frustration with Marion, one of *ILC*'s managing partners. I asked her for ways to improve my batting average. Marion looked at me, smiled, and said, "Tom, it's really very simple. Although highly qualified, your most recent series of candidates have not passed the airplane test." Well, I thought I was familiar with all of the candidate evaluation methods, but I had never heard of that one, so I asked her to explain.

She set the stage for me. She is at the departure gate. Her flight is called and she boards the aircraft. As she takes her seat she says good morning to the young man sitting next to her. The plane leaves the gate, heads for the runway, and the pilot announces they are third in line for takeoff. After twenty minutes, the pilot announces that a weather problem at their destination has delayed their departure and, since all the gates are full, they will have to sit on the tarmac and wait. At this point Marion and the young man strike up a conversation. They chat for the two hours it takes for the plane to finally take off and interact for the two-hour duration of the flight. As they deplane, Marion and the young man shake hands and wish each other well.

How does she feel about this young man after sitting next to him for almost five hours? Has it been a positive, pleasant, and enjoyable experience? Or were they five of the most painful hours of her life? That is the airplane test. Whenever she interviews a candidate, she imagines what it would be like to spend time with him or her under those circumstances.

Regardless of the strength of the résumé or how well the candidate tests for the position, in the end it comes down to personality, specifically things like listening skills, empathy, sense of humor, appropriateness, manners, courtesy, energy, and enthusiasm. Are you the kind of person Marion wants on her team? The results of the airplane test will do much to help her answer that question.

63. Extra Preparations

The importance of proper interview preparation cannot be overemphasized. For reasons discussed in "The Audition" in section III, sales interviews are unique and require preparations above and beyond the norm. Here are the extra steps you should take to ensure your readiness for a sales interview.

- **Get ready for the question "Why sales?"** This is actually three questions rolled into one. Why do you want sales? Why do you want to sell (that product or in that industry)? Why do you want to sell for (the company with which you are interviewing)? Although the answer to the first one is relatively constant, the next two call for specific insights. For example, if you are interviewing with *GENERAL MEDICAL SYSTEMS (GMS)*, be prepared for "Why do you want to sell in the medical diagnostic equipment industry?" and "Why do you want to work for *GMS*?" Keep in mind that these three questions will not necessarily be asked in sequence or be asked that directly. However, they will most certainly be asked, in one form or another.

- **Double up on your research.** If you are like most military personnel, you don't know much about the sales process in the worlds of business and industry. You have little or no experience with sales as your primary profession. It is therefore important to increase your level of knowledge in two areas: knowledge of self and knowledge of the position.

- **Fine-tune your self-knowledge.** Entering a sales interview without a thorough understanding of your salesperson-like qualities and motivators would be a big mistake. Take the time to research yourself. What is it about you that makes sales an option?

- **Ramp up your reading.** One of the best ways to learn more about sales and selling is through reading. I recommend these titles: *The New Strategic Selling: The Unique Sales System Proven Successful By the World's Best Companies* by Robert B. Miller and Stephen E. Heiman with Tad Tuleja; *The New Solution Selling: The Revolutionary Sales Process That is Changing the Way People Sell*, by Keith M. Eades; *How to Become a Rainmaker: The People Who Get and Keep Customers*, by Jeffrey J. Fox; *How to Master the Art of Selling*, by Tom Hopkins; *The 25 Sales Habits of Highly Successful Salespeople*, by Stephan Schiffman; *Swim With the Sharks Without Being Eaten Alive: Outsell, Outmanage, Outmotivate, and Outnegotiate Your Competition*, by Harvey Mackay; *Professional Selling: A Trust-Based Approach,* by Thomas N. Ingram et al.; and *Little Red Book of Selling: 12.5 Principles of Sales Greatness*, by Jeffrey Gitomer. Reading one or more of these books enhances your preparations in two ways: your vocabulary and subject-matter knowledge is improved, and you will have a great response when the interviewer inquires about your reading habits.

- **Seek out information interviews.** Simply reading about the subject is not good enough. You would benefit from some real-world insight. The information interview is an excellent way to gain this information. Do you know anyone with sales experience in the business or industrial sectors? If you are focused on one particular industry, whom do you know in that industry? Perhaps they have frequent dealings with sales reps. For example, if you are considering a sales position in medical technology, do you know any doctors, nurses, or therapists? Spending time with these insiders can provide you with a worthwhile glimpse into sales personnel and the sales profession.

- **Prepare for negative interviews.** As discussed earlier in this section ("What's with That Tie?"), some interviewers employ the negative interview technique as a way of screening candidates. They turn up the heat in the interview to a level that approximates the realities of the job. Although most interviews include some degree of this tactic, sales interviewers are notorious for using the negative interview approach. Playing the role of the disinterested or rude customer during the interview and observing the candidate's reaction gives them valuable insight as to how you will handle similar situations in the actual job. It is important to prepare for the negative interview.

- **Get ready to *close* the sale.** Since interviewing is actually a form of selling, the interviewer can appraise many of the candidate's sales attributes during the interview. One of the most important attributes of a successful sales rep is his or her ability to *close the sale* or *ask for the order*. Regardless of the type of job for which you are interviewing, it is important to state your desire for the position. In a sales interview this is more than just important; it is critical. You must show the interviewer your willingness and ability to close.

- **Consider specialized sales training.** Unless you have had recruiting duty, it is unlikely that your military career has afforded you any specific training in sales. Many military recruiters are sent to the Xerox Professional Sales Skills course before they assume those responsibilities. You could invest in sales training courses such as the ones offered by Dale Carnegie, the Sales Training Institute, and the Prime Resource Group.

- **Practice, practice, practice.** Getting a few practice sales interviews under your belt before you walk in the door for the real deal will enhance your chances. There are two types of practice interviews. One option is to ask someone to simulate a sales interview for you. Ideally, this person would be a friend or acquaintance who has experience in sales. The second option involves practicing during an actual interview. This requires more effort but offers the additional benefit of real-world experience and feedback. Here's how:

There are certain businesses that, due to high turnover, are constantly seeking new sales reps. Financial services and insurance companies fall into this category. It is relatively easy to generate a sales interview with them. The irony is that as easy as it is to get the interview, you would think that the interviewing process would be equally painless. Not so. They run you through the meat grinder. You will come out of it with a definite understanding of the sales interviewing process and be better prepared for the interviews you really want. If this tactic interests you, then contact one of those companies and tell them that you want to sell. If you are able to generate an interview, take it seriously and do your best. Why? Some people who use this approach discover that this occupation is actually a good fit for them.

Incorporating this guidance into your preparations will improve your odds of success. Even if you are not interviewing for sales, this extra effort adds considerable value, especially in a highly competitive field or during tough economic conditions.

Interviewing is salesmanship and most sales interview preparations can be applied to any interview.

SECTION VII.
INTERVIEWS—VARIETY AND FUNCTION

Interviews come in many shapes and sizes. They can be categorized and labeled, but no two are ever the same. Although you can never be certain of what will actually occur during the interview, you can at least arm yourself in advance with the fundamentals.

The activities that precede and follow this event are just as important as the event itself, and they deserve special attention.

In the following chapters you will:

- Prepare a checklist.
- Take an etiquette lesson.
- Investigate the interview varieties.
- Find out what's for lunch.
- Defend yourself from rejection.
- Get your first offer.
- Process the paperwork.
- Use your decision matrix.

64. Interview and Etiquette Checklist

Congratulations. You received a call from the *XYZ* Company. The résumé you submitted several weeks ago has defied the odds, passed through several filters, made its way to a hiring manager's desk, and you have been asked to come to the site for an interview.

Being well prepared for the interview itself is critical, but there are several issues to consider before the interview takes place.

Much like the rules of etiquette that exist for society in general, organizations tend to have their own standards of acceptable behavior. You are familiar with military service etiquette, and when you join a civilian organization you will discover a new, albeit similar, set of rules. During your transition, it is important to keep in mind an additional set—those that define job search etiquette.

The rules of etiquette in a job search deal with behavior. Certain behaviors are expected and others may or may not be acceptable, depending on the circumstances. When we combine the expected behaviors with common sense and common courtesy, we end up with a useful interview checklist:

- **Confirm the appointment.** Do this twenty-four hours or one working day in advance. Make sure you know the date, the time, and the location of the interview. Try to find out how long you should expect to be there. An hour? Half a day? The entire day? Also, make sure you have the appropriate phone numbers in case you have to call.
- **Anticipate the paperwork.** Determine what you need, gather it together, organize it, and make sure you have the appropriate container (e.g., a briefcase, portfolio, binder, or pocket notebook). Copies of your résumé, reference list, performance evaluations, and education records are among the documents that might be requested. Also, bring some writing materials in case you need to take notes.
- **Know the players.** If you know the name or names of the interviewers in advance, confirm the pronunciation and spelling. This comes in handy both during and after the interview.

- **Verify your destination.** Make sure you know how to get there. If time and circumstances permit, take an advance trip. Scout the location, parking options, traffic patterns, and walking distances. Waiting until the day of the interview to discover a construction delay could be costly. *Never* arrive late.
- **Clear your calendar.** If possible, keep your schedule free of any other commitments. The interview might run over or you could be asked to stay longer. Explaining that you have someplace else to be could create an awkward situation.
- **Do not arrive late.** Showing up late, regardless of the reasons, not only casts doubt on your reliability, but also labels you as discourteous or rude. If unforeseen circumstances arise and you will be arriving late, do everything in your power to call ahead of time to explain.
- **Do not arrive too early.** Time your arrival so you are fifteen minutes early. That is about when they start looking for you. Any earlier and you could create an awkward situation. They might not know what to do with you while you are waiting.
- **Dress appropriately.** Arriving at the interview only to discover that you are not properly attired is embarrassing for both parties. Although traditional business attire is appropriate most of the time, circumstances may dictate otherwise. If this issue is unclear, seek guidance from your point of contact at the company. When in doubt, take the safe course. Being overdressed in your conservative interview suit is preferable to the alternative. Make sure all of the pieces are in good repair, clean, and fit you well. If dry cleaning is necessary, be certain that everything will get back from the cleaners in time. For more on this subject, see "Uniform of the Day" in section IV.
- **Turn off or silence your cell phone.** Short of a family emergency, there is no excuse for an interruption of that sort during the interview. This includes the audible notification that alerts you to a new text or e-mail.
- **Announce your arrival.** Walk up to the receptionist, smile, shake hands, introduce yourself, state that you have an appointment with Mr. or Ms. So-and-so at 9:00 a.m., offer your business card or résumé, and wait for instructions.
- **Be patient.** This is a double standard. Although you cannot be late, they are allowed to keep you waiting. Keep smiling. Make eye contact with the receptionist. Try not to fidget, sigh, or look perturbed. After about thirty minutes, ask the receptionist for a glass of water or directions to the lavatory. The hint will be taken.

- **Remember the importance of body language.** The behaviors here—expected, acceptable, and otherwise—are many. The first chapter in section VI, "Body Language," covers this in detail.
- **Be courteous and polite.** Everyone you meet in an interview expects and deserves common courtesy and respect. Although the guard at the gate and the front office receptionist are not part of your interview agenda, you should expect that their opinions of you will be solicited.
- **Anticipate the necessary follow-up activity.** Make sure you are aware of any post-interview expectations on the part of the interviewers. You might be asked for additional materials, a modified résumé, to complete an application form, or to provide references. Whatever the case, do it and do it in a timely and accurate manner. Additionally, send follow-up letters or e-mails. More on this later in this section.
- **Communicate well.** Call when you say you will. Return calls promptly. Make your voicemail message short and to the point. If you use their voicemail, always include your phone number and the date and time you called. Communicating via e-mail may or may not be appropriate. Find out in advance.

This advice may seem like a simple combination of basic common sense, politeness, and personal and professional courtesy, but it is very important. There is much about the interviewing process that is out of your control. It does not do you any good to worry about those issues. However, you do have control over the steps leading up to the interview. Putting in a little extra effort and exercising some caution will pay dividends.

65. Interviews—Purpose, Process, and Form

Although the word "interview" is repeated dozens of times throughout this book, you must not allow your increasing familiarity with the word to become complacency regarding its importance. An interview is a critical component of almost every job search and it usually takes a series of successful ones to generate an offer. Let's review the basics.

Purpose. An interview is a two-way interaction in which both parties check each other out to see if each can meet the needs and expectations of the other. In an employment interview, the organization evaluates the candidate's qualifications, potential, interest level, and requirements. The candidate in turn evaluates the organization's ability to satisfy his or her needs. The primary evaluation tools are questions and answers, the importance of which is stressed throughout this book.

Most interviews are done face-to-face and occur only after a certain amount of filtering has occurred. As discussed in section I, this pre-interview filtering is important for several reasons. Since a personal interview is time consuming and costly for both parties, it makes sense to schedule it only after the obvious mismatches have been eliminated. This filtering process not only saves time and money for both parties but also increases the odds of a successful interview, making it more likely that an offer will be extended and more likely that it will be accepted.

The mutual evaluation process that occurs during an interview has both objective and subjective elements; however most of the objective evaluation is often completed before the interview occurs. An interviewer does not need to meet you to see if you are properly trained or educated for the job, or to determine if the salary and location work for you. Likewise, you do not need to sit down with the interviewer to figure out if the location and the money meet your needs. Although most of this objective screening occurs in advance, it will continue to some degree during the interview. Remember that:

Even if the entire interview feels like objective evaluation, it is mostly subjectivity that determines the outcome.

Subjectivity has its roots in personality and fit. Consider the identification and impact of things like interpersonal skills, communication, chemistry, personality, attitude, friendliness, style, mannerisms, and expression of interest. None of those come into play before the interview, but most of them are revealed when face time begins. Throughout the interview, no matter what the interviewer is asking or saying, he or she is thinking, *Is this the kind of person we want on our team? Can we make and keep this person happy?*

Similarly, the candidate is thinking, *Are these my kind of people? Is this an organization where I can be productive and happy?* The answers to each of those questions rely heavily on subjective rather than objective criteria.

Varieties. Although similar in purpose, interviews come in a variety of forms. Here are some of the most common ones and a brief discussion of each.

- **Information interview.** This falls outside the mission of normal employment interview. The goal is information, not a job. This type of interview is an excellent way to learn about a job, a company, an industry, or a career path before deciding whether or not to pursue it as part of your search. Asking friends, associates, family members, and others for help is a good way to generate an information interview. Prepare well and do your best—even though this is not technically a job interview, it might lead to one someday.
- **Initial** (or first level or screening). This is typically the first thing that happens after a résumé generates interest. It is usually conducted over the phone (see "Can You Hear Me Now?" in the next chapter) or in a neutral setting such as a hotel room, coffee shop, base education office, or family services center. Another common location for initial interviews is the job fair or hiring conference, where hundreds of short initial interviews occur throughout the day. See "An Employment Perfect Storm" (section IV) for additional information.
- **Follow-up** (or second level or site visit or callback). A follow-up interview is the reward for a successful initial interview. Generally it is scheduled at a mutually convenient time and takes place at the potential job site. It can last from an hour or two to two full days. In most cases the company covers all of the associated travel expenses. There is usually a slate of interviews with several people. These people may include your boss-to-be, coworkers, a human resource representative, and subordinates. A tour of the facility and/or the local area is often included. In most cases the decision to extend an offer is made as a result of the information obtained and the interviews conducted during that visit.
- **Social interview.** This variety is designed to see how you handle yourself in a public and/or in a social setting. The most common versions include a meal, typically lunch or dinner, and sometimes there is a cocktail reception in the mix. It may be just you and your new boss or a coworker, or there could be several additional people involved. There is more on this subject later in "Let's Do Lunch."
- **Negative interview.** Although this is a technique rather than a category of interview, it deserves your attention. See "What's with That Tie?" in section VI.

- **Group interview.** A group interview consists of multiple candidates being interviewed or observed at the same time. Not only are you and your competition being evaluated but you are also checking each other out. Sometimes the group interview is combined with the social interview, which gives the employer the opportunity to see how you interact with peers and competitors.
- **Panel interview.** A panel interview puts one candidate in front of multiple interviewers at the same time. This tends to be a high-stress, rapid-fire, taxing event. The panel measures the candidate's ability to handle stress and think on his or her feet. The members pay particular attention to the candidate's ability to involve and engage the entire panel, not just the member who happens to be asking or answering a question.
- **Day-in-the-field** (or ride-along). In most cases the interview process is complete after the follow-up interview. However, some companies add another step. The interviews may have been held at a facility, but the actual job requires a significant amount of time away from that facility. If this requirement is inherent in the job, then it is important for the candidate to also experience that aspect of the job. One way to accomplish that is to have the candidate spend a day in the field with someone who is already doing the job. Some companies schedule this before making an offer and others do it after the offer is made but before the candidate's response. Regardless, the candidate is more likely to make the right decision having experienced firsthand that aspect of the job. Interviews for jobs such as sales, consulting, and technical rep are likely to include this step.
- **Client approval.** If you are interviewing with a contractor or consulting firm and the position requires you to spend most of your time with a specific client, you may need to be approved by that client before you can be hired. This means an extra round of interviews at the client site.
- **Testing/evaluation/case studies.** Many companies will set aside a portion of a site visit for formal testing or evaluation. The purpose is to measure aptitude or intelligence as it applies to the job. Although not an interview per se, it is helpful in determining the potential for a solid fit. If the purpose of the test is knowledge-based then you should be forewarned and can prepare accordingly, but there is little you can do in the way of preparation for aptitude or personality testing.

- **Profiling.** Some companies collect historical personal performance data to build a profile of what constitutes a successful employee and what jobs are most likely to utilize the talents of a particular candidate profile. These companies will hire a behavioral analysis company to do a profiling session with you before an offer is extended. This usually takes the form of a question and response survey, either online or via telephone.

Regardless of the form, setting, length, or technique, keep in mind:

An interview is a forum in which two parties exchange the information necessary to determine if each party's professional needs can be satisfied by the other.

66. Can You Hear Me Now?

Most initial interviews are conducted in neutral settings, and few settings are as neutral as a telephone conversation. Companies use telephone interviews for several reasons. Any geographic separation between the parties is neutralized and the cost in time and money is minimized. It is also an easy way to add personality to the résumé. For those reasons you should expect that many of your initial interviews will likely be conducted on the telephone. Telephone interviews can be tricky, however, and deserve special attention. Here are the guidelines.

- **Schedule and confirm.** Telephone interviews are scheduled events. Expect an advance call to arrange a mutually convenient day and time. Address any time zone differences. Ask for the amount of time to be allotted, determine who is to initiate the call, and verify the phone number to be used. Confirm that the employer has everything needed from you to conduct the interview.
- **Homework.** As with all interviews, you must prepare in advance. Research the company. Learn something about the interviewer, if possible. Be knowledgeable about the specific position for which you are being considered.

- **Self-knowledge.** Review the results of the exercises in sections II and V ("Lifetime Tasks and Skills Inventory" and "Tell 'Em What They Want to Hear," respectively) to enhance your ability to emphasize your positive attributes that are most relevant to the job.

- **Questions.** Compose a set of questions. Select them with two things in mind: you want to gather information about the opportunity, and you want to demonstrate your interest in the job. Avoid questions that are selfish in nature (salary, benefits, or relocation costs, for example). Save those for later in the process.

- **Environment.** Decide in advance where you want to be when the phone call takes place. Pick a quiet, comfortable spot where you are unlikely to be interrupted. A desk or table is important because you will be taking notes.

- **Technology.** If you are using a cell phone, make sure it is fully charged. To be safe, keep your charger handy and sit near an electrical outlet. Confirm in advance that you have a strong, reliable signal. If you have call-waiting, temporarily deactivate it. If this is not possible, plan to ignore it.

- **Materials.** Make sure you have access to a glass of water, your résumé, your list of questions, background information on the company, and writing materials. Using your computer to take notes is risky. The interviewer might hear the keystrokes in the background and suspect that you are multitasking rather than focusing on the interview.

- **Punctuality.** Being late for an interview is often the kiss of death, and this rule also applies to phone interviews. Be ready to make or receive the call at the scheduled time. End any other incoming calls as quickly as possible. Keep the line free—the interviewer will not be happy with a busy signal or voicemail prompt.

- **Patience.** If the interview time arrives but the call does not, stay near the phone and wait. If the phone fails to ring during the time you have set aside, call the person and offer to reschedule. Likewise, offer to reschedule if you are initiating the call and the interviewer is unavailable. Resist the temptation to be accusatory. Allow for the possibility that the error is yours, even if that is not the case. Perhaps you are being tested.

- **Introductions.** Once you and the interviewer are on the phone, introduce yourself. The interviewer should return the introduction. If this is a multiperson conference call, it is appropriate to ask for introductions to the other individuals who are participating.

- **Body language?** In a telephone interview, your body language is out of play, as is that of the interviewer. Your words, both their meaning and their delivery, are the only tools at your disposal, so choose them wisely. Having a strong handshake and maintaining eye contact are irrelevant now, but you should still conduct the interview as if you were face-to-face. The fact that you are focused on the conversation, nodding, and smiling will come through in your voice.

- **Enunciation.** Speak clearly and more slowly than you normally would. Also, resist the temptation to use the speaker phone. Hands-free is comfortable, but the risks of bad audio or loss of privacy override any added convenience.

- **Rapport.** This is critical. Whether or not the interviewer likes you has a major effect on the outcome. Your natural enthusiasm, sense of humor, and inquisitiveness will serve you well. If given the chance, try to get the interviewer to talk a little bit about his or her background. Do not go overboard—remember who is interviewing whom.

- **Closing the deal.** To succeed in any interview, you must state your level of interest and ask for the next step. Since the preferred outcome of a phone interview is often a personal visit to the company (sometimes called a site visit or second-level interview), you should ask for this visit in a clear, polite, and sincere manner. Conversely, if you are not interested in the opportunity, let the interviewer know why. Perhaps you are misreading something, or maybe there is another position available for which you are better suited.

- **Follow up.** A telephone interview requires the same follow-up as any interview. Timely and well-worded correspondence is an excellent way to express both your level of interest and your gratitude for the interviewer's time and consideration. Chapter 69 offers a more detailed discussion of this topic.

A successful telephone interview is one in which the interviewer not only *hears* your words but also processes them to your best advantage.

67. Let's Do Lunch

When most people think about interview situations, they visualize an office environment, a tour of the company's facilities, or perhaps a neutral setting such as

a hotel conference room or a telephone call. Although these examples are accurate in the normal sense, a surprising number of interviews are conducted in social situations. Let's discuss a frequent setting for a social interview: lunch.

How do you handle an interview that includes a meal? Conventional wisdom says that your mouth has but one purpose during an interview—talking. However, since you cannot just sit there and watch the interviewer eat, it would be a good idea to anticipate this situation and prepare for it. Considering the following questions will help.

- **Is it really an interview?** Sometimes the interviewer tells you that the meal is not part of the interviewing process so relax and enjoy your lunch. Do not fall for it. Any interaction you have with any representative of a company before an offer is extended is part of the evaluation process.
- **What should you order?** Keep several things in mind. Some foods can be a challenge to eat. For example, think twice before ordering soup, certain salads, shellfish in the shell, or tacos. Avoid foods with unwanted after-effects, such as garlic, onions, spinach, and beans. Stay away from pricey items. Although the lobster and filet mignon is tempting and the interviewer selected it, ordering those foods might send a bad signal.
- **Conversation?** This can be a challenge. In normal social situations it is expected that both parties will initiate and respond conversationally. However, in a social interview, the host is in control. He or she proposes the topics and you go along. This does not mean you should sit there mute unless you are responding to a question. It is important to respond, engage, be attentive, ask questions, actively listen, and appear interested. Stay on point and allow the host to change the subject when he or she is ready to do so. A certain amount of dead air is fine, but watch out for extended periods of silence. Should that be the case, it will be incumbent on you to initiate some conversation. Here is an opportunity to get the interviewer to talk about himself or herself.
- **How about alcoholic beverages?** Regarding lunch, this is easy—never order an alcoholic beverage, even if your host does. However if it is a dinner inter-

view, you may follow the lead of the host. Assuming you drink alcohol, one drink with your meal is acceptable; more than one is risky behavior. If you do not drink alcohol, or simply prefer not to, politely decline the drink.

- **What happens when the server brings the check?** Who pays? The host always pays. Although it is a rare occurrence, should you, the interviewee, suggest a lunch setting or invite the interviewer to lunch, then you should offer to pick up the check. Otherwise, your only obligation is to say thanks.

- **Any additional pointers?** Your water glass is the one positioned above your knife. Your bread plate is the one to your left. Your napkin belongs in your lap when you are seated and on the seat of your chair when you are not. Take small bites. Turn off your cell phone. A follow-up letter is appropriate. Although this discussion was focused on lunch interviews, you can apply the same guidance to other social interview situations, such as cocktail parties and dinners. For more information on this subject, read *Don't Slurp Your Soup: A Basic Guide to Business Etiquette*, by Elizabeth Craig.

68. Post-Interview Follow-Up Procedures

You worked hard to generate an interview. You prepared thoroughly. You walked in the door and did your best. The interview is over. What now? Sit around and wait for the phone to ring or the envelope to arrive in the mailbox? No way. You are now in the post-interview phase, and your work continues. Let's review the steps you should take once the interview is complete to ensure you have applied the appropriate finishing touches.

- **Performance.** How do you think you did? Take some time to jot down your thoughts while the event is still fresh in your mind. How did you handle the questions? What would you change and what would you do differently next time? These lessons learned add value to the interview you just completed and to the ones you will have in the future.

- **Names/addresses/phone numbers.** If you did not obtain this information prior to your departure, contact an administrative person at the company as soon as possible. Keep reading and you will see why this is important.

- **How you feel.** Do you want this job? Do you want to take the next step?

Would you seriously consider an offer? On the other hand, maybe it would be best to cut things loose.

- **Decision matrix.** In section IV you designed a decision matrix to use as a job search tool. Add this company. How does this opportunity appear to stack up against your *BENCHMARK* company and any other companies you have seen? Take what you learned during the interview and apply it to your decision matrix. The last chapter in this section provides guidance on how to do this effectively.

- **Follow-up letters.** They have two themes: your level of interest and words of appreciation for the interviewers' time and attention. If you are interested in the opportunity, they are mandatory. If you are not, the *thank you* message is still appropriate (more on this in the next chapter). Refer to the contact information you obtained before or during the interview to ensure that all names and addresses are correct.

- **Application forms.** Many companies will send you home with an application form. Completing it thoroughly, neatly, and accurately, and returning it promptly sends a strong signal of interest. Not doing so will send the opposite signal. For more information on this, see "Application Forms—Thank Goodness I Made a Copy" in section IV.

- **Timelines/deadlines.** It is possible that you will need to know your status by a certain date. Perhaps you will be deploying for three months. Maybe another company has given you a deadline to respond to an offer. Make sure all parties are aware of your timelines and decision dates.

- **Contact info.** Will your contact information change, even temporarily, during your search? Travel and vacation plans might impact your mailing address and phone numbers. Keep the company in the loop.

All successful interviews have their roots in preparation. However, no matter how well prepared you are *before* the interview and how well you perform *during* the interview, what you do *after* the interview will also influence the result. Do not make the mistake of assuming that just because both parties are smiling when the interview is complete you have accomplished your mission. Communication is the key. Although a company might frustrate you by what appears to be a lack of communication, do not give them a reason to feel the same way about you. Until the job offer is in your hands, there is still work to be done.

69. Until the Paperwork Is Done

Every successful job search involves a large amount of paperwork. Résumés, reference lists, and cover letters are all pre-interview preparations. There is also a very important piece of correspondence that comes into play in the post-interview phase: the follow-up letter.

During the interviewing phase of your search, get in the habit of following up each interview with correspondence that relays to the interviewer your true feelings about the opportunity. A well-written follow-up letter does three things:

1.   It expresses appreciation for the interviewer's time and consideration.
2.   It states your level of interest in the organization and position.
3.   It causes you to be remembered.

The following Q & A will help you understand its significance.

- **Is a follow-up letter the same thing as a thank-you letter?** Only if you remember the importance of expressing your level of interest in the job while also thanking the interviewer for his or her time and consideration.
- **Should I send a follow-up letter if I have no further interest in the job?** Yes, you should be grateful for the interviewer's time and you should share this gratitude with him or her. Although you have no further interest in that position, perhaps there are other positions.
- **When should the follow-up letter be sent?** Do so at the earliest opportunity. Timeliness is very important, especially given the high likelihood that you have competition for the job.
- **Is there a standard structure, format, or length?** Use standard business letter structure and format. Unless you have been asked to provide additional information, one page is sufficient.
- **How about using hand-written thank-you notes instead?** Although some would argue that these notes are more personal, most organizations view a follow-up letter as business correspondence. Therefore, the computer-generated standard business letter is preferred. Additionally, a follow-up letter is a de facto writing sample and should be letter-perfect, error-free, and grammatically correct.

- **Can it be e-mailed as an alternative to normal mail?** Different corporate cultures reflect different expectations. One clue is to look at the interviewer's business card. If an e-mail address is listed, it is probably safe to use it. It is best to ask the interviewer if he or she is comfortable communicating via e-mail. If you use e-mail, I suggest you compose the letter in a Word document and then cut and paste it into the e-mail. Attaching it to an e-mail is risky because many e-mail servers block messages that include attachments.

- **Other than saying "thanks" and "I am interested," what else is included?** Provide a bit of information that will make the reader remember you and the interview. Maybe there was something you forgot to mention and you can do it now. Perhaps you were unable to answer a question effectively. Your follow-up letter can fill in the blanks.

- **If there were multiple interviewers, should I send multiple letters?** In general, a separate letter to each individual is preferred. Sometimes this can be impractical. For example, during an all-day visit to a company you could meet with a dozen people. Should you send a dozen letters? Maybe yes, maybe no. One approach is to send follow-up letters to the most powerful people (e.g., your potential boss, the facility manager, and the HR representative) and in those letters make mention of all the others.

- **Is _Dear Mr. Jones_ or _Dear Bob_ the proper salutation?** Although interviewing etiquette allows for the use of first names in conversation after you have been introduced, it is safer to stick with the titles in written correspondence, at least until after you have joined the company. If this feels too formal to you, then go with the name or title that was used during the interview.

- **Is a follow-up letter appropriate for a telephone interview?** Yes. A telephone interview should receive no less attention, in either preparation or follow-up, than any other interview.

Now that the questions have been answered, let's take a look at a sample.

Let's review Jeff's letter. In the first paragraph Jeff thanks the interviewer for his time and attention. In the second paragraph he expresses his high level of interest in the position and makes a case for his qualifications. The next paragraph affords him the opportunity to provide additional information in the form of an enclosure to the letter. Finally, in the fourth paragraph, he takes the bold step of definitively asking for the next step in the process.

Jeffrey A. Jones

1322 East Nittany Street
State College. PA 18745

(814) 676-1633 (H)
jjones@psu.mba.edu

August 15, 2006

Mr. Robert Pearson
Vice President, Quality Assurance
Caterpillar Equipment Corporation
1800 Main Street, Suite 1976
Downingtown, PA 19388-1488

Dear Mr. Pearson:

Please accept my gratitude for the time you spent with me yesterday morning. The information you provided on both your company and your quality management programs was enlightening. The time I spent in your production and maintenance facilities was particularly valuable. I now have a much better understanding of the responsibilities of the Manager of Quality Assurance and how that function relates to the overall mission and the rest of the Quality Team.

Mr. Pearson, I am very interested in continuing the interviewing process for your Manager of Quality Assurance position. I believe the combination of my MBA in Operations Management and my demonstrated success in leadership, maintenance management, and quality assurance as a naval officer has me well prepared for the responsibilities of that position.

During my tour of the facility, I spoke with Ms. Kathy Ryan about her role as Lead Quality Engineer. She explained to me how much time she is dedicating to your ISO 9000 certification process. Enclosed you will find a copy of my Operations Research Thesis on that subject. Perhaps you and Ms. Ryan will find some of my research and conclusions helpful.

May I return to your facility to continue the interviewing process? Final exams begin in two weeks, but I am available any day between now and then. Please let me know if you need any additional information. I look forward to your call. Thank you very much for your time and consideration.

Sincerely,

Jeff Jones

Encl: Masters Thesis

The only thing missing from Jeff's letter is an attempt to repair any errors or omissions he made during his interview. Perhaps he did not make any (highly unlikely) or they were minor and not worth mentioning (we will give him the benefit of the doubt). All in all, it is a very good letter in that it passes an important test. Upon reading it, will there be any doubt in the mind of Mr. Pearson that Jeff is appreciative of the opportunity to interview and that he has a high level of interest in the position?

The moral of the story? Pay as much attention to the quality of your post-interview paperwork as you do to your interview preparations, and you will maximize your odds of success.

70. Dear John

The interview is over. You ask the human resource manager when you will hear something and are told that you should know your status in two weeks. A letter arrives two weeks later. You open it with a mixture of apprehension and optimism and read the following:

> *We regret to inform you that we are unable to offer you a position at this time. Although the management team was impressed with your background, we have concluded that your skill set is not compatible with our requirements. We have identified another candidate who appears to be a better fit for our opening. We will keep your résumé on file and contact you in the event a more appropriate position becomes available. We enjoyed meeting you and wish you well.*

Meet the dreaded **Dear John** letter. Not at all the result you expected. Your level of disappointment will vary depending on your level of interest. Being rejected from the job of your dreams is one thing; losing one in which you had little interest is easier to swallow. In any event, you might like to know why you were rejected and if you have any recourse.

Regarding recourse, probably not. *No* almost always means *no*. For reasons discussed later, it is doubtful you will ever know the actual reasons for rejection. It is impossible to challenge or overcome objections which are unidentified. You can ask, but you will probably not be told. Your chances of finding out improve if you have an inside connection. If you decide to not take *no* for an answer, it is important to stay positive and professional in your approach. Do not get defensive, indignant, or accusatory. Stay humble. Be appreciative. Ask for help. The odds are against you, but maybe your persistence will pay off and you will be able to overcome the objection and eliminate the real reason for rejection. It can happen. Remember Dan, aka my dad's old Buick, in chapter 62?

Regarding the reason for rejection, note the language in the letter: "your skill set is not compatible with the requirements of the position." That must be the reason, correct? Probably not. Your résumé indicated the minimum skill set or the interview would have never happened. There must be another reason and perhaps you could counter it. Whether that is an option or not, knowing the cause of the rejection could be a good lesson learned for future interviews.

Does the company owe you a more specific explanation? No. Years ago companies were forthcoming with concrete reasons for rejection, but as our society has become increasingly litigious in nature, the willingness to share rejection feedback has all but vanished. Rather than risk a lawsuit for reasons that could be interpreted as discriminatory, a company will use the terminology above. If they are feeling generous, they might substitute the phrase "another individual was better suited for the position," which is code for they liked another person more than they liked you—a legal form of discrimination.

The actual reasons for rejection fall into two categories: ones that were within your control and ones that were beyond your control. Let's review several examples of each.

- **You failed to show sufficient interest in the position.** This is a classic. Maybe you truly were not interested and it showed. Maybe you were very interested and failed to let it show. Regardless of how you feel, the perceptions of the interviewers become their reality.
- **You are overqualified for the position.** This one is often used as a polite way of showing you the door—complimenting you as they send you on your way. Sometimes it is genuine. If the interviewer senses that the job will bore you or that you will become impatient, he or she can legitimately label you as overqualified or unqualified for the position.
- **You are unqualified.** As important as a well-written résumé is in any successful job search, sometimes it can oversell. Perhaps you presented your collection of qualifications accurately, but the interview exposed problems in the depth of some of those qualifications. This does not necessarily mean that you misrepresented yourself. Sometimes the potential employer is guilty of a little wishful thinking when reading a résumé.
- **They liked someone else better.** This one gets used quite often. Why? It is cut and dried. How can you argue with it? People either like you or they do not. If they do not, there is nothing you can do to change it.
- **You were beaten out for the position.** As long as there are great jobs and great candidates for those jobs, you will have competition. As good as you know you are, it would be a mistake to assume that you are the only qualified candidate for the job.
- **Although you did well, the *yes* votes were not unanimous.** Rarely is the decision to offer or not in the hands of one person acting alone. In most cases there are many people in the interviewing process and they all have some input regarding the final decision. Whether they vote on or off the record,

their votes will be counted. In some cases, consensus or a majority decision is enough. In other cases, it is all or nothing.

- **You failed to sell yourself for the position.** As you leave the interview, ask yourself what impressions you left in the minds of the interviewers. Do they see you in the job for which you are being considered, doing it well, and with a big smile on your face? If so, congratulations. If not, then *Dear John.*

- **You displayed inappropriate behavior or breached interviewing etiquette.** Were you on time? Dressed appropriately? Polite and courteous? Did you treat everyone you met with respect and courtesy, or just those people in the powerful positions?

- **You were not prepared for the interview.** How much homework did you do? Were you knowledgeable about the company? The industry? The position? The company's competitors? Yourself?

- **The position was filled before you got to the interview.** This happens frequently. Many companies would rather go ahead with the interview than cancel out on you at the last minute. Why? Well, it might be too late to recover most of the money they have already invested in the interview process. Going forward with the interview does two things for them. First, they can file you away for future openings. Second, it's good for PR—although you will not be working for that company you are more likely to continue to use their products.

- **You focused too much on you and not enough on them.** Human beings are by nature selfish—they care about themselves, their needs, and the needs of their dependents. No one expects you to deny your selfish side, but you need to be time sensitive about it. Showing that self-interest too early in the interviewing process will increase the odds of rejection. When is it safe to broach those selfish issues such as vacation time, holidays, benefits, and the like? After the job offer is on the table.

- **You seemed more interested in the future than the present.** Let's say you asked twenty questions during the interview. Five of them concerned the position at hand and the rest were focused on the jobs to come. Sounds like you view the initial position as simply a stepping-stone. Is that the signal you meant to send?

★

Although it is rare for a company to share the actual reasons with the rejected candidate, they do keep track of this information. Organizations such as college placement centers, TAP/ACAP offices, and placement firms are given access to this data. Although rarely individual-specific, the consolidated information is provided as a way of better preparing future candidates for interviews.

Throughout my career I have tracked the reasons candidates were rejected. Here are the top thirty, in no particular order:

1. Arriving for the interview too late or too early.
2. Poor self-knowledge.
3. Too much ego or a know-it-all attitude.
4. Body language issues, e.g., eye contact, handshake, and posture.
5. Poor performance in an academic setting.
6. Signs of inflexibility or rigidity.
7. Vague or nonspecific answers to questions.
8. Apparent insensitivity or intolerance.
9. Too much *I*, *me*, and *my* and not enough *we*, *us*, and *our*.
10. Too much *we*, *us*, *our* and not enough *I*, *me*, and *my*.
11. Lack of involvement in extracurricular or community activities.
12. Inappropriate personal appearance.
13. Disappointing questions, either in quantity, scope, or depth.
14. Little sense of humor.
15. Insufficient research on the company.
16. Low self-esteem or lack of confidence.
17. Poor examples of goal setting and achievement.
18. Inability to relate previous experiences to the job.
19. Apparent lack of enthusiasm for or interest in the job.
20. Too much focus on benefits and money.
21. Too restricted on travel or relocation frequency.
22. Little thought given to career planning.
23. Too aggressive or unrealistic career goals.
24. Lack of understanding of the profit goal.
25. Negative attitude toward previous employer or coworkers.
26. Seems to give up too easily.
27. Admits to few or any failures, weaknesses, or disappointments.

28. Lack of specific examples to validate points.
29. Nervousness.
30. Too rigid, stiff, or military in bearing or presentation.

Note that some of these are within your power to control, while many of them are not. With proper preparation and strong self-knowledge, you can minimize the chances that they will be used against you. In most cases it is a combination of reasons, as opposed to a single one, that will cause your downfall. So, what can you do? Learn from your mistakes, think positive, be prepared, control the controllable, and accept the fact that the rest is out of your hands. Nobody is perfect—you might get away with one or two of the above, especially if the interviewer likes you.

71. Your Decision Matrix (Part Two—Usage)

In section IV you were encouraged to design your decision matrix and use it throughout your search as a way to keep track of interview activity and comparison shop. When you reach the point where you have one or more offers on the table it is time to put this tool to work.

To illustrate this functionality, let's assume Companies X, Y, and Z have extended offers and see how you can use the matrix to assist in the decision process. After reviewing each of these offers and comparing them to *BENCHMARK*, you fill in the matrix as follows:

Congratulations! With four offers on the table, including the fictitious *BENCHMARK*, you have some choices to make. Based on the scores, your choice is easy: Company Z, correct? Maybe not.

Attributes:	Weight	Benchmark	CompanyX	CompanyY	CompanyZ
Growth Potential	10	10	8	10	7
Job Satisfaction	10	10	8	10	5
Quality of Life	9	9	7	9	7
Compensation	8	8	6	8	8
Initial Location	7	7	3	1	7
Future Location(s)	7	7	7	4	7
Co-workers	6	6	6	4	6
Benefits	5	5	5	2	5
TOTAL:	62	62	50	48	52

Look at how close the X, Y, and Z scores are to each other. Also, compare each of the scores to the *BENCHMARK* equivalent to see how they stack up. Sometimes maximum scores in lower weighted attributes can skew the data. For example, Company Z excels in the last five criteria but fares poorly in the areas most important to you. Conversely, Company Y has the lowest total, yet receives the maximum scores in your most important areas.

Here is another way to use this tool. Notice the lightly shaded areas on the matrix.

These shaded areas indicate attributes that are noticeably out of line with *BENCHMARK*. Could these be deal-breakers for you? The best test is to ask the question, *Is this deficiency tolerable or, better yet, fixable once I join the company?* If the answer is yes, then it is not a deal-breaker. If the answer is no, and it is relatively important to you, then you will have to walk away from the offer.

In the end, even after all of this objective and analytical decision-making, other things not on the matrix are likely to override the numbers. Gut feel, subjectivity, instinct, and emotion come to mind. Does this mean that the entire benchmarking and decision matrix design and utilization has been a waste of time? Not at all.

The *process* is more important than the numbers. The value comes from determining in advance what is important to you, keeping track of the data, comparing apples to apples, getting organized, and trying to stay objective during what is a highly subjective and emotional time of your life. Pay attention to the final numbers, but pay more attention to the process that produced them.

Additionally, you can use your decision matrix to treat the symptoms of that dreaded job-hunting disease called **One-offer-itis**, which is discussed in section VIII.

As you use your decision matrix you will discover that no opportunity ever matches up exactly with the *BENCHMARK* criteria. It would be both naive and very frustrating to conduct your search with that expectation. Why? Consider the following lesson from my past.

Several years ago, Debbie, the director of human resources at one of my client companies, was sharing with me the results of the interviews she had just completed with several of my candidates. I was a bit nervous because this was a new client—one I had been courting for months—and, in addition to offering exceptional opportunities, it had the reputation of being extremely picky. I selected the best possible candidates for her schedule and hoped for positive feedback.

Although she seemed pleased with her interviews, Debbie remarked that none of the candidates were perfect. Seeing the look of disappointment on my face, she smiled and told me she was actually very happy with that result. As my expression changed from concern to confusion, she added that I should not be disappointed because she makes it a point to automatically reject all the perfect candidates she encounters.

She explained further by saying that, since by their very nature humans are imperfect, her danger signal goes off when the perfect candidate comes along. She knows there are imperfections but they remain unseen or undiscovered. Rather than risk that these imperfections are major in nature and would cause serious problems when they ultimately do appear, she will reject the candidate and eliminate the risk. She added that she always hires imperfect candidates, as long as the imperfections are identified in advance and deemed either tolerable or, better yet, correctable through training, coaching, and career development.

If we accept the premise that the perfect candidate does not exist, then it is important to consider the corollary—there are no perfect jobs either. Like the perfect candidate, the existence of the perfect job is also fiction. If you find perfection it means you have not looked deeply enough. So, what should you do? Just as the employer will hire a less-than-perfect candidate, you could accept a less-than-perfect offer, if the imperfections are tolerable or, better yet, correctable or short-lived once you have joined the company.

Perfection—an unrealistic expectation on the part of both hiring managers and job seekers.

SECTION VIII.
OFFER, DECISION, AND LAUNCH

The reward for a successful search is a job offer, but not just any job offer. It needs to be one that you want to accept. It is also much more than just your potential paycheck. The amount is important, but there are other factors to consider before making the decision.

This decision is one of the biggest ones of your life, and it would be nice to get it right the first time. You would also be wise to consider what happens after you launch your new career. The following chapters address those issues and more.

As you read them, you will:

- Take the plunge.
- Feel the shifting of power.
- Learn how to decipher an offer.
- Rev your engine.
- Prepare for negotiation.
- Use your decision matrix.
- Dodge a few bullets.
- Launch your new career.
- Learn how to stay on course.

72. Learning How to Swim

There is no avoiding it. Sometimes in life you just have to take the plunge.

Back in high school, during the summer before my senior year, my friend Ken and I were enjoying a day at the beach and contemplating our college plans. "College" is a poor choice of words because we were both hopeful of being accepted to one of the service academies, especially the Naval Academy, since it was only an hour away from where we lived. Ken said something that day that took me completely by surprise—even if he were accepted, he might not go. When I asked why, his answer shocked me: he did not know how to swim.

At first I thought he was kidding. We had been going to the beach together since we were ten years old. He was always in the water, loved to play on the canvas rafts, and was quite a good body surfer. How could he not be able to swim? He pointed out that regardless of his affinity for the water, he had no ability to self-propel when he could not touch bottom. That is a problem for a future naval officer. However, since Ken was a natural athlete, I knew this problem was fixable. Before the summer was over he would learn to swim.

First came the how-to books on swimming. Then the old Johnny Weissmuller and Esther Williams movies in which swimming was a central theme. Stories of Mark Spitz and his seven gold medals. Some new gear—swim goggles and trunks. A couple of instructional videos. Observation and visualization. Lessons on strokes, breathing, and kicking in the shallow end of the community pool. Finally, with Labor Day weekend marking the end of the summer, we went out into the bay on a friend's boat. We put out enough anchor line to know that the water was at least ten feet deep. Ken put on his goggles, stood on the bow, hesitated, and . . . .

This story is a metaphor for many events in our lives. When we set out to do something that we have never done before, there is much we can do in the way of preparation for the event. In the end, however, there is a moment of hesitation before the decision to act. All the research, practice, advice, preparation, visualization, and equipment become secondary to the fact that, in the end, if you want to learn how to swim, you have to take the plunge and get wet.

Getting ready for the plunge also applies to career change. This is especially true for most people in the military. Due to the free-will aspect of the decision, the military-to-civilian transition is much different than receiving permanent change of station (PCS) orders and changing duty stations. The hesitation to take the plunge occurs twice. The first time is just before that initial interview. The second time occurs at the end of the search when it is time to reply to a job offer. Have I prepared well enough? Do I know what I am getting into? Have I done enough research? Have I talked to enough companies? Can I do this job? Am I ready? Am I making the right choice?

What to do? At some point you have to give yourself credit for your preparations. Believe in yourself. Know that if you hold out for 100 percent of the data before you act it will be too late, accept the fact that nothing valuable is risk-free, and jump. The water might be colder or warmer than you expected, there could be a riptide, the salt might get in your eyes, but your training and instincts will kick in and you will reach your destination, one way or the other.

Oh, I almost forgot. Ken took the plunge, swam a couple of laps around the boat, finished senior year, and opted for dry land—choosing instead to attend the Military Academy at West Point. He completed a successful career as an armor officer, started a second one with the federal government, and he is still a pretty darn good body surfer.

73. The Power Shift

Every successful job search involves a shifting balance of power. Understanding the way the power shifts during the interviewing process can be a valuable tool for anyone looking for a new job.

From the beginning to the end of the job search process, a series of choices are made. Initially, both parties—the candidate and the potential employer—share a balance of power. The candidate researches an opportunity and chooses whether or not to approach the employer. The employer reviews the résumé and chooses whether or not to interview the candidate. Assuming both parties have sufficient interest to take the next step, the balance of power will never be equal again.

Once the organization decides to interview the candidate, the power shifts to the organization. Why? Although either party can curtail the process at any time, it is the potential employer that controls the progressive steps leading to an offer. Assuming the candidate remains interested, he or she must continuously work hard to survive the cut. However, the longer a candidate remains under consideration, the more power he or she gains, and the more likely an offer will be extended.

In the early stages of the selection process, the organization has little invested. A screening interview is relatively inexpensive. However, the subsequent steps— follow-up interviews, airline tickets, hotel bills, testing, managers' time and attention, and reference checks—begin to add up in terms of money and time invested. It is during these steps that the power begins to shift from the organization to the candidate. The candidate's goal is to shift the power completely to his or her side of the table.

This power shift is complete when the candidate, not the organization, controls the outcome. How do you know when this has occurred? Although there may be hints along the way, the surest indicator is an offer of employment on the table. At that point, it is the candidate's decision to say yes or no.

For most organizations, the candidate selection process is a careful and thorough one. Before making an offer, the organization wants to be as confident as possible that this is the right person for the job and the job is right for the person. Upon reaching that conclusion, and given a sense that the odds of acceptance are high, the job offer will be extended.

From the perspective of the job seeker, something equally important has occurred in parallel with the organization's process of selection. As the organization evaluates the candidate, the candidate has the same opportunity to appraise the organization. By the time the organization makes the offer, the candidate should know whether or not he or she wants to accept it. Thus, the power shift is complete and the candidate gets to decide.

With an offer on the table, the decision is totally yours—now it is your turn to say yes or no.

In summary, if the opportunity truly interests you, do what it takes, within the bounds of truthfulness, to survive the cut. The power will gradually shift to your court. When the power shift is complete and the job offer is extended, the final decision is yours.

74. Job Offer—The Message and the Makeup

In section I we discussed your theoretical monetary value to a company. With an actual offer on the table, the theory becomes reality. A job offer represents the culmination of a successful job-hunting process. The first thing that jumps to mind when we hear the term "job offer" is money. How much is this organization going to pay me? There is no argument as to the importance of the paycheck, but to fully understand the significance of a job offer, we must look at a picture much bigger than the W-2.

- **The message.** What does it mean when a company makes you an offer? Several things come to mind. They have firsthand knowledge of you. They have evaluated your experience, education, personality, strengths, weaknesses, potential, and character and decided that you are the kind of person they want on their team. They like you. They feel you are worth the investment of time and money necessary to help you succeed and that your short-term and long-term success will add value to the organization. Their estimate of this short-term value is reflected in the amount of money they have offered you. Finally, they have sensed your high level of interest and that you would like to join them.

  As you can see, there is much supposition on the part of the potential employer to validate the feelings reflected in the previous paragraph. Any quality interviewing process allows both the potential employer and potential employee to evaluate each other. Both parties should take the time necessary to evaluate each party's ability to meet the needs of the other, short and long term. Be wary of an organization that offers you a job after a short or cursory interviewing process. Are they simply trying to plug a hole with a warm body, or are they interested in both your experience and your potential?

  If you have received a job offer from an organization that has taken the time to thoroughly evaluate both its ability to meet your needs and also your ability to meet theirs, then it is definitely an offer worth considering.

- **The makeup.** A job offer usually contains several important elements. You should look for a title or a short summary of responsibilities. Many offers will also include the job location and the name and title of the individual to whom you will report. The actual dollar amount of the offer should also be stated. Sometimes a start date will be mentioned, and frequently the offer will include a response date. On occasion there will be other elements included. For example, some offers address benefits, bonuses, performance/salary review cycles, confidentiality or non disclosure agreements, or non compete agreements. In most cases, however, these and other items of a legal nature, if relevant, are typically covered in a document separate from the offer.

- **Written or verbal?** An offer can be either verbal or written and will frequently come to you in both forms. Although a verbal offer might not feel as firm or official, rest assured that it carries as much weight as the written version. Most companies prefer to make a verbal offer first and then follow it up with the written version. There are two reasons for this sequence. One, they are pleased to be extending you the offer and, by extending it to you verbally, they can both express that sentiment and also get your real-time reaction. Two, a verbal discussion of the offer can sometimes lead to changes to or even cancelation of the written version prior to sending it to you.

- **Contingency offers.** It is an unusual offer that does not contain at least one contingency. Some of the common ones deal with drug screening, background checks, reference checks, and start date. Less common are the ones that are tied to either the approval of a client or the awarding of a specific contract. In the former case your employment is contingent on whether or not the client to which you will be assigned approves you, either via résumé review or personal screening. In the latter case the employer has included you (in the form of your résumé) in a contract bid. Should the contract be awarded, the contingency is removed and your offer stands. However if the contract is not awarded then the job offer is rescinded.

There is nothing illegal, unethical, or nefarious about contingency offers. In fact they are quite common when the job is with a government contractor or consulting firm. If that particular type of work appeals to you then you should be prepared for that possibility. If it turns out that the job you want to accept comes with a contingency then go ahead and accept it as such, but with one caveat—your acceptance also includes a contingency, which you may or may not choose to share with the employer.

Normally when you accept an offer you are 100 percent committed and you cease all job search efforts and decline any further interviews or offers. When you accept a contingency offer you do so with every intent to honor that acceptance in anticipation of the removal of the contingency, but in this case you do not curtail your job search. Pursue other opportunities and continue interviewing. You need a back-up plan in case that contingency is not removed.

- **Employment contracts.** Although not all that common, some employers require the new hire to sign an employment contract. There is nothing wrong with this but it does add an additional layer to your decision-making process. Since a contract is a legally enforceable document, you must be clear on the terms before you sign. Having the contract reviewed by an attorney or a similarly knowledgeable advocate before you sign it is highly recommended.
- **Additional considerations.** Be wary of an offer that comes with a very short response time. This tactic could reflect a corporate culture that might be cause for concern. If you are given less than five working days to make a decision then you should be suspicious of the employer's motives. There might be a legitimate reason for the short response time, but perhaps your new boss is simply trying to close the deal quickly. The most onerous version of this tactic is the *exploding offer*, in which case the employer extends the offer and tells you that it is only valid until the end of the day or for twenty-four hours. Another version of this is the "let's see who blinks first" tactic. Although there is only one opening, the company offers it to two people at the same time and tells both candidates that the first one to say yes gets the job.

Given the proper understanding of the information and issues mentioned above, congratulations are in order—you have the offer. Now, what are you going to do with it? You have three courses of action: you can accept it, reject it, or negotiate it. Before we get into how to respond to an offer, let's discuss several factors that may affect your decision. The next five chapters will elaborate.

75. The REV Factor

At some point in your job search, you will find yourself staring at an offer, or perhaps several offers, and you will need to make a decision. Analyzing the opportunity involves both subjective and objective criteria, and each individual uses his

or her own list of evaluators. There is one very important decision factor that should be on everyone's list but is often overlooked—résumé enhancement value, or REV.

When an organization decides that an individual is the person it wants on its team, an offer of employment is extended. When an individual decides that he or she wants to commit to the organization, the offer is accepted. Neither party enters into this relationship lightly. Both parties see the short- and long-term benefits of the match. A good analogy is a marriage. There is a proposal, an acceptance, and a pledge of *till death we do part*. Unfortunately, many marriages fail. Although neither party entered into the covenant expecting failure, unsuccessful marriages are a fact of life.

A reputable company will not offer permanent employment unless the prospects for long-term commitment are excellent. In turn, the person accepting the offer enters the relationship confident of mutual benefits well into the future. Sadly, as in some marriages, the predictions do not always come true.

Although neither party dwells upon it, or brings it up at all, both parties know up front that the odds are against a long-term relationship. Nearly half of all career commitments will fail in the first five years. The organization fails to provide for the long-term needs of the individual, and the individual is forced to look outside the organization. Or, the individual fails to live up to the expectations of the organization. In either case, assuming the shortcomings have been addressed and no internal fix is viable, it is in the best interest of both parties to end the relationship. Sometimes failure has nothing to do with the break-up. Individuals grow in different directions, change their priorities, or experience major changes in their personal situations. Organizations go through transition, react to market conditions, expand, contract, or change their focus.

Accordingly, although most organizations and individuals hope for long-term success, they both understand and accept that the relationship will not be everlasting. Organizations control their risk through continuous recruiting, career development programs, and succession planning. It is therefore important for individuals to do some succession planning of their own. One of the best techniques is to add a surprisingly little-used tool to the offer evaluation process—the REV factor.

As you evaluate an offer it is important to remember that even when your job search is complete, your résumé is not. It remains a work in progress, and it will continue to change as your career develops. It is highly likely that someday you will update it and use it again. When you do, what will it say about you? Have you enhanced your marketability? Is your experience transferable to other companies or industries? Does your employer have name recognition value? If so, then taking that job and working for that company will add value to your résumé and the REV is high. If not, you may look back and wonder if your choice of that job was a wise one.

Regarding name recognition value, many people fall into the branded consumer products trap. Although everyone is familiar with Motorola, Coca-Cola, and Apple, do those companies have better REV than ones like Stryker, Cintas, and Lazard? All six of those companies are world-class leaders in their respective fields, but consumers cannot buy products produced by the latter group at their neighborhood superstore. The companies in the first group, however, purchase the goods or services of those in the latter group every day. So, depending on your target audience, the REV of working for any of the six would be high.

In addition to the name of the company when determining REV, consider the work content and nature of your responsibilities. Assuming you are successful in your endeavors, can you transfer your talent and that success to other organizations? What tools have you added to your toolbox, how well do they work, and are they applicable beyond the scope of your present employer?

No matter how thorough you are in the offer evaluation process, there is always an element of risk. If you are fortunate you will accept an offer from a company where both the long-term and short-term prospects are outstanding, beat the odds, and find yourself retiring from that company twenty or more years later. If, however, you find yourself in the job market again, you will be happy that you also took into account the REV factor of that opportunity before accepting it.

76. The High Jumpers

Congratulations. Your search was successful and you have narrowed your choices down to two job offers. Although the opportunities are similar, the salary offers are significantly different. One of the companies has offered you $65,000 and the other one has made an offer of $75,000. Add to that the fact that the offers are equal with regard to cost of living, benefits, job satisfaction, and corporate culture, and your choice is a no-brainer. Like most people, you will take the extra $10,000 and run. Wait; not so fast.

Here's the story of two high jumpers from the D.C. area, twin brothers Nick and Brian, sons of one of my shipmates when I was on active duty. Two of the best athletes on their high school track team, Nick and Brian had both jumped  personal bests of six feet nine during their senior year. In addition to their track-and-field prowess, they were both very good students. This success generated a lot of interest among college recruiters. Although, like many twins, Nick and Brian had done just about everything together throughout their lives, they decided that attending different colleges would be best for both of them.

Since sophomore year, both brothers had been receiving interest from various track powerhouses throughout the country. Nick was leaning toward attending a school in the Pac-10 Conference with a reputation of developing world-class athletes, not to mention that it was a nationally ranked school of business. Brian found himself becoming more and more interested in a Southeastern Conference school known for its pre-med program and several NCAA championships in recent years. Both schools offered athletic scholarships and each brother found the academic and social benefits as appealing as the monetary ones.

In recruiting Nick, the track coach at the Pac-10 school told him that he estimated that Nick would be capable of jumping seven feet during his freshman year. Brian's coach, on the other hand, told him that his target for Brian was six feet eleven by the end of his first college season. As a result, both brothers were headed to college with goals of significant improvement over their high school careers. Following high school graduation, Nick headed west and Brian packed his bags for the southeast.

They stayed in touch throughout the year, but Nick and Brian did not see each other again until May. Although separated for nine months, the mysterious bonds that connect twins had not deteriorated. In fact, they had both gone off to college with identical personal bests in the high jump and returned with the same result—both of them had improved to 6 feet 11 1/2 inches during their freshman year. You would expect this to be cause for joy, but it was not. The relationship was strained. Brian's spirits were high, but Nick was morose. Why? Although they had both improved, Brian felt like celebrating and Nick felt like a failure.

Before you jump on that highest offer, you would be wise to consider the expectations that come with it. Although there are many factors that affect the amount of money that a potential employer will offer you, it is important to remember that when you accept an offer, you are confident in your ability to live up to the expectations that accompany that paycheck. Taking the $75,000 offer means that you will add $75,000 of value to your employer in the following twelve months. Your employer expects that from you. Similarly, accepting the $65,000 offer carries with it an expectation of the equivalent value added.

What are these expectations? Before accepting an offer, regardless of the amount, you should get a sense of how the employer will measure your performance or contributions throughout the year. Sometimes both the measuring stick and the scoreboard are clear. Maybe the job carries with it a sales or production quota. Perhaps you will be expected to increase production capacity by a certain percentage. Quite often performance goals are related to cost containment or reduction.

The issue becomes more difficult when there are no specifically stated goals. For example, consider this description of the position you are about to accept:

Build your team, train your team, and lead your team to accomplish the mission; increase efficiency and reduce cost while maintaining a safe working environment and enhancing quality assurance.

Before committing, you would be wise to discuss with your potential boss his or her expectations and how your performance and the performance of the team will be measured.

Let's go back to your choice of the $65,000 or $75,000 jobs. In either case, consider a scenario in which your contributions for the first year on the job are judged by your employer to be $70,000. In one case, you are a hero—you exceeded expectations and added more value than was expected. In the other case, you are a disappointment—you did not live up to expectations. Picture yourself sitting down with your boss for your first annual performance and salary review. In which situation would you rather be?

Whether we are talking about clearing the high bar or measuring performance on the job, keep in mind the importance of expectations. One way to improve is to set the bar higher at each step along the way, but resist the tendency to set it too high, especially when doing so puts it out of reach, regardless of how hard you try. Exceed the expectations and be a hero. Fall short and be prepared to update your résumé.

77. Will You Marry Me?

Made any big decisions lately? Purchased a car? Made your first mortgage payment? Decided to leave military service and pursue a civilian career? Made or accepted a marriage proposal? For many of you, those are among the biggest decisions you will ever make. Comparing two of these events will provide some valuable insight into the career transition process.

Compatibility, mutual respect, common interests, long-term commitment, growth potential—sound familiar? It should. We could be discussing a couple in the process of deciding if they want to marry. We could also be discussing an individual and an organization that are investigating the prospects of a mutually beneficial professional career. There are many parallels between courtship and job searching: interviewing and dating; offers of employment and proposals of marriage; acceptances or rejections; start dates and wedding dates. Although the similarities are noteworthy, there is a point at which the analogy breaks down, and if you are not careful, the relationship falls apart before it has a chance to get started.

Consider the tale of David and Kathy. They have been dating for several months, enjoy each other's company, and find themselves in a relationship that seems to get stronger every day. David decides to take the plunge. He buys the ring and makes a reservation at a fine restaurant. Over champagne, he looks into her eyes and says, "Kathy, will you marry me?"

After pausing a couple of seconds to catch her breath, Kathy responds, "Oh, David, what a surprise. When do I have to give you my answer?"

David is taken aback. He replies, "Well, I hoped you would accept my proposal now. But, if you are not ready, please think about it for a while."

Kathy responds, "That's great, David. Thanks. I really do need more time. You are a very nice guy and we have had some wonderful times, but I am not ready to stop dating yet. I need to meet some more guys and shop around a little bit, just to be sure. Of course, if no one better comes along, then your proposal will be just fine."

At first David is surprised and a little shocked. Then disappointment and a touch of resentment surface. Carefully choosing his words, he says, "Well, Kathy, this is not at all the response I was expecting. Given all the time we have spent together and how well we have come to know each other, I thought that both of us were ready to commit. Obviously, I got that wrong. Sure, I am disappointed, but I respect your need to date other people for a while. Perhaps you will find someone else. I guess I should also keep dating. Although I doubt it will happen, I will let you know if I happen to find someone else I would rather marry."

Now it is Kathy's turn to be surprised and she says, "Oh no, David, I did not mean that I want you to keep dating. You know that I am the right woman for you, otherwise you would not have proposed. I simply want to hold on to your proposal while I continue to date other men. After all, you could turn out to be the one for me."

Much like a courtship, the interviewing process gives both parties a chance to thoroughly check each other out. A reputable company will spend a significant amount of time with an individual before offering employment. This period of time is mutually beneficial in that the individual has an equal opportunity to investigate the company. When the company makes the job offer, they are saying that of all the candidates they have considered, they want you. You are the best person for the job and they feel that the job and career potential will be right for you. They want you on their team and they sensed that you also want this. They expect your answer. What will you tell them? Well, you might be tempted to respond like Kathy did: "When can I get back to you?"

Although employers are willing to give you a reasonable amount of time to respond to an offer, they would not want this courtesy to be abused. How much time do you need and why do you need it? Are there questions you have for them that might require a few days to get an answer? Do you need to discuss the offer with family members or advisers? Perhaps some negotiation is appropriate and that will take some time.

Most companies will find these issues reasonable and will allow you the time necessary to resolve them. One week is typical. If you need more than that, then there are other issues present—ones outside of their control and likely to produce little sympathy. You, like Kathy, feel the need to date around a little more before committing. And, also like Kathy, you would like this company to hold the offer open for you while you continue your comparison shopping. Supply and demand also influence this issue—the larger the number of qualified candidates from which to choose, the shorter the response time on the offer.

Everyone needs to comparison shop, especially for the big-ticket items. Would you buy the first car you test drove? Put a contract on the first house you saw? Marry the first person you dated? Accept the only job offer you have at the time? Maybe yes, maybe no. It depends on how much research you did in advance. How organized and thoughtful have you been in your search? How much data have you been able to compile? Keep in mind that the reward for successful interviewing is a job offer. How will you respond? If you are wise, not like Kathy did.

Balance your need to be thorough against the company's need to know where you stand. They have probably identified a back-up candidate and will not want to risk losing both of you. If you are sincerely interested in the opportunity but expect to hear from one or two additional companies before deciding, then use the offer you have as leverage with the other companies. Tell them that you need to respond to an excellent opportunity within a week or two but that you would prefer to hear from them prior to that deadline.

Once a response date has been agreed upon, resist the temptation to ask for an extension. It has been my experience that 90 percent of all offers with extended deadlines are ultimately rejected. Employers also know this and they react accordingly. Even if they grant the extension, expect that they have reactivated the candidate search process for the job they have offered you. Think about this—how would you feel if they called to tell you they found someone they like better and your offer is canceled?

Yes, there is a dance going on here, and it is hard to dance on shaky ground, but consider this:

Balancing or juggling multiple leads and job offers may be difficult, but do not complain too loudly—it is a problem you want to have.

Multiple offers are great, but you can only accept one. You should never make that commitment unless you intend to honor it, nor should you string a company along for any reason if the likelihood of accepting its offer is low. Just make sure that your decision and response process does not damage your relationship with your new employer before you have even started.

78. One-offer-itis

Although the career transition, interviewing, and job-search process is a universal one, the execution varies significantly from person to person and from organiza-tion to organization. One common denominator is the need to comparison shop. A company will always prefer to have multiple candidates for each opening and job seekers want more than one offer when decision day comes around. Regard-ing the latter, we can learn a lot about comparison shopping in your job search by examining the way it would work in a perfect world. Let's pretend you live in Utopia. Here is what you can expect.

- **Week One.** You do your research and identify the ten companies for which you would most like to work. You submit your résumé to each of those companies.
- **Week Three.** You hear back from all ten companies and all ten schedule phone interviews for the following week.
- **Week Four.** You nail the phone interviews and each of the companies asks you to schedule an on-site interview during Weeks Five and Six.
- **Week Seven.** Ten fat envelopes arrive in your mailbox, each containing an at-tractive job offer and a request for a decision in two weeks or less.
- **Week Eight.** Just before the weekend you pick up the phone and make ten calls, declining nine of your offers and accepting the one you really want.

Hello! Time to wake up and rejoin the real world. Although the Utopian ideal is not a bad plan to set for yourself, the realities of the job market and the job search are much more likely to produce the following result. You receive your first job offer on the Monday of Week Five and that company wants your response by the end of Week Six.

On the surface, that's not such a bad situation, given the fact that you got an offer and that a one- or two-week decision timeline is rather common. The problem lies beneath the surface—something just does not feel right. Although there could be other explanations, you have most likely caught one of the two dreaded job hunter's diseases—**One-offer-itis** or, a related strain, **First-offer-itis.**

Here are the symptoms. It is your first offer or it is the only offer you have on the table at that time. It seems like a good opportunity, but with no points of comparison, how do you know for sure? Some people say you should never take your first offer, but what if you decline it and it turns out that it was your best one? Perhaps you have other interviews scheduled after this offer expires. You wonder if you can get an extension. Will asking send a bad signal?

Everyone should expect to catch one, if not both, of these diseases during their search. Unfortunately, short of simply walking away from the offer, they are not curable, nor are there any inoculations. They can, however, be treated. One of the best treatments is prevention or, in the case of job hunting, preparation.

If you find yourself suffering from the symptoms of one-offer-itis, you can use the decision matrix and the *BENCHMARK* tools discussed in sections IV and VII to reduce and perhaps even eliminate the discomfort. Although you cannot compare your solitary job offer to another actual job offer, you can compare it to *BENCHMARK* or previous offers you have obtained. Your decision matrix allows you to keep track of previous or current interviewing activity and it also contains the attributes of your perfect job offer—the one you obtained from *BENCH-MARK.*

Here is what you do. Let's say that you have just received an offer from the *XYZ* Company, one that will expire before any others are likely to present themselves. Whether this is the first offer your search has produced or the only one on your plate at the time, add it to your decision matrix by adding *XYZ* to the top of the first empty column. Beneath the name, assign to it the scores you deem appropriate as you compare its attributes to those you assigned to *BENCHMARK.* When you have filled in all the blanks (and applied any weighting factors, if you designed them into your matrix), see how well *XYZ* stacks up against *BENCH-MARK.* Warning: no opportunity will ever appear as good as *BENCHMARK,* because you designed *BENCHMARK* to be perfect and you do not live in Utopia, remember?

The next step is to highlight those attributes of *XYZ* that fail to measure up to those of *BENCHMARK*. For the sake of discussion, let's say your matrix uses ten decision criteria and *XYZ* fails to live up to *BENCHMARK* in three of those areas. For each of those three, ask yourself this question: is that deficit tolerable or, better yet, correctable once I join the company?

If any one of your responses is a *no*, you will have to decline *XYZ*'s offer and continue your search. However, if you end up with three *yes* responses, your job search might just be over. Although the *XYZ* opportunity is not perfect, it may be as close as you will get in the real world. For an example of what a decision matrix might look like at the end of that exercise, see the illustration at the end of section VII.

Perfection, or the lack thereof, is a two-way street. Never forget that when *XYZ* offered you that job, they did so in spite of the fact that you are not the perfect candidate for the job. In the process of interviewing you, they discovered your imperfections and decided that those imperfections were tolerable or, better yet, correctable once they had you on the team. You would be wise to take a similar view.

79. Salary Negotiation

Salary discussions become an issue twice in your interactions with a potential employer. Initially, companies use salary expectations as a filter—they must make sure that your salary requirements are in line with what they intend to pay. If not, there is no need to proceed. There is not much in the way of negotiation at this point. Either your expectations and their range overlap or they do not.

Unlike a military salary, which is based on time in service, time in grade, a salary in the corporate sector is a measure of value added. More specifically, it is a prediction of the value that you will add to the organization during the review period, typically one year. This is particularly difficult when we are talking about starting salaries since no one knows for sure what value you can add until you have actually worked there for a while. For a further explanation of this, see "How Much Are You Worth?" in section I.

Assuming that you continue the interviewing process beyond the initial filtering stage, pass the tests, interview successfully, and receive a formal offer, salary negotiation can enter the picture again. Here are some things to keep in mind should you find yourself navigating those waters.

What is the corporate culture? Although you are within your rights to attempt to negotiate the starting salary, there is no requirement for your potential employer to do so. You can ask but they can refuse. Corporate culture comes into play. Some companies fully expect to negotiate and the first offer they make is not necessarily their last. This will often be the case when the job itself requires effective negotiation skills, such as sales, development, marketing, etc. Other companies are like the old Saturn dealerships. You get their first, last, and best price upfront. Take it or leave it.

It would be helpful to have advanced information on the company's culture on this issue. Maybe your research gave you some indication. Your Uncle Harry or Aunt Mary may be able to provide some guidance. Perhaps the person who initially interviewed you, the one who became your advocate, could help. Absent any other sources, you might have to ask the person who extended the offer if it is negotiable, but, as you will see later in this chapter, that approach requires a delicate touch.

What is your leverage? Why are you asking for a higher offer? Let me guess— you *want* more. Well, we all want more, but that is not good enough. Asking a company for more money means that you feel you can add value in excess of what they are offering. How do you know that? How do they know that? Where is your proof? You need leverage and *wanting* is simply not good enough. Do you have higher offers from other companies to do similar work? Have you made appropriate cost of living adjustments? Is there something in your background that they have failed to take into consideration? *No, my degree is not complete, but it will be by the time I start work.* How about your current salary? Is that leverage? Maybe, but be careful. Let's say you are a helicopter pilot and the army pays you an additional $600 per month for that skill. If you are interviewing to be the pilot of the Channel 9 *Eye in the Sky,* you have leverage. On the other hand, the plant manager at the chemical processing plant has no interest in your stick skills.

How much room is there? Most companies will assign ranges to the starting salaries for their various openings. This allows them to take into account the level of experience and years of education, among other things. It also allows them some flexibility when it comes time to review performance and adjust salary. Most companies attempt to bring you on board near the midpoint of the range. Why? The person they want in the job is too good to hire at the bottom of the range. On the other hand, bringing someone in at the top of the range means that there is no way to increase their salary until they are promoted. Since you are unlikely to be promoted until you have been there for a couple of years, your salary is in effect frozen until then. This may sound familiar: "John, you have been doing outstanding work for the past twelve months, but since you will not be promoted for a while, we can't give you any more money."

How far apart are you? Here is a good rule of thumb. If there is more than a 10 percent difference in the offer they have made and the offer that you would accept, then perhaps you should not be interviewing for this job in the first place. Normally this issue gets resolved much earlier in the process because of that initial filter I mentioned in the first paragraph.

Are you negotiating in good faith? Negotiating in good faith is essential. It must be done in an honest and ethical manner. What does this mean? Simply stated, it means both parties very much want the deal to go through, and both parties are working toward that goal. Here is an example. Let's say *XYZ* Company has offered you a job at $60,000. You counteroffer at $66,000 and they agree. You call them back a couple of days later and decline the offer because you decided the job was not right for you. Whoa. Bad faith. When you asked for the additional $6,000 you were in effect saying, *This is a great match and the only deal-breaker is the money, and if you fix the money by raising it by $6,000 then I am coming to work for you.* Moral—do not ask for more money until and unless *all* the other issues are resolved and you are ready to accept the offer.

When should you ask? One of the biggest mistakes job seekers make during salary negotiation is to put their counteroffer on the table too close to the end of the decision timeline. For example, if you and the company have agreed that you will respond to the offer by October 1, it is bad form to call on October 1 and ask for more money. Assuming they are of a mind to negotiate, the process required to modify and approve the offer may take several days. A last-minute counteroffer shows naiveté or a lack of professionalism, putting your offer at risk.

Should you even try? Here is another marriage analogy. A man and a woman are dating. The man asks the woman to marry him. She says yes. All the arrangements are made and the details fall into place. But what if he had never proposed? Or, what if she had declined? No need to worry about the date, the invitations, flowers, the attendants, etc. Receiving and accepting a job offer is like considering a marriage. Resolve the big issue first and worry about the details later. The big issue: are you and the company right for each other and is this opportunity a great way to start what both parties hope is a long-term relationship? If not, then the aforementioned details, including salary, do not really matter.

Whom should you ask? Having an offer means you have impressed many people and created several advocates in the company. If negotiating your offer becomes appropriate, with whom should you discuss it? Your best bet is your future boss. He or she wants you on the team, has gone to bat for you, and has strongly recommended and/or approved your offer. Hopefully your boss will go to bat for you again. As a matter of courtesy, you should also keep your contact in the human resources department in the loop.

Have you set the stage properly? When a company makes an offer they are telling you in no uncertain terms that they want you. The company believes you are the right person for the job and you have sent strong signals of interest. Asking for more money tells them that all is not well, so be careful how you ask. It is important to let them know that you are close to joining the team. You are excited and enthusiastic about the opportunity. However, there is one area in which *you need their help*. Words to that effect are critical. They will want to help you solve this problem. You let them know that you are ready to commit if they can up the ante. Using whatever leverage you have, you explain to them why you believe their initial offer undervalues your worth to them and ask them if there is any room for negotiation. You should be ready to propose a counteroffer, one that you are prepared to accept.

Does your reasoning pass this test? There are three possible responses to your request for more money: they say yes, they say no, or they meet you someplace in between. Here is a test for you: if this is really the right opportunity, then you should be prepared to accept regardless of their response. Think about it. The first possibility is a no-brainer, assuming you are indeed negotiating in good faith. They offered, you countered, they agreed, negotiation complete—go to work. As to the second and third possibilities, let's revisit our $60,000 example. They offer $60,000, you counter at $66,000, they come back with $63,000, and you decline. If you are walking away from the opportunity because of $3,000 then this was not a good fit anyway. Do the math. $3,000 divided by twelve paychecks, less federal, state, and local taxes, works out to about $180 per month. If the difference between yes and no is $180 per month, then it is most likely a mismatch anyway. Even if the company does not budge from $60,000 and the delta becomes $360 per month, the same logic applies. Factor in one 10 percent salary increase and the spread evaporates.

As you can see, there are rules, but they are not so simple. Diligence is required when navigating these waters. Set your course on reasonable expectations, let good faith be your polar star, use sincerity as your rudder, and your voyage will end successfully.

80. Responding to Offers— The Right Way

A successful job search is measured by the number of interviews you've generated and the number of offers you've collected, similar to those notches on the gunslinger's holster, correct? No, not at all.

Having an offer you want to accept is the mark of a successful job search.

It's all about quality, not quantity. Furthermore, as you learned at the end of section VII, quality does not mean perfect—there is no such thing.

Let's say that after all of your hard work you have your offer of choice on the table, and you are very close to accepting it. There is a correct way to do so and a recommended procedure to follow. Following this procedure will make the process go smoothly, help you get off on the right foot with your new employer, and minimize the possibility of unintentionally damaging your reputation before you begin your new job. For the sake of this discussion, assume you ended up with three offers—X, Y, and Z—and you are leaning toward offer Y.

- **Timing.** You update your decision matrix and take the weekend to review X, Y, and Z. You go to bed Sunday evening with a strong leaning toward Y. You wake up Monday morning and decide to take the plunge—Y it is. According to the Y offer letter, you owe them an answer by the end of the week, so you wait until Friday to let them know, right? No. Sure, you do not have to let them know until Friday, but why delay? Do not make them wait until the last minute to hear the good news. Tell them now. *Interviewing empathy,* as discussed in chapter 55 ("Tell 'Em What They Want to Hear"), still matters. Think of the positive signal you send your new employer when your acceptance arrives earlier than expected.

- **Regret.** Accepting offer Y means that you will also have to decline offers X and Z. That could be difficult. You did well with those companies and they want you on their team. You might have established a positive relationship with some of the people there. Turning them down will be hard. You do not want to disappoint, and no one likes to deliver bad news. It may help you to remember that it is highly likely there is a replacement candidate waiting in the wings, and they will get over missing out on their first choice.

- **Sequence.** If you are accepting and declining offers at the same time, it is critical that you do so in the correct order—**accept the one you want before you decline the ones that you do not.** There are two reasons for this. First, although the possibility is remote, what if just after you decline X and Z you call Y to deliver the good news only to be told that due to unforeseen circumstances your offer had been rescinded? Ouch. You just went from three offers to zero offers in record time. Be sure to lock in the one you want first and you will eliminate that risk. Second, when you speak with X and Z to let them know you are declining, you should expect some blowback. They might twist your arm, or sweeten the pot, or maybe even beat you up a little bit. Because you have already accepted an offer, you are able to say, "Although my decision was very difficult and I am flattered by your interest, I have already made a sincere commitment to another company." When they hear the word "commitment" they will most likely respect your decision, back off, take their lumps, and wish you well. Your file is closed with a positive note. Who knows, your paths may cross again someday.

- **Point of contact.** You should deliver your acceptance to your new boss. If that person is unknown to you or unreachable, then you should call your contact in the human resources department with the news and ask him or her for additional guidance on how to make sure your new boss is in the loop. When declining the offer, delivering the news to your human resources contact is sufficient.

- **Verbal.** All of the information above needs to be in the form of live conversation, delivered either in person or over the phone. Accepting live is easy, but there is a temptation to deliver bad news via voicemail or e-mail. Do not make that mistake.

- **Written.** Once you have accomplished the tasks verbally, be sure to back up those conversations with written verification and confirmation of what was discussed in person or on the phone. Mail, fax, or e-mail this letter to the people with whom you had the verbal exchange. Many offers include an acceptance form for you to sign and date and include with your letter.

- **Start date.** The start date is frequently cited in the offer letter. If that is not the case then you should state your preference in the same sentence in which you are accepting the offer. You are much more likely to get what you want by doing it this way, rather than being stuck with what Company Y has in mind or getting into a potentially uncomfortable negotiation over the start date.

- **Negotiate?** Speaking of negotiation, now—i.e., the day you are calling to accept—is not the time. Accepting an offer means that all terms are already acceptable. If that is not the case, then you must address those issues well in advance of your decision date. See the previous chapter for guidance.

- **Loose ends.** Although you have accepted Y and declined X and Z, you may not have delivered all the news. Remember to close the loop with any additional companies that consider you to be an active candidate for employment. Also, do not forget about Uncle Harry and Aunt Mary (section IV). All the people in your search network, your references, and everyone else who has provided assistance need to know where you stand. This would also be a great time to say *thank you.*

81. Lift Off and Stay on Course

Finally! I know it feels great to get to this part of your journey—congratulations. Your search is over. You have accepted the offer and confirmed your start date. The thank-you phone calls have been made and the similarly themed letters have been mailed. You have taken care of all of the necessary paperwork and logistics to support your out-processing and your move. The first step of a new journey is just around the corner.

That journey begins with the first day on the job and continues as you get the first week, month, and year under your belt. It will be a time of mixed emotions. Relief and stress. Excitement and apprehension. Wonder and fear. Optimism and self-doubt. Affirmation and surprise. Happiness and melancholy. All of this is normal and to be expected.

Although you have much to learn and there will be twists and turns and potholes and detours, you should expect success. I have helped thousands of people launch similar journeys and for almost all of them, this has indeed been the case. There have been many lessons learned as those careers were launched, and the following information will help you stay on course.

- Re-confirm the start date a week or two in advance to be certain that all parties are in sync.
- Take care of as much of your personal, family and household start-up requirements in advance of your start date as possible. You do not want to have to ask your manager for time off to meet with the cable guy, or wait for the refrigerator to be delivered, or enroll your children in school during your first week on the job.
- Make sure that you have completed any prior-to-reporting-to-work expectations, such as a physical exam or drug test.
- Contact your manager to see if there is any job-related material or subject matter reading that you can do in advance of your start date.
- Ask the personnel office if you can take care of any of the new employee paperwork prior to your first day on the job.
- Do not be surprised if you have feelings of uncertainty about your decision. This is normal and mostly temporary. It comes from a combination of the nervousness associated with starting a new job and the buyer's remorse that often accompanies choices that have big financial consequences and lead to significant changes in your working environment.
- Make sure you will be properly attired when you show up for work. Do not hesitate to ask about dress codes before your first day. There is no point in investing in a work wardrobe that you cannot wear.
- Verify in advance to whom you should report on your first day, where you should report, and the time you are to be there.
- Arrive early, say hello, smile, introduce yourself, ask questions, and stay late.
- Observe, take notes, listen, learn, and ask for help.
- Do not expect the same level of after-work social interaction as you experienced when you reported to a new assignment in the military. Those opportunities will be there, but you need to be patient and a bit more proactive than in the past.
- After a few weeks, look for company-sponsored volunteer activity such as Adopt-a-Road or Habitat for Humanity. This is a great way to meet new

people and get to know them better. Similarly, joining the company softball team or bowling league can be a good way to break the ice.

- Remember your family. This is a stressful time for them also. Try to get them settled in to your new home and community when you can do it together rather than having them fend for themselves because you are too busy at work.

- Although it may be six to twelve months before your first formal performance review, do not be shy about asking for periodic informal evaluations. Let your boss know you care and that you want to make sure you are on the right track.

- Keep a personal journal of your progress and contributions, especially those that can be measured or quantified. Write them down as they occur and be specific. This information will come in handy at your first review.

- No matter how good or valid they may be, do not attempt to implement your ideas too soon. Adding value is important, but doing so gradually will be less likely to raise eyebrows or cause resentment.

- Stay in touch with your current mentors and look for opportunities to develop new ones.

- Do not be surprised if you feel underutilized for the first month or two. This is a start-up and break-in period for both you and your employer. You may be used to a work pace and tempo that is far different from your new one, especially early on.

- However, if boredom or a lack of challenge continues for too long, there might be a problem. The military is very good when it comes to making sure you know what you should be doing and when you should be doing it. Standard operating procedures, plans of the day, checklists, and the organizational manuals were convenient and helpful, but did you get a little too used to them? Civilian companies are less likely to use similar tools, relying more on your ability to recognize what needs to be done, figure out how to do it, and then make it happen. If you are bored, go to your boss and say, "I need your help. I feel like I am missing something. I seem to get my work done early in the day and find myself with nothing to do. I know this is not right. Please, tell me what I am missing."

- It is also possible that the lack of work is intentional. Many companies would rather ease you into the new job slowly than blast you with a fire hose.

- Balance the positives of being the eager beaver with the negatives of biting off more than you can chew.

- If you are unclear as to how much or how little initiative is appropriate at any particular juncture, err on the side of the former. Your boss would much rather reel you in because you are trying to do too much than let out the line because you are doing too little.
- Try to avoid office politics, cliques, and turf wars. Ease into the social aspects of the workplace gradually.
- Be prepared for the possibility of a feeling of resentment or skepticism among some of your new peers or coworkers. This is a fairly common reaction when someone from outside the company enters the mix. Trust that your personality and professionalism will gradually overcome those feelings.
- Bumps in the road are inevitable. Problems with coworkers, a rocky relationship with your boss, difficulty adjusting to the job, and similar issues are not uncommon. Should they arise, give them a day or so to resolve themselves. If that does not happen, schedule a meeting with your manager. If that is awkward or difficult, reach out to someone in the human resources department. You might also have to seek outside assistance or advice. Contact Uncle Harry or Aunt Mary or one of your mentors. At this point, many people seek out the services of a professional, such as a counselor or career coach, and the next chapter will elaborate.

Bottom line—this will be one of the most challenging times in your life, but also one of the most enjoyable. There are several contradictions in the above bullets, but that is to be expected. Each individual will have a unique set of experiences and react to them differently. You will succeed if you remember to work hard, work smart, be fair and honest, add value, take care of your people, make a difference, treat others with respect, and ask for help if you need it.

82. A Personal Trainer for Your Career

Perhaps you are familiar with personal trainers and the impact they can have on physical fitness. Some people do perfectly well in the gym without any professional guidance. Others need expertise and/or the external motivation to accomplish their fitness goals. A career coach is like a personal trainer, only the focus is on *career* fitness, *job* health, and *professional* well-being. Having that expertise on speed dial is not only comforting but also critical in times of career transition or crisis.

Should you have a career coach in your professional development arsenal? Maybe. Have you ever needed, or will you ever need, an accountant? An attorney? A personal trainer? Situations change and individual circumstances dictate whether or not professional assistance is needed or you can go it alone. If you decide to tap into the expertise and wisdom of a career coach, make sure you select the right one. Military-to-civilian transition, job hunting, and post-military career development is unique to veterans. You could benefit from a career coach who is intimately familiar with that experience and the special circumstances that surround it. Better yet, find one who wore the uniform and experienced that transition at a personal level.

So, how do you find that person? A personal referral is always your best bet. You can also do a quick Internet search by typing this phrase into the search engine: *"military to civilian" and "career coach"* (quotation marks included). Visit the websites to find someone who appears to have the requisite qualifications mentioned above. Make contact and schedule a short telephone call. The career coach will determine whether or not he or she can assist you, and you will decide if you want that assistance if it is offered. Included in this call will be a discussion of the fee for service.

If you do not have the resources to invest in a career coach, you may be able to receive some of that same assistance for free. In section IV there is a discussion of placement companies that specialize in military personnel. One of the ways the best of those firms distinguish themselves is the quality of the candidate recruiters they employ. A knowledgeable, experienced, ethical, and professional candidate recruiter, especially one with prior military service, will function as a de facto career coach. He or she will help you prepare and attempt to match you up with the right company. Because that company is the client in the relationship, it pays the fee, and there is no charge to you.

As you may recall from section II, I started my post-navy career as a recruiter for a placement company. It was an ideal job for me. The teamwork, the independence, and the financial rewards were great, but the best part was assisting my candidates as they made the transition and conducted their job searches. Although I did not place all of my candidates—some of them found the right jobs on their own—I know I helped every single one in one way or another. That experience led me to my current occupation—career coach—and influenced me to write this book.

Assisting others in their professional development is not only my expertise but also my passion. Career coaching is my profession and I focus on the needs of my clients. My relationship with my clients falls into two categories—short- and long-term engagements. The short-term engagements are tactical in nature and focus on a specific goal or issue, such as writing a résumé, preparing for a performance review, or discussing how to deal with a difficult boss or colleague. Many short-term engagements evolve into long-term relationships. These are strategic in nature and involve more big-picture issues, such as military-to-civilian transition, continuing professional development, and career planning.

Another way to look at this is to consider a flywheel. When at rest on its axle, it adds no value to its environment. To do its job it must be moving. To get it up to speed and spinning takes a lot of energy, but once it is up and running it only needs a little tap on a regular basis to keep it that way. If for some reason it needs to go in the other direction, two big applications of force are needed. One to stop it from spinning in its current direction and then another to get it moving again in the new direction. That is what a career coach does for a client, where the flywheel represents the client's professional development. Together the coach and the client apply the necessary energy to get the wheel moving, keep it moving, and if necessary, change direction.

Here is an example from my experience as a career coach. Remember Mark, the roller-coaster junkie in section I? He is one of my clients. As promised, you can turn to the next chapter—the final chapter in this book—for an update on his story.

83. Has the Ride Lost Its Thrill?

After Mark took the job with *API*, we continued our career coaching sessions. Once each month we would spend an hour on the phone reviewing the previous month and setting goals for the next one. I learned that Mark enjoyed his new job as a project manager. His learning curve started out a bit steep but he settled in and worked hard. His contributions made an impact and his value added was apparent, as witnessed in his performance reviews. In fact, during his second review his manager mentioned that Mark's name had come up earlier that week during a senior staff meeting as someone who had the potential to be fast-tracked into the company's ELDP—Executive Leadership Development Program—in the next two to three years.

Mark's reaction was mixed. On the one hand he was elated. He was familiar with the ELDP and knew that all of the top executives in the *API* organization had participated in that program. However Mark also knew that those people shared another common denominator, one that he lacked: they all had MBAs. Before he could raise that point, Mark's boss told him that there was one glitch. When compared to the other ELDP nominees, his lack of a graduate degree in business would hurt his chances.

Sensing disappointment, Mark's manager reminded him that the company benefits included a tuition reimbursement package. He also mentioned several schools in the area that offered weekend or evening MBA programs. If Mark could get started in the fall he could complete the degree in three years, maybe less. Mark expressed his gratitude and asked his manager if he could take the weekend to mull it over. His manager told him to take as much time as he needed, talk it over with his family, and get back to him. They agreed that if Mark decided to pursue this avenue his manager would nominate him to the ELDP selection committee.

Although we were not scheduled to chat again for several weeks, Mark called me that evening. He filled me in on this new development and the details. I congratulated him and asked him to tell me how he felt about the ELDP, especially the MBA part. Mark replied that he was interested in the opportunity and flattered to be considered, but he was also conflicted. He explained that he was not sure he could make the sacrifices required to make it work. He reminded me of our coaching session several years earlier in which we discussed the promotion he had been offered at his previous company and the associated move to Chicago—a sacrifice he was unwilling to make. Although this opportunity would not require relocation, it would have a serious impact on his quality of life.

He had researched the local universities and found two that would allow him to complete an MBA in three years or less. One of them was an executive program in which once each month for twenty-four months he would attend classes Friday through Sunday. The Friday requirement was problematic, but he expected he could accommodate most of that by taking vacation days. The second school offered an evening program for which he would have to attend class at least two nights per week for almost three years.

Although both of these could be accomplished on a mostly not-to-interfere basis with respect to his job—a requirement for tuition reimbursement—neither of them could avoid interfering with his personal life. Mark and his wife were very involved in their children's schooling, sports, and club activities, most of which occurred in the evenings and on weekends. The two of them were also youth ministers in their church, a commitment that frequently involved more than just Sundays.

I asked him to put aside for a minute the impact this opportunity would have on his quality of life and instead focus on the professional development side of the equation. Mark understood how obtaining an MBA and going through the leadership development program would enhance his chances of becoming a company executive, but he also admitted that he was not sure that he wanted to work in the executive "ivory tower." When I asked him to explain, he mentioned a classmate of his, Joe, another naval aviator and F/A-18 pilot, with whom he had recently reconnected at a class reunion. Although Joe had done well in the navy—he had attained the rank of admiral and commanded a carrier battle group—his success had come at a price. Joe loved to fly and every promotion meant less stick time. In fact, since he made admiral there had been no stick time. That was an eye-opener for Mark.

He explained to me that he loved working on the operational side of the business at *API*. Making things happen, getting things done, customer experience, quality assurance—code for riding the rides—and process improvement were the aspects of the job that motivated him. Although completing ELDP would enhance his professional profile it would most certainly also move him from operations to strategy and finance, and he did not find that prospect very appealing. I asked him to explain what job would be appealing. He took a couple of seconds to answer and when he did, he was laughing. "That's an easy one, Tom. I would design roller coasters."

"Just kidding," he added, and then he explained. For a couple of years now he had his sights set on becoming general manager of one of the company's theme parks, especially one with plenty of coasters. Unlike the corporate executives in the ivory tower, the park general managers were not necessarily products of the

ELDP and very few of them had MBAs. I told Mark that I understood and agreed with his logic, but I was concerned about the potential downside of declining the ELDP. He shared my concern but felt that the culture at *API* was one that would not hold that against him. Yes, he was cutting off the path to the ivory tower, but for the sake of his quality of life, the trade-off was worth it.

It has been about a year since that conversation. As this book was about to go to press, Mark called me to say that he was on the short list to be the general manager of *API*'s newest amusement park, which just happened to also be the future home of the Super Hornet—the fastest and longest roller-coaster ride in the world.

AFTERWORD

My father and grandfather were woodworking craftsmen. I grew up with phrases like "the right tool for the job" and "measure twice, cut once." Although my lack of woodworking skills is obvious in the lopsided planter lamp I made in high school shop, I have found that these maxims also apply to the craft of my profession.

During thirty years of assisting people as they left the service, I learned that the interviewing and career transition process is a craft, and, like any craft, it can be mastered. Learning a craft requires several things: aptitude, commitment, the right tools, practice, and an experienced teacher, to name the most important ones.

I wrote this book to assist individuals in career transition. Moving from one job or career to another requires much in the way of preparation, practice, research, and execution. This transition is a plan and a process—a series of connecting steps strung together in a logical manner. There are many tools available to you as you accomplish each of the steps. Initially, like the apprentice craftsman, you practice, become familiar with your tools, discover which ones are appropriate for the task at hand, keep them well-honed, and gradually become more skilled. Eventually, you use your tools, apply your craft, seek help if you need it, and continue your professional development.

Congratulations. You now have your own transition toolbox. Carry it with you in your new job and career. One more thing. My father and grandfather were right—*take care of your tools and they will take care of you.*

ACKNOWLEDGMENTS

A riddle: What do a turtle sitting on a fence post and this book have in common?

Answer: You know there was a lot of help involved.

The idea for this book was in the back of my mind for many years. The reality of the book is a result of the inspiration and assistance of several very important people. Like that turtle, I had help, and, but for that help, there would be no *Out of Uniform*. I welcome this opportunity to acknowledge them and say thank you.

Paul Kreider: He comes first because he was the first, i.e., he wrote the first worthwhile book in the military-to-civilian transition genre. I recommended it throughout my career, although always with the caveat: "Read this book; it is the best one out there, at least until I get around to writing one." Thanks, Paul, for the inspiration, the support, and the wine.

The Writers Bloc of Brunswick County, NC: I thank you all for accepting me into your group and for your encouragement, high standards, constructive criticism, and support.

My Manuscript Peer Review Group: Debbie and Al Artale, Linda Bolan, Susan and Dan Christman, Roy Cranford, Skid Heyworth, Glen Hatzai, Terry Jemison, Ben LoBalbo, Tom Mays, Mike McGovern, John Peake, Loren Pearson, Bob Ravener, John Rudder, Ken Shearer, Mark Smith, and Lou Terhar. I knew that subjecting the manuscript to these people would open it up to a diverse set of reactions and many changes, but the subsequent barrage of comments, suggestions, and constructive criticism resulted in a much better book. Thank you.

Captain Josh Glover, USMC: Not only for providing a much-needed user's perspective, but also for the sacrifices you made in the service of our nation, I thank you.

CDC partners and wives: Terry & Marilyn, Ben & Cindy, Mike & Julie. I am grateful for the support, tolerance, and, most of all, 33+ years of friendship and camaraderie.

Scott Sullivan: I have little ability when it comes to graphic arts, illustration, and drawing. Fortunately my friend and neighbor is extremely talented in those areas and generous with his time. Thanks, Scott, for the visuals that appear throughout this book.

Charlie & Lois Smith: Friends and neighbors. Thanks, Charlie, for the photograph. You did quite well considering the limited subject matter. Lois gets credit also—yes, the wine definitely helped.

Elizabeth Demers: Senior editor at Potomac Books. Thank you for taking a shot on an unpublished, un-agented writer when others would not.

Mark Smith: Meeting Mark was accidental and fortuitous. He endorsed the concept of the book, encouraged me to join the Writers Bloc, and pushed me to continue writing. I struggled with transitions and sequence, but his significant contributions helped overcome that obstacle. Thank you, my friend.

Loren & Rob Pearson: Our dearest friends. The use of their family cottage on the Maine coast allowed me to accomplish months of work in two weeks. Although I am grateful for their generosity, it is their friendship for which I am most thankful.

Taylor Wolfe & Blair Wolfe: Fine writers but even finer daughters. Thanks for your support and input, especially your efforts to make sure that my conventional wisdom was updated in a way to keep it relevant for contemporary readership.

Julie Wolfe: The best for last. My strongest critic, my biggest supporter, my muse, my best friend, and the love of my life—my wife. Without her the book would forever remain in the back of my mind. Thank you.

KEYWORD INDEX

academic, 11, 16, 20, 93, 195

Army Career and Alumni Program (ACAP), 120, 124, 195

acronyms, 98

adversary, 159

advocate, 113, 159, 206, 217

airplane test, 169

alcohol, 186

alumni associations, 5, 58, 119, 124

application forms, 94, 110, 179, 188

audition, 83

Aunt Mary, 115, 217, 222

availability, 15, 17, 35, 56, 102

BENCHMARK, 11, 13, 89, 188, 196, 215

benefits, 23, 30, 44, 89, 184, 194, 205

BIGCO, 44

body language, 13, 92, 151, 185, 195

bottom line, 66, 76

bullets, 100

bumps in the road, 225

camaraderie, 142

career coach, 113, 226

caution, 18, 51, 65, 97, 117, 120, 135, 154

cell phones, 57, 115, 166, 178, 187

cheerleaders, 138

classifieds, 46, 58, 118

close, the, 152, 172, 185, 206

communicate, 127, 179, 180, 188, 190

compensation, 9, 16, 22, 44, 89

competitive, 81

competition, 84, 136

consulting, 69, 158, 169, 182

contractors, 71

cover letter, 94, 101, 105

culture, 30, 44, 53, 89, 131, 143, 190, 217

day-in-the-field, 182

Dear John, 191

decision, 31, 33, 43, 131

decision matrix, 89, 188, 196, 220

documentation, 93, 177

education, 6, 11, 15, 31, 74, 97

empathy, 132, 140, 145, 148, 168, 220

engineer, 7, 19, 67, 79

errors, 100, 102, 107, 112, 115, 191

etiquette, 177, 187, 190, 194

eye contact, 13, 92, 151, 178, 185, 195

expenses, 25, 69, 94, 121, 181

exploding offer, 206

filters, 14, 26, 28, 56, 102, 180, 216

first-offer-itis, 214
follow-up, 107, 110, 114, 179, 181, 187
follow-up letter, 94, 111, 185, 188, 189
for the right opportunity (FRO), 27

GI Bill, 23, 32
grade point average, 11, 20

handshake, 152, 185, 195
headhunters, 54, 80, 120, 121
hiring conferences, 56, 124

individual contributor, 23, 61, 146
Internet, 54, 58, 116, 117, 134
interview, 35, 79, 114, 147, 149, 175
interviewers, 8, 21, 63, 138, 155, 159

job fairs, 74, 124, 181
job offer, 13, 90, 132, 196, 204, 212

keyword, 15, 98
knowledge, 92, 135, 148, 171
knowledge pie, 136

learning curve, 10, 44, 50, 65, 72
leave, 17, 55, 57
lift off, 222
likeability, 81
location, 31, 53, 57, 89, 180, 204

manager, 39, 64, 66, 146
money, 16, 22, 30, 76, 122, 204, 217
motivation, 32, 77, 121, 171, 225

negative interview, 156, 171, 181
negotiation, 18, 52, 213, 216, 222
networking, 58, 116, 120, 127, 222

objective, 43, 48, 97, 100, 107, 112, 121
one-offer-itis, 197, 214

paperwork, 93, 177, 189, 222
performance, 12, 21, 40, 93, 187, 195, 211
personal information, 98, 109
personality, 12, 82, 136, 139, 170, 180
placement companies, 120, 121, 125, 226
post-interview, 94, 179, 187, 189
potential, 12, 21, 52, 72, 93, 98, 204, 211
power shift, 202
preemptive strike, 138, 140
pre-interview, 180, 189
preparations, 36, 76, 83, 87, 129, 170, 188
professional guidance, 76, 95
professional societies, 124
profiling, 14, 183

quality, 15, 30, 53, 127, 133, 220
quality of life (QOL), 30, 53, 145, 168
quality of work (QOW), 30, 145
questions, 131, 161, 168, 170, 184, 212

recruiters, 12, 27, 63, 80, 122, 172, 226
references, 93, 102, 108, 109, 177, 222
rejection, 13, 111, 126, 131, 141, 192, 193
relocation, 16, 25, 45, 90, 195
remote, 11, 53
research, 33, 35, 41, 54, 133, 171, 183, 195
response date, 95, 205, 213
résumé, 46, 65, 72, 90, 93, 95, 105, 125
resume enhancement value (REV), 45, 207
ride-a-long, 182

salary, 16, 22, 27, 44, 52, 69, 71, 89, 216
sales, 23, 78, 80, 81, 85, 170, 182
sales quotient (SQ), 81
self-education, 7, 8, 48
self-employment, 75, 76, 77

self-knowledge, 8, 41, 83, 92, 135, 171, 184
seven seconds test, 96
site visits, 68, 156, 181, 185
size, 43, 58, 79, 95
skepticism, 84, 225
SMALLCO, 44
social interviews, 153, 181, 182, 186
social networking, 92, 116, 118, 119, 127
start date, 17, 34, 102, 205, 211, 222
stereotype, 8, 44

Transition Assistance Program (TAP), 120, 124, 195
task and skills inventory, 41
team leader, 23, 39, 61, 66
team member, 23, 61
thank you, 92, 110, 111, 187, 188, 222
timeline, 34, 55, 92, 97, 98, 188, 214, 218
too much information (TMI), 146
toolbox, 65, 89, 107, 133, 208
tools, 65, 89, 107, 133, 208, 231

training, 11, 32, 39, 44, 51, 72, 90, 97, 172
travel, 15, 18, 30, 45, 57, 69, 90, 102, 195

Uncle Harry, 115, 217, 222
uniform, 9, 17, 113, 178, 236

value added, 45, 52, 72, 121, 123, 136, 216
voicemail, 92, 165, 179, 184, 221
veterans service organizations (VSOs), 119

wages, 22
wallflowers, 138
wardrobe, 113, 114, 115, 213
weaknesses, 135, 141, 195, 204
white space, 99, 100
work ethic, 8, 13, 51, 81, 108
work with people, 62
working hours, 16, 30, 52, 75, 76, 90, 143, 165
writing sample, 94, 100, 107, 111

ABOUT THE AUTHOR

Tom Wolfe is a recognized expert in the field of career transition. Prior to serving as the candidate strategies editor and career coach at Bradley-Morris, Inc., he was a senior partner at Career Development Corporation, where he provided guidance to separating military personnel. Tom graduated from the U.S. Naval Academy, served as a surface warfare officer in the navy, and completed tours of duty as a flag aide, communications officer, and administrative department head. His work has appeared in such publications as *Civilian Job News*, *Stars and Stripes*, and *G.I. Jobs*. Tom lives in North Carolina with his wife, Julie, and their Chesapeake Bay retriever, Maggie.